Racial Politics in Contemporary Brazil

RACIAL

POLITICS

IN

CONTEMPORARY

BRAZIL

❁

Edited by Michael Hanchard

Duke University Press   Durham and London

1999

© 1999 Duke University Press

All rights reserved   Printed in the United States of America

on acid-free paper ∞

Typeset in Adobe Garamond with Twentieth Century display

by Tseng Information Systems, Inc.

Library of Congress Cataloging-in-Publication Data

appear on the last printed page of this book.

CONTENTS

Michael Hanchard

INTRODUCTION

The conference "Racial Politics in Contemporary Brazil," held at the Institute of Latin American Studies at the University of Texas, Austin, 8–10 April 1993, was part of a three-year project on racial identity, inequality, and politics in Latin America funded by the Ford and Rockefeller Foundations. This edited volume represents the culmination of the Ford Foundation–Brazil's portion of the project, which was devoted to Afro-Brazilian politics and social movements. Originally conceived through a collaboration between myself and anthropologist Greg Urban—and further developed with suggestions from colleagues Richard Graham, Aline Helg, and Sandra Lauderdale Graham—the project synthesized various regionally oriented analyses of race relations into a more national perspective. Together, we sought to contribute to the burgeoning discussions about race in a democratizing Brazil.

This book should be read within the context of both this epoch in Brazilian society, and the study of its race relations patterns and dynamics. Its overarching aim is to add to the scholarship and discussion of Afro-Brazilians not only as cultural subjects or victims of racial slavery (a dominant tendency in the literature, which will be examined briefly below), but also as active though unequally situated participants in national politics, society, and cultural practices. The term *racial politics* encompasses the role of social constructions of race and racial difference in formal, institutional politics as well as in the political interactions of daily life.

Given the emergent literature on a variety of topics connected to racial difference in Brazil—from racial classification and categorization to labor market inequality, residential segregation, and the intersections of gender, race, and sexuality—no single monograph or multiauthor work could satisfactorily cover the many questions and issues now being debated. Nonetheless, the scholarly and activist texts assembled here share a common concern: to investigate the dynamics of racial difference, identity-formation, and inequality as an ongoing process in Brazil that is constantly altering—as well as being influenced by—the economy, the political sphere, and civil society.

One of the consequences of the authoritarian rule in Brazil between 1964 and 1986, in addition to the political and moral impacts of a dictatorship, was the repression—sometimes brutal—of dissent. This included scholarship and critical debate that not only questioned the military's power, but also rendered suspect Brazil's national and international reputation as a racially egalitarian society. Racial discrimination, therefore, was a taboo subject. A positive outcome, among many, of the return to civilian rule was the public and scholarly consideration of the roles of race and color as organizing principles of difference and inequality. The new topics and debates that emerged after the period of democratic opening (*abertura*) led, in turn, to the challenging of old paradigms and theorems.

In Brazil, as in all other societies of the late–twentieth century, there are *multiple* axes of social inequality. The centering of racial difference at the core of scholarly inquiry into Brazil is not done at the expense of other factors, like social class, region, gender, or state power. For the specialists assembled here, the manifold consequences of racial inequality—political, economic, cultural, and social—cannot be answered by monocausal explanations (race versus class arguments, for example). Subjects as seemingly disparate as labor wage differentials, residential segregation, trends in Brazilian political philosophy and social theory, and the earning power of white professional women in the labor force are connected by the myriad ways in which racial difference consciously and unconsciously aids in the determination of where people are employed and where they are not; where people decide to live and with whom; and lastly, what the nation's greatest minds imagine, conceptualize, and articulate when debating issues of fundamental importance to their national community.

Though the emphasis here is decidedly within the social sciences (the scholarly contributions hail largely from sociology, political science, and history), many of the methodologies, themes, and issues utilized in the following chapters emanate from other disciplines and knowledge formations: gender and women's studies, social theory, literature, and philosophy. The combination of qualitative and quantitative methodologies in a single volume should prove useful for students interested in regional, national, and cross-national variations of Brazilian racial patterns.

BRAZILIAN RACE RELATIONS: A BRIEF OVERVIEW

The vast literature on Brazilian slavery, race relations, Afro-Brazilian religions, racial identity, and racial inequality requires far more detail and nuance than these introductory pages allow. Readers unfamiliar with such literature would be best served by referring to several general sources on these and related topics, as well as their attendant debates (Skidmore 1993; Andrews 1991; Azevedo 1975; Nogueira 1955; Moura 1988).

Six years before the election of Tancredo Neves as the first civilian president since the military coup of 1964, in a seminal essay on Afro–Latin American politics, Pierre-Michel Fontaine (1980) would write that "standard texts on economics, politics, political economy, or even sometimes sociology tend to ignore the African presence and its implications, in spite of millions of blacks, *morenos* (browns), mulattoes and *zambos* (mixtures of blacks and Indians) in Latin America." Relating Fontaine's analysis specifically to Brazil, the African presence could signify three related but distinct modes of influence that the slave trade had on economic, cultural, and political development. In economic terms, the slave trade's undeniable role in colonial, monarchial, and ultimately republican prosperity has received significant attention from both Brazilian and foreign commentators. Conversely, resistance to the oppressive conditions under enslavement is also well documented in scholarly work, and is often utilized by contemporary black activists as a political signpost for collective action in present-day Brazil. Brazil had the single largest outlaw slave community in the world, the *quilombo* of Palmares (Carneiro 1958), and among the greatest number of outlaw slave societies of any slaveholding system in the hemisphere.

There is a rich literature on the nexus of African Brazilian and national identity. Like many other Latin American nation-states, Brazilian folklore has long subsumed the notion of racial difference under the rubric of national identity, which in itself was part of a regional response to national and racial hierarchies prevalent in the industrialized West (Davis 1966; Stepan 1991). The influences of West African religious practices evident in Brazilian Catholicism and in its syncretic religions—Umbanda, Candomblé, and Afoxe, among others—represent the most visible and coherent constellations of African-derived cosmological systems in the Americas, rivaled only by those in Haiti and Cuba. These practices have shaped virtually everything in Brazilian national culture, from sexual mores, to notions of community, death, and afterlife, to consideration of employment and marriage opportunities (Prandi 1991; Braga 1992).

The widespread influence of West African civilizations on Brazilian society and culture was largely attributed to the relatively easy acceptance by Portuguese colonizers of religions, cuisine, and other cultural practices transmitted by African Brazilian slaves. Such interpretations became the basis of Luso-tropicalism and Gilberto Freyre's conceptualization of "racial democracy." At its core, the myth or ideology of racial democracy was a response to the biologically rooted notions of racial difference and hierarchy that were popular at the turn of the century, which Latin American intellectuals in many countries sought to refute (Viotti 1985). Freyre, like José Vasconcelos of Mexico and José Martí of Cuba, answered Anglo-Saxon claims of Latin American inferiority by emphasizing the culturally—rather than biologically—based origins of "racial" differences and celebrating those differences as a positive feature of national development. Similar to Vasconcelos and Martí as well, Freyre equated miscegenation with the subsequent civic equality of racially distinct groups and the fusion of indigenous, European, and African "races" into a superior, brown-skinned, mulatto nation.

In successfully exposing the pseudo-scientism of Brazilian intellectuals such as Nina Rodrigues, who upheld the Spencerian notion that miscegenation would create a doomed race of mongrels, Freyre identified the contribution of various African Brazilian influences in realms as diverse as mining and sexuality, and encouraged further study. As with any pioneering intellectual figure, Freyre impacted future scholarship on Afro-Braziliana; it either had to assimilate or attempt to refute his thesis of Luso-tropicalism.

Subsequent generations of scholarship focused overwhelmingly on African survivals in Brazilian culture, the syncretic character of Brazilian religious practices, and the emergence of Afro-Brazilian forms of cultural expression, especially in what can be termed the corporal arts (samba, *capoeira,* spirit possession, and ritual dance), as elements of popular culture (Bastide 1978; Verger 1964; Elbein dos Santos and dos Santos, 1984). In both popular and scholarly works inside and outside of Brazil, Freyrean Luso-tropicalism became the ideological cornerstone for a common belief in Brazilian racial exceptionalism: the idea that Brazil, unlike other multiracial polities (Hanchard 1994), was not a land of racial inequalities. The scholarly and political consequences of Freyre's exceptionalist beliefs are encapsulated in the following questions: Why bother to study or presume racial inequality in a place where it is nonexistent? Why should nonwhites struggle for civil rights in a society based on miscegenation and racial egalitarianism?

Much of the literature through the 1940s implicitly responded to such questions by eliding or ignoring them. Concurrently, incidents and writings that challenged the dominant interpretation of Brazilian society as atypical in relation to the United States as well as the rest of the Americas were often met with ridicule and marginalization (Ramos 1957). Indeed, Brazil was considered a laboratory for racial egalitarianism not only by Brazilians, but also by U.S. African Americans and white U.S. scholars who sought to contrast it to the United States (Hellwig 1992). Brazil's self-image as a racially unbiased nation was so pervasive that, by the 1950s, it was known throughout the world as a "racial democracy." The United Nations Educational, Scientific, and Cultural Organization (UNESCO) sponsored a research project on Brazilian race relations in that same decade to determine, among other things, if there were object lessons that the rest of the world could learn, particularly after World War II.

The results of this vast research project, however—which involved several of Brazil's most respected social scientists (Fernandes and Bastide 1959; Cardoso and Ianni 1960), including the nation's current president—exposed racial prejudice in the land of racial democracy, a nation that had produced neither concentration camps nor legally codified segregation. The Brazilian military forcibly closed down the department of sociology at the University of São Paulo during the initial phase of the dictatorship and repressed any public discussion of Brazilian racial politics that placed the country in an unfavorable light. This action effectively postponed scholarly consideration of Brazilian racial dynamics until the return to civilian rule in 1985. At the same time, the Freyrean model was upheld and propagated by the dictatorship and most civilian elites because it was far less threatening, and it emphasized cultural mélange and integration, along with the tracing of familial, racial, and ethnic "roots" or genealogies, rather than sociopolitical conflict or discord.

The intellectual legacy of the São Paulo school of sociology was one in which racial discrimination was recognized as a structural result of capitalist development and slavery. In contrast to Freyre and his adherents, Florestan Fernandes (1969) identified racial inequality in Brazilian society. Fernandes believed that racism, a powerful albeit unacknowledged feature of Brazilian society, was an epiphenomenon of dependent capitalism. As such, it was a transitional phenomenon or intervening variable in the process of capitalist development that would wither away, much like Marx's capitalist state, only with the dismantling of capitalism.

One of Fernandes's key contributions was his examination of the Frente Negra Brasileira, the second black political party in the hemisphere, which existed between 1931 and 1937. Its political life was cut short by the second Getúlio Vargas regime, which outlawed all political parties and organizations based on racial affiliations, presumably in response to rising fascism in western Europe, even though the curtailment of political opposition was the more immediate benefit of this prohibition. Yet the party's raison d'être, advocating racial equality for Afro-Brazilians, persisted long after its demise. Like Palmares, scholars and activists have written about the Frente and its epoch as a lost opportunity for Afro-Brazilian mobilization, and of the possibility of reviving its legacy of organized resistance.

The Frente's history is well documented in studies of São Paulo during the period (Fernandes and Bastide 1959; Andrews 1991), dissertations, and participant testimony (Leite and Cuti 1992). As an organization, it encountered problems inherent in Brazil's political culture of the time, as well as difficulties specific to social movements more generally. The indifference of the Brazilian state and white elites to the demand for equal rights and recognition of racial discrimination against Afro-Brazilians represented the first constraint; ideological differences, limited resources, and an inability to generate a mass-based movement along racial lines constituted the internal paradoxes of the organization.

The implications of the Frente's successes and failures for an examination of Afro-Brazilian politics, however, persist. The major impediment to the nationwide success of the Frente—how does one spawn a movement based not only on a recognition of racial inequality, but also on a common racial identity in a society where there is presumably no such thing?—has been a recurrent theme in both Afro-Brazilian movement politics and Brazilian society as a whole. This is due to the absence, in Brazil, of subjective but nonetheless consistent lines of demarcation separating white, black, mulatto, and numerous other phenotypical classifications (such as Jim Crow, ethnic cantons, or apartheid). In this respect, Brazil is an anomaly in relation to the United States, South Africa, and even so-called plural societies like Trinidad and British Guyana.

By the 1970s, scholars and activists began to openly question not only the racial democracy myth, but the perspectives of the São Paulo school as well. Fernandes himself would ultimately revise his own position on the role of Afro-Brazilian social movements in São Paulo in relation to Brazilian capitalism (1989). What can be characterized as the third generation of race relations literature in Brazil emerged during this period.

Working mostly from census data and quantitative studies, scholars such as Nelson do Valle Silva and Carlos Hasenbalg sought to debunk the racial democracy myth perpetrated by the first wave of scholars of Brazilian race relations, but also to treat racial discrimination as a feature of social life that was materially based and not a secondary phenomenon of another sociological variable, like class, region, or education. For these and other scholars, racism was not an "archaic" ideology summoned on occasions of intergroup conflict, as Fernandes suggested, but an ever-present reality in Brazilian society. It was a significant indicator in assessing levels of education, employment opportunities, health, and even marriage choices. Racism in Brazilian society had been transformed in the transition from slavery to abolition, and complemented the shift from slave to wage labor to effectively "disqualify blacks from objective market competition" (Hasenbalg 1979, 1985).

This research occurred within the context, during the dictatorship, of a reemergence of black movements in Brazil, along with other modes of protest, organization, and mobilization that did not fit into the existing models of political parties, trade unions, and interest groups. Referring to the black movement, Ivanir dos Santos, a nongovernmental advocate for street children and Partido dos Trabalhadores (PT) member, writes in his contribution to this volume that "they are not disorganized, they are just sectors that have a different form of organization." The political and personal experiences of Benedita da Silva, Thereza Santos, and Ivanir dos Santos as black activists in the Brazilian public sphere are testaments to Santos's dictum. Samba schools, churches *terreiros de Candomblé,* and other religious and cultural sites operated as centers for political mobilization (Mitchell 1977; Prandi 1991). With the increasing focus on the nexus of inequality and race in the postdictatorship era, strategic alliances developed in the 1980s between certain Afro-Brazilian movements and scholars working on various topics related to questions of inequality.

Evidence of the difficulties of racial classification reappeared in scholarly debates after 1986, leading several Brazilian and non-Brazilian scholars to maintain, as Nogueira and others did in the 1950s, that the major difference between Brazil and multiracial societies like the United States was that Brazilian society emphasized phenotypic rather than "racial" distinctions. In other words, a mark of color held prominence over a mark of origin. Recent evidence suggests that contemporary students of race must examine neat distinctions between phenotype and race as a means of differentiating Brazil from other multiracial polities.

One of the phenomena related to racial identification in Brazil explored by Charles Wood (1991), Peggy Lovell (1992), and Howard Winant (1994) is the changing content of phenotypical categories. Where earlier in this century *moreno* meant a brown-skinned person, it has now come to mean a white person with brown or brunette hair. Yvonne Maggie (1988) found that both whites and nonwhites rarely refer to *pretos* (black) or *pardos* (brown) as black.

Brazilians prefer to use descriptions that emphasize the numerous, often arbitrary distinctions on the Brazilian color continuum, such as *escurinho* (very dark) or *clarinho* (a little light-skinned), rather than oppositional categories like *branco e preto* or *negro e branco.* These categories are reserved for strangers, people once removed in a social setting. They are never used to refer to friends or those one directly interacts with, for fear of insulting them.

The increase in the number of people in the mulatto and white categories between the 1955 and 1980 census does not indicate the literal "disappearance" of "purely black" peoples in Brazil, but shifts in how people identify themselves and lean toward an identification with whiteness, an attachment to the idea of "being white." Wood's findings imply, among other things, that while the predicates of racial democracy have been rebutted, the steady and increasing turn toward white phenotypic ascription means that the belief in whitening advocated by Gilberto Freyre and other Luso-tropicalists in the 1920s has remained steadfast among Brazilians.

Exchanges such as the one between sociologist Edward Telles, a contributor to this volume, and the anthropologist Marvin Harris, represent distinct methodological and generational perspectives on the salience of color versus race in Brazil. In the journal *Social Forces,* Harris (1993, 1995) reaffirmed his initial argument concerning the salience of *moreno* as a racial identity by conducting a survey in Rio de Contas in northeastern Brazil, thirty-seven years after his previous study there. Harris utilized this data to critique the decision by the Instituto Brasileiro de Geografica Estatistica (IBGE) to discard the *moreno* category in favor of *pardo,* which encompasses mulattoes and *morenos.* Telles (1995) responded in support of the IGBE's decision, due to the ambiguity of the term *moreno* alluded to above, and questioned the applicability of Harris's findings to the rest of Brazil.

At least two points remain unresolved from this and other exchanges about racial identity in Brazil: the degree and variability of racial self-identification, coupled with the demonstrated empirical evidence that *pardos, pretos,* and mulattoes have unequal access to education, health care, employment, housing, and other quality-of-life indexes in Brazil. Moreover, contrary to many popular as well as academic claims, phenotypic self-identification does not operate as a free-floating signifier for Brazilians, but within long-standing parameters of white and black, with qualified but none-theless oppositional meanings attached to both phenotypic cate-gorizations.

Part of the argument about the facets of Brazil's racial dynamics was that the existence of a phenotypical continuum, rather than hypodescent, made it difficult to categorically define "whites" and "blacks" according to skin color (Nogueira 1955). In addition, the purported existence of a "mulatto escape hatch" (Degler 1971) — the thesis that mulattoes, the result of miscegenation, evade the stigma of racial difference and are sociologically better off than their darker-skinned counterparts — made categorization more fluid and ambiguous than in other multiracial polities. A mulatto in one re-gion of Brazil could be white in another region, while a *branco da Bahia* (Bahian white) would not necessarily be considered white in Santa Catarina, a southern state with a largely German population. Further, the attendant ideology of *embranqueamento* (whitening) —whereby social class ascension and/or money could allow dark, clearly nonwhite individuals to "become" white—supposedly re-futed the assertions of a fixed, castelike status for Afro-Brazilians. Internationally known soccer star Pelé, for example, epitomized *embranqueamento* because of his standing as a national hero.

The connection between phenotype and meaning is related to what Harold Hoetink (1967) has referred to as psychosomatic norm images of blackness that trigger negative stereotypes that people act on. As Hoetink argues, negative depictions of darker-skinned African-descended peoples are common to both Iberian and Anglo-American race relations paradigms in Latin America and the Caribbean.

Earlier work by Carlos Hasenbalg and Nelson do Valle Silva (1988) suggests that such comparisons have some validity. After an assessment of quality-of-life indicators such as health, educa-tion, and wage earning based on the 1980 census, they concluded that the differences between blacks and mulattoes are negligible. As Silva (1985) argues, "Mulattoes do not behave differently from Blacks [*sic*], nor does race play a negligible role in the process of income attainment. In fact it was found that Blacks and mulattoes are almost equally discriminated against. . . . This clearly contra-dicts the idea of a 'mulatto escape-hatch' being the essence of Bra-zilian race relations." Hasenbalg and Silva have subsequently used the category nonwhite to include blacks and mulattoes (yellow and undeclared were excluded). While Thomas Skidmore (1985, 20) believes that the escape hatch thesis might be plausible in theory, there is no evidence to suggest that "the person of mixed blood got preferential treatment." Skidmore (1993) and George Reid Andrews (1991) note further that from a comparative viewpoint, Brazil has become more racially polarized since World War II than the United States when one considers demographic statistics along white/nonwhite racial lines.

In response, many Brazilianists have countered that the analysis of scholars such as Skidmore and myself are biased by perspectives on racial conflict developed in the United States, a more bipolar context in which to examine racial dynamics, identity, and inequality than the more culturally hybrid and phenotypically multipolar Brazil. Such claims resonate, to a point. No scholar, I believe, enters the field, conducts interviews, or works in archives without bearing some of the norms and values of both professional and personal experiences. Thus, understandings of race may be just one of many possible normative influences on a study of a society that is not one's own.[1]

Yet the reverse is also true: that norms and values influence the development and sociology of knowledge of scholars working in their own countries. In the 1990s, when such "American" topics like affirmative action, residential segregation, and police violence against black youth are covered and debated in national and local newspapers and at conferences in Brazil, it is clear (at least to me) that such issues are not peculiar to any one nation but symptomatic of societies with racial inequality. It is less important to discern the origin of such topics and debates than to understand why they are occurring in Brazil at the time of this writing. Only through comparative, cross-national research do both similarities and differences, as well as subjective understandings of those similarities and differences, become apparent.

From this perspective, Brazil is not unlike other polities with African-derived populations. Even those with histories of formal apartheid have legacies of miscegenation along with cultural explanations that either condemn or condone the practice, depending on the dominant norms. Even more broadly, such data and interpretations suggest that the use of terms like bipolar and multipolar to categorize multiracial societies often obscures common features between the two; distinctions between race and color, intermarriage, racial violence; and other phenomena. Conversely, differences between societies are exaggerated as the terms become explanatory variables, rather than reflections of actually existing societies that require scholarly investigation and explanation. As Skidmore (1993) has remarked, for example, the increasing Latino population in the United States since the 1960s has meant that there are demographically significant sectors of the U.S. population that do not fit into white or black categories, rendering the biracial definition of racial classification there less valid.

Undoubtedly, the research of sociologists into the demographic indicators of racial inequality in the 1980s has become the "material" basis for most subsequent examinations, both interpretive and quantitative. While the identification of socioeconomic and other forms of racial inequality provide empirical evidence of racial discrimination in Brazil, the recognition of inequality, by itself, tells us little about people's reaction to it. In one of the few review essays concerning research into Afro–Latin America, Fontaine (1980) noted that Afro-Brazilian studies literature does not "deal with political institutions, behavior or attitudes, or with elections, electoral behavior, or political parties, or even public policy." Missing from the emerging portrait are scholarly accounts of Afro-Brazilian agency in contemporary national life in response to the varied material, symbolic, and cultural forms of racial inequality and identification, though recent contributions by Robin Sherriff (1994), Francine Winddance Twine (1996), and Denise Ferreira da Silva (1989, 1992) help.

This blank space is not necessarily attributable to inherent shortcomings in one quantitative approach or another. Rather, it reflects a need for the complementary development of scholarship on the consequences of racial inequality for white and nonwhite Brazilians alike, and its effect on group and national consciousness as an impetus or impediment to collective action. In calling for a comprehensive political economy approach to the study of Afro–Latin America, Fontaine (1980, 132–33) asserted "a need to explore the notion of power in the relation between the races, the relation between ethnicity and race . . . the very meaning of race in an officially assimilationist society, the dominant Brazilian vision of blackness,

Africa, and Africanity, and the socioeconomic and political implications thereof."

One might also add to Fontaine's proscriptive insights the necessity of understanding the cultural, normative, and gendered implications of these power dynamics as they help structure the lives and experiences of Afro-Brazilians. The need for more wide-ranging, interdisciplinary work as well as monograph studies into the implications of racial inequalities remains a challenge for students of Brazil. Interpretive analyses have not kept pace with the development of quantitative (largely demographic) approaches to racial inequality. One indication of this is that the very first nationally based survey on racial attitudes and behavior, conducted in 1996, was undertaken by the research organ of the *Folha de São Paulo* newspaper.

NEW TRENDS

Unlike the regional studies literatures of Southeast Asia, eastern and western Europe, and Africa, Latin American studies as a whole has only recently utilized interdisciplinary, comparative, and more theoretically innovative approaches to investigate racial dynamics. Since the mid-1980s, there has been a resurgence in scholarship on Afro-Latin or Afro–New World populations, done mainly by scholars of race relations and national identity (Helg 1995; Wade 1993; Wright 1990; Hale 1994). With varying degrees of success and investment in theoretical innovation, such works reflect the attempts of scholars to broaden the purview of race in Latin America by developing a race-centered focus in their analysis. It is too early to gauge the impact such work will have on race relations research, but there are younger scholars in early stages of their research who are employing more interpretive approaches in an effort to explain the multiple significances of "hard" indicators of inequality.

As the above review of recent literature indicates, the politics of racial difference in Brazil permeates most facets of social life. Thus, while more regionally and nationally focused analysis of the mechanisms of discrimination and inequality in such traditionally studied areas as residential segregation and labor market segmentation is necessary, research into the everyday forms of racial discrimination that influence issues such as socialization, self-esteem, and personal identity is crucial. In this respect, Brazil may be one of the most understudied multiracial polities in terms of everyday racism, given the plethora of literature on Afro-Brazilian culture. For this reason alone, given the manifold ways in which such politics informs institutional and personal practices, conscious and unconscious behavior, the limitations of the race versus class debates within Brazil (or anywhere else) should be quite apparent. Within this literature, there needs to be a greater linkage of empirical and quantitative analysis of racial dynamics, and more interpretive work of race and racial difference, not only in Brazil, but in comparative perspective as well.

Nineteen-eighty-eight was a significant year for the Brazilian republic, Afro-Brazilian activists, and Afro-Brazilian studies. It marked the centennial of the abolition of slavery in Brazil, the year of the first civilian constitution since the dictatorship, and the first time ever in the Brazilian republic that racism was categorized as a constitutional crime punishable by imprisonment. After a year-long national consideration of the ongoing histories of racially motivated violence against nonwhite street children, the treatment of Afro-Brazilian women (mulattas and *negras*) as objects of domestic and sexual labor, wage discrepancies between whites and nonwhites of similar occupational status, and the daily indignities experienced by people on the basis of their color, Brazil no longer appeared dissimilar from other polities with African-derived populations. Brazil could no longer be preserved in a glass case with the words "special status" among multiracial polities inscribed.

Brazilian President Fernando Henrique Cardoso's (1994) acknowledgment of the need for state activity around and recognition of racial inequality punctuated the resonance of 1988 in subsequent national politics; racism and Afro-Brazilians pursuit of civil rights remained topics of national concern. The quincentennial celebration of Zumbi of Palmares, as well as an international conference on affirmative action in 1996, provided further proof of the increasing saliency of race issues at the century's end. Cardoso— a former student of Fernandes who, with Octavio Ianni (1960), authored an important study on racial attitudes and behavior in Florianopolis—not only made explicit references to Afro-Brazilian social inequalities, but also appointed Pelé and several other noted

Afro-Brazilians affiliated with the *movimento negro* to government positions.

The renewed attention to race at the state level can be viewed, in part, within the broader context of a *global* shift in the paradigms of race and ethnicity, which necessitates that a comparative perspective be imposed on the racial realities of Brazil. In the Americas, for example, indigenous peoples have found it politically expedient to forge coalitions among themselves, turning *indio,* once a pejorative term, into an organizing principle for various indigenous groups. Like Afro-Brazilians (as well as other Afro–Latino Americans), previously "ethnic" indigenous groups are now situating themselves within a transnational community outside the conventional boundaries of the territorial nation. In Ecuador, Guatemala, Peru, and elsewhere, indigenous activists utilize a language of pan-ethnicity vis-à-vis the state and *ladinos* in general (Hale 1994). These phenomena suggest heightened racial consciousness between indigenous peoples, contrary to earlier discussions of diffuse racial differences in the region (Eckstein 1989) or fugitive ethnicities (Young 1976).

As the contributors to this volume attest to, contemporary racial dynamics inform questions of personal, collective, as well as national identity; the distribution of resources and services; and the very manner in which Brazilians conceive and act on their Brazilianness. While not losing sight of their historical antecedents, the stress on the contemporary nature of these problems also points to the shift from paradigms that emphasize the more anthropological dimensions of racial interactions and the African (or, for that matter, European) survivals amid New World culture in Brazil, to ones that focus on inequality and collective identity as it relates to political action by a specific social group.

The myriad forms that the dynamics of racial inequality assume lead us to the a priori need for interdisciplinary perspectives, if not approaches that, when assembled together, these articles attempt to provide. For a subject like Brazilian racial politics, this approach is not new; while it ascribes to some contemporary notion of traversing disciplinary boundaries, it also recognizes the long-standing, transcendent character of Brazilian, Latin American, and regional studies more generally. At a moment in the U.S. academy when area studies have come under withering attack, it is important to reemphasize that contributions such as this book have potential repercussions far beyond their immediate objects of analysis—to places, theorems, and paradigms quite unlike themselves.

THE CONTRIBUTIONS

Taken together, the essays in this volume place contemporary racial politics in Brazil in regional, national, and cross-national contexts. Richard Graham's article opens this book with a look at current debates in light of the past. Graham notes that most Afro-Brazilians were free *before* abolition, a point lost on many scholars of Brazilian history and slavery. In documenting the manner in which black and brown Brazilians were discriminated against before abolition in 1888, Graham complicates a facile line of demarcation between slavery and freedom. The interactions between African- and Brazilian-born slaves, as well as between the manumitted and the enslaved, provide a glimpse of the differential treatment accorded to Brazilians of African descent, and how distinct groups among this population were perceived and treated by the Brazilian elite, who encoded their beliefs into law and societal practice to ensure that these populations could not garner political power and threaten the existing social order. In other words, the shift from slave to wage labor after 1888 was not the only moment in the history of the Brazilian nation when either the municipal or national government utilized race as a device to distribute resources, rights, and when necessary, coercion. Graham's opening essay lends insight into the evolving and shifting relationships between racial difference, the state, and social class in both monarchal and republican Brazil.

My contribution, "Black Cinderella? Race and the Public Sphere in Brazil," seizes some of the history of racial prejudice and discrimination in Brazil with a comparative analysis of racial inequality in Latin America. Long considered an exception to national race relations patterns in the region, I suggest that Brazil is, in many ways, similar to other multiracial societies in the hemisphere. The example of race-related violence is used to underscore the ways in which that country's public sphere is both unmistakably Brazilian with distinct patterns of racial prejudice and consciousness, while also similar, in some respects at least, to its purported opposite to the North: the United States.

Edward Telles's article on residential segregation in present-day Brazil is an example of another understudied theme (segregation) that is, itself, the outgrowth of broader patterns of inequality. Not only does he uncover the existence of white/nonwhite segregation, but higher rates of residential segregation between blacks and browns than between blacks and whites as well. For Telles, residential segregation is another impediment to the racial mobilization of blacks and browns, in addition to the ideology of racial democracy and whitening. At the same time, however, Telles suggests that in cities like Rio de Janeiro and Belo Horizonte, where segregation increases with income, racial awareness may increase among blacks and browns as a result of structured residential segregation.

Telles adds to research by Raquel Rolnik (1989) in showing that neighborhoods and communities are also bounded by racial difference, contrary to earlier works that emphasized the inability of scholars to identify neighborhoods by race (with the exception of upper-class areas), particularly among the urban poor. The interrelationship of race, residential segregation, and political power can be linked to broader ruminations on the politics and production of space in political and social theory, and the role of subaltern groups in dominant social spaces (Lefebvre 1991; Virilio 1977). Afro-Brazilians clearly can be considered in light of this literature, as locales like Alto das Pombas in Salvador, Bahia, Bixiga in the city of São Paulo, and Zona Norte in Rio de Janeiro all bear the mark of subaltern communities of people who have made a formerly exclusive or uninhabited space their own. As in other multiracial societies, racial prejudice and discrimination has spatial and territorial dimensions in Brazil as well. The connections between race, otherness, and spatial distance are evident in the literal English translation of the title of Gilberto Freyre's classic text, *Casa Grande e Senzala* (1946). Rather than *The Masters and the Slaves*, as the book is entitled in English, it actually translates as *Big House and Shanty.*

Telles's ideas are an interesting juxtaposition against the contribution of Howard Winant. Like Telles, Winant is concerned with the politics and parameters of racial identity, but in a decidedly interpretive, poststructuralist vein. Winant echoes one of the wider aims of the conference and volume in terms of the need to bring theoretical innovations to bear on the new racial politics and dynamics of Brazil. In his comparative analysis, Winant argues that in both the United States and Brazil, the denial of democracy was racially based. He utilizes this claim to develop the notion that there are increasing similarities between the two countries, which have always been considered leagues apart in terms of their racial dilemmas, though this has in no way inhibited endless comparisons between the two. Winant also suggests that the "color line" in the United States has been deeply eroded by a growing "multiculturalism," so that it now appears closer to the earlier Brazilian self-image of a pluralist society than a dichotomous one.

This is fairly contentious in the face of the timeworn tendency to view Brazilian-U.S. race relations as a study of static opposites, with all fluidity belonging to the former and rigidity to the latter, a tendency repeated often by contemporary observers (Sansone 1996). This assertion echoes Winant's more general theoretical thrust in the area of racial theory: that the United States has neither a monopoly on nor is a template for racial inequality within the hemisphere. As the first postcolonial region of the world, all former colonies within the hemisphere exhibit variations on certain dynamics, processes, and patterns that, in turn, interact with other forces and variables in the society and region.

This is exemplified as well in the Foucauldian analysis of Michael Mitchell, who in his reflections on the Brazilian intellectual Miguel Reale, links elite preoccupation with modernity and modernization to matters of race. Mitchell notes how neatly the discourses of Brazilian racism and conservative modernization fit, a point often overlooked in discussions of Brazilian racial politics. Equations of whiteness with civilization and technological advancement, and blackness with backwardness and waste, have some of their roots in the Brazilian context of Reale's writings. The denigration of Afro-Brazilians as productive members of society is deeply informed by the desire to mold Brazil into the image of a European nation; as described by Reale, Afro-Brazilians were the antithesis of modernity and, hence, impediments to prospects for Brazilian modernization. It was no accident, then, for Mitchell that Reale's treatises on race and modernity were well received by Brazilian elites, particularly those in the military after 1964, who consulted with

Reale on matters of public policy. Reminiscent of Emilia da Costa Viotti's dictum (1985, 238) that "in order to explain people's perceptions of racial patterns one would have to look outside the narrow frame of race relations," Mitchell's analysis suggests that ideas about racial difference in Brazil are profoundly influenced by ideas about modernity itself. Here, Mitchell's mode of reasoning mirrors other works on Brazil and Latin America more broadly, as debates about sexuality, mental health, and physical hygiene were all constructed, in one form or another, in racial terms (Stepan 1991; Chalhoub 1996).

The manner in which the politics of racial difference cuts across many social dynamics is presented with no greater clarity than in Peggy Lovell's demographic reading of income earnings for white and nonwhite women. Lovell's findings, based on analysis of census and other data, provide stark evidence of continued earning inequality for black women. Though black women made absolute gains in terms of earned income between 1960 and 1980, they lagged behind white women. Once again, the importance of the "whitening ideal" appears to be its objective material advantage for whites vis-à-vis nonwhite groups, rather than any benefit for those who are not viewed as white but may aspire to be so.

Her results represent a structural basis for understanding the distinct axes of inequality that separate the black women's movement from white feminists. In the words of Sueli Carneiro, an activist in São Paulo, the black women's movement is at the intersection of the women's movement and the *movimento negro*. The conjunction of race and gender issues has necessitated dual strategies for Afro-Brazilian women activists. With the emergence of Afro-Brazilian women's groups across the country, such as Geledes in São Paulo and Agbara Dudu in Rio de Janeiro, this underexamined dimension of the *movimento negro* warrants further study.

Carlos Hasenbalg, who has long called for renewed research and expanded focus on Brazilian race relations, makes an important contribution to this volume with coauthor Nelson do Valle Silva by pointing toward particular avenues of investigation into the process and nature of racial inequality in Brazil, going well beyond the more conventional quantitative analysis of quality-of-life indicators. For example, they highlight civil rights and treatment by police as areas pertinent to new democracy issues.

Hasenbalg and Silva's essay also compares the Afro-Brazilian social movements of the 1930s with their 1970s' counterparts to assess their success, respectively, at mass mobilization. The variations in political regimes along with ideological shifts in the black movement, according to Hasenbalg and Silva, account for the different success levels of mass mobilization between the two periods. At the same time, a fundamental problem is exposed in studying Afro-Brazilian social movements: the virtually complete absence of studies of political attitudes and behavior with respect to race. Hasenbalg and Silva state that Afro-Brazilian activism as well as elite- and state-generated responses to such activism have remained within a fairly restrictive circle of elite discourse, rather than being part of a fuller spectrum of popular exchange and debate. As the coauthors note, "We know much more about what the elite think about these items, whether they be white or black, than we know about the general public."

The relationship between political elites and masses has been a source of curiosity for as long as men and women have analyzed and participated in politics. The complexities of this relationship were manifested in the Afro-Brazilian movements of the 1970s and 1980s by the emergence and formation of an Afro-Brazilian political elite from the confines of academic and quasi-academic research centers, and not from the favela or other locale of Afro-Brazilian community (Hanchard 1994). As a consequence, it is difficult to discern the extent of congruence between Afro-Brazilian activists and their "constituents" in the same way that other racially based social movements with high levels of constituency support have had obvious conjunctions of activist and constituent interests (McAdam 1981; Morris 1984). Hasenbalg and Silva's call for increased studies of the nexus of race and political behavior, then, is prescriptive. Future studies could provide us with greater knowledge about how Brazilians think about elections, both in terms of voting patterns and campaign rhetoric, and racial difference.

The implications of the role of racial difference in electoral campaigns were exemplified in Benedita da Silva's unsuccessful race for mayor of Rio de Janeiro in 1992. The explicit discussion of racial discrimination during the campaign—and the equation in the mass media of social disorder, violence, and street crime with a victory by da Silva (Tavares 1992)—reveal the way in which Afro-

Brazilians are portrayed as criminal elements or, in da Silva's case, a bearer of disorder.

The Afro-Brazilian activists and politicians present at the conference have directly experienced and acted on the intertwined, but often conflictual relationship between the *movimento negro brasileiro* and party politics, between a politics of culturalism and cultural politics. Most important, they can shed light on a political process generally alluded to, but rarely detailed in the literature on Brazilian racial interactions—that is, the process and prospects of Afro-Brazilian political mobilization.

As conference participants, Benedita da Silva, Thereza Santos, and Ivanir dos Santos provided insights into the more quotidian aspects of racial politics in Brazil, insights with profound political and theoretical implications. Poverty, racial discrimination, gender, community, and family were the building blocks for their racial identities, as evidenced in their participation in conference discussions and contributions to this volume.

In addition to the interventions noted above, da Silva's article addresses a recurrent tension within Afro-Brazilian politics, what she characterizes as issues of identity versus political claims and strategies, and the limitations of social movement and political party politics for Afro-Brazilians.

In the same vein, Thereza Santos, a cultural activist in São Paulo, attests to the need for autonomy within Afro-Brazilian politics. Historically, her position is a reiteration of the claims of the Frentistas of the 1930s as well as the founders of the Movimento Negro Unificado in 1978. Her contribution also discusses the internalization of beliefs of racial and gendered inferiority crucial to the reproduction and maintenance of racial hegemony.

Ivanir dos Santos—a PT militant, coordinator of da Silva's mayoral campaign, and a leading activist within the movement to protect the rights of Brazil's street children—points to the workings of intraparty politics around racial issues as a microcosm of racial politics writ large. The PT was the first political party in Brazil to formally create a black nucleus. This was in recognition of the dual role played by Afro-Brazilian *petistas,* as well as the grudging acceptance of a nondeterministic view of social and economic relationships in a multiracial polity like Brazil. Indeed, the impact of Afro-Brazilian activists within political parties in changing platforms on racial matters still goes unrecognized within the accounts of political party development and transformation in the postdictatorship era (Stepan 1989).

The activities of Benedita da Silva as a *favelada* and community organizer, Ivanir dos Santos as an advocate for the rights of street children, and Thereza Santos as a cultural activist and creator of projects for the formation of black consciousness all indicate the multiple axes of political mobilization as an outgrowth of manifold forms of social inequality.

Each activist's narrative gives evidence of individuals who have surmounted incredible odds to become leading figures in Afro-Brazilian politics, political parties, governmental institutions, and in da Silva's career, national politics as well. Yet their accounts provide us with much more, I believe, because of their insights into the difficulties, successes, and failures of the black movement in placing their concerns in national debate and political platforms. Readers will obtain a glimpse of how Afro-Brazilian activists assume multiple roles in their activism and daily life that reflect not only their positions as blacks in Brazil, but as women, feminists, workers, politicians, and a panoply of other social identities.

Most scholarly work inside and outside Brazil has yet to acknowledge the influence of black activists in pro-democracy social movements, or how the agendas of black activists have helped transform party and labor politics. Afro-Brazilian activism during and after the dictatorship remains largely understudied by students of Brazilian or Latin American social movements, democratic transitions, political identity, or cultural politics. Unfortunately, this situation is not new for the study of the relationship between racial difference and democracy in Brazil.

A chasm exists between students of racial difference, racism, and racial inequality in Latin America and those who study other phenomena in the region, even though many questions that apply to oppositional political parties and social formations in Brazil after the dictatorship would apply to the *movimento negro*. Parties such as the PT have had to reformulate their arguments about the role of the state and the primacy of class struggle in the face of mounting evidence of state- and economy-generated racial inequality in Brazil.

Questions concerning the fate of social movements in the transformation from antidemocratic to pro-democratic rule, or correlations between the role of racial difference in the disintegration or encouragement of democratic reforms, could be posed in an examination of Afro-Brazilian social movements and their relation to the Brazilian state and civil society. Such questions, however, will remain unanswered as long as an intellectual division of labor persists between scholars who research issues of race and those who either ignore or dismiss the subject altogether in pursuit of seemingly "broader" phenomena.

Perhaps most important, readers of these personal accounts can explore an internal debate within various segments of the black movement that rarely finds its way into either scholarly or party documents; namely, the role of the Brazilian Left itself in impeding the discussion of racism, as witnessed by these individuals in their party-related activities both during and after the dictatorship. While there has been discussion of discriminatory practices in labor markets, mating and courtship, the distribution of state violence, and various other aspects of Brazilian life, there has been little scholarly consideration of the impact of racism on the Brazilian Left. This history, and the struggles of activists to alter it, is recounted most explicitly in the personal testimony of Thereza Santos, but it is present in both dos Santos and da Silva's contributions as well.

It should be obvious by now that the struggles and experiences of these activists are crucial for a fuller, more complex understanding of the relationship between the Brazilian state and Brazilian society, between theories of democracy and citizenship and their use and application by real people. In Brazil, like most former slaveholding societies, citizenship and public rights have been structured as much by racial or gendered difference as they have been by legal covenant. For this reason, the struggles of Afro-Brazilians in the most recent democratic epoch are key barometers for economic and political democracy in Brazil. Similar to other multiracial polities, this fight for racial equality is inextricably linked to the fate of Brazilian democracy for people of all colors.

Collectively, the contributions of these activists provide a sense of Afro-Brazilian identities and mobilization that cannot be surmised by survey data. This is not to suggest that survey data on race in Brazil are unimportant, but to reemphasize the need for increased qualitative work to correspond with the proliferation of quantitative data on racial inequality in Brazil. It is also to call attention to the need for dialogue between activists and academicians to understand the distance between academic and political debate. As noted earlier, the scholarly "findings" of racial inequality in the 1980s and 1990s would be inconceivable without a prior identification of its sources by activists and scholars in the 1970s and before.

Hopefully, this book will provide the backdrop for further reflection and inquiry into Brazil's special status as a multiracial polity, not only among conference participants, but also for students and scholars in general. In this sense, this is a continuation of the efforts of other students of Brazil, like Pierre-Michel Fontaine (1985) and Randal Johnson (1984), who have also used conference forums to address issues of race, politics, and culture in Brazilian life.

Although Brazil's racial dynamics may be unique, most societies and political systems have certain patterns, peculiarities, and idiosyncrasies that distinguish them from other nation-states. The allegedly more subtle brand of Brazilian racism speaks to the idiosyncrasies of the Brazilian case, not the absence of racism itself or the lack of more violent, overt forms of discrimination and prejudice. In short, it is the degree and combination of race-related phenomena that distinguish Brazil and other similarly constituted polities from each other. While the derogation of blackness can be found in numerous societies, it manifests itself differently in each context.

Dialogue between Brazilian and U.S. scholars, and more crucially, between Brazilian activists and Brazilian scholars, could lead to the development of scholarship that broadens our perspective on the problematics of race in contemporary Brazil. Moreover, it could help fuse theory, strategy, and practice in affecting social and political change in a society that has long been considered a racial paradise, and that is only now being confronted with a racial reality that does conform to its national self-image.

NOTES

1   Unfortunately, charges and countercharges of American or Brazilian influence and biases in the study of racial and national identity in Brazil

have rarely been viewed within the broader context of the intricacies of outsider/insider status among foreign- and native-born commentators in the Americas. João José Reis (1993) and others have provided insightful analysis on the role that Brazil has played within the U.S. scholarly imagination as both laboratory for race relations and antidote to the apartheid of the pre–civil rights United States. Brazilian and United States scholars have written historical interpretations of the social, material, and cultural conditions of racial slavery in Brazil, and have examined the comparative implications of such conditions with great care. At the same time, however, it should be remembered that some of the best commentaries on racial and social inequalities in the United States have been written by foreigners residing in and/or traveling through that country; for instance, Alexis de Tocqueville's *Democracy in America,* Gunnar Myrdal's *An American Dilemma* or José Martí's numerous essays on the United States, "Coney Island" being perhaps the most incisive.

In thinking about this comparatively, the more important consideration here is the cultural construction of "truths" concerning a particular nation-state, region, or topic, and the function that such constructed truths perform in the arguments of defenders and detractors alike. Why have Myrdal's or Tocqueville's claims about the limitations of U.S. liberalism and republicanism with respect to race been largely seen as tangential, rather than central to the construction and evolution of U.S. notions of democracy by many U.S. commentators? Why were Martí's writings labeled scandalous by the U.S. state and the Spanish crown when they were composed in the language of late-nineteenth-century liberal nationalism? Thus, while the outsider/insider status of a particular author or commentator would seem to be a secondary, even superficial consideration, the determination of outsider/insider status by national intellectuals is a significant factor in an examination of who gets to subject the nation to criticism and who does not. Against this backdrop, the vehicle of critique (the outsider) becomes inseparable from the content or nature of the criticism itself, and provides a justification for dismissal. Charges and countercharges between the United States and the Soviet Union during the Cold War generally followed such logic, as accusations of state totalitarianism levied by the former against the latter were often met with retorts about the existence of racial domination, amounting to a rhetorical nullification of the respective antagonist's claims without acknowledgement, admission, or rectification of the charges themselves.

REFERENCES

Andrews, G. R. 1991. *Blacks and Whites in São Paulo, Brazil, 1888–1988.* Madison: University of Wisconsin Press.

Azevedo, T. d. 1975. *Democracia Racial: Ideología é Realidade.* Petropolis, Brazil: Editora Vozes.

Bastide, R. 1978. *The African Religions of Brazil: Toward a Sociology of the Interpenetration of Civilizations.* Baltimore, Md.: Johns Hopkins University Press.

Bastide, R., and F. Fernandes. 1959. *Brancos e Negros em São Paulo.* São Paulo: Companhia Editora Nacional.

Braga, J. 1992. Candomblé: Força e resistência. *Afro-Asia* (Bahia), no. 15: 13–17.

Cardoso, F. H. 1994. *Maos A Obra Brasil: Proposta de Governo,* 238–40. Brasília: s:s.ed.

Cardoso, F. H., and O. Ianni. 1960. *Cor e mobilidade social em Floriánópolis: Aspectos das Relações entre negros e brancos numa Comunidade do Brasil Meridional.* São Paulo: Companhia Editora Nacional.

Carneiro, E. 1958. *O Quilombo dos Palmares.* 2d ed. São Paulo: Companhia Editora Nacional.

Chalhoub, S. 1996. *Cidade Febril: Cortiços e Epidemias na Corte Imperial.* São Paulo: Companhia das Letras.

Davis, H. E. 1966. *Latin American Social Thought: The History of Its Development since Independence, with Selected Readings.* Washington, D.C.: University Press of Washington.

Degler, C. N. 1971. *Neither Black nor White: Slavery and Race Relations in Brazil and the United States.* New York: Macmillan.

Eckstein, S. 1989. *Power and Popular Protest: Latin American Social Movements.* Berkeley: University of California Press.

Elbein dos Santos, J., and D. M. dos Santos. 1984. Religion and Black Culture. In *Africa in Latin America,* ed. M. M. Fraginals. New York: Holmes and Meir.

Fernandes, F. 1969. *The Negro in Brazilian Society.* New York: Columbia University Press.

———. 1989. *Significado do Protesto Negro.* Vol. 33, *Coleção polemicas do nosso tempo.* São Paulo: Autores Associados.

Ferreira da Silva, D. 1989. Revisitando a "Democracia Racial": Raça é Identidade Nacional no Pensamento Brasileiro. *Estudos Afro-Asiáticos* (Rio de Janeiro: Conjunto Universitario Candido Mendes) 16 (March): 157–70.

Ferreira da Silva, D., and M. Lima. 1992. Raça, Género e Mercado de

Trabalho. *Estudos Afro-Asiáticos* (Rio de Janeiro: Conjunto Universitario Candido Mendes), no. 23 (December): 97–112.

Fontaine, P.-M. 1980. Research in the Political Economy of Afro-Latin America. *Latin American Research Review* 15, no. 2: 111–42.

———, ed. 1985. *Race, Class, and Power in Brazil.* Los Angeles: University of California, Los Angeles, Center for Afro-American Studies.

Freyre, G. 1946. *The Masters and the Slaves.* New York: Alfred A. Knopf.

Hale, C., Jr. 1994. *Resistance and Contradiction: Miskitu Indians and the Nicaraguan State, 1894–1987.* Stanford, Calif.: Stanford University Press.

Hanchard, M. 1994. *Orpheus and Power: The Movimento Negro of Rio de Janeiro and São Paulo, Brazil, 1945–1988.* Princeton, N.J.: Princeton University Press.

Harris, M., J. G. Consorte, J. Lang, and B. Byrne. 1993. Who are the Whites? Imposed Census Categories and the Racial Demography of Brazil. *Social Forces* 72, no. 2 (December): 451–62.

———. 1995. A Reply to Telles—Who are the Morenas? *Social Forces* 73, no. 4: 1613.

Hasenbalg, C. A. 1979. *Discriminação e Desigualdades Raciais no Brasil.* Rio de Janeiro: Graal.

———. 1985. Race and Socioeconomic Inequalities in Brazil. In *Race, Class, and Power in Brazil,* ed. P.-M. Fontaine, 25–41. Los Angeles: University of California, Los Angeles, Center for Afro-American Studies.

Hasenbalg, C., and N. d. V. Silva. 1988. *Estructura Social, Mobilidade e Raça.* São Paulo: Vertice e IUPERJ.

Helg, A. 1995. *Our Rightful Share: The Afro-Cuban Struggle for Equality, 1886–1912.* Chapel Hill: University of North Carolina Press.

Hellwig, D. 1992. *African-American Reflections on Brazil's Racial Paradise.* Philadelphia, Pa.: Temple University Press.

Hoetink, H. 1967. *Caribbean Race Relations: A Study of Two Variants.* London: Oxford University Press.

Johnson, R. 1984. *Cinema Novo.* Austin: University of Texas Press.

Lefebvre, H. 1991. *The Production of Space.* Cambridge, Mass.: Blackwell.

Leite, J. C., and Cuti. 1992. *E disse o velho militante José Correia.* São Paulo: Seçretaria Municipal de Cultura.

Lovell, P. A. 1992. Development and Racial Inequality in Brazil: Wage Discrimination in Urban Labor Markets, 1960–1980. Paper presented at the Peopling of the Americas Conference, Veracruz, Mexico.

Maggie, Y. 1988. O que se cala quando se fala do negro no Brasil. Mimeo, June.

Martí, José. 1975. "Two Views of Coney Island." In *Inside the Monster: Writings on the United States and American Imperialism.* Trans. Elinor Randall. Ed. Philip S. Foner. New York: Monthly Review Press.

McAdam, D. 1981. *Political Process and the Development of Black Insurgency, 1930–1970.* Chicago, Ill.: University of Chicago Press.

Mitchell, M. 1977. Racial Consciousness and the Political Attitudes and Behavior of Blacks in São Paulo, Brazil. Ph.D. diss., University of Michigan.

Morris, A. 1984. *The Origins of the Civil Rights Movement.* New York: Free Press.

Moura, C. 1988. *Sociologa do Negro Brasiliero.* São Paulo: Atica.

Myrdal, G. 1962. *An American Dilemma: The Negro Problem and Modern Democracy.* New York: Harper and Row.

Nogueira, O. 1955. Preconceito de Marca e preconceito racial de origem. In *Anais do XXXI Congresso Internacional de Americanistas,* 409–34. São Paulo: Editors Anhembi.

Prandi, R. 1991. *Os candomblés de São Paulo.* São Paulo: Editora HUCI-TEC.

Ramos, G. 1957. *Introdução Crítica a Sociedade Brasileira.* Rio de Janeiro: Editora Andes.

Reis, J. J. 1993. *Slave Rebellion in Brazil: The Muslim Uprising of 1835 in Bahia.* Trans. A. Brahel. Baltimore, Md.: Johns Hopkins University Press.

Rolnik, R. 1989. Territorios negros nas cidades brasileiras (Ethnicidade e cidade em São Paulo e no Rio de Janeiro). *Estudos Afro-Asiáticos* (Rio de Janeiro: Conjunto Universitario Candido Mendes), no. 17: 29–41.

Sansone, L. 1996. As Relações Raciais em *Casa-Grande and Senzala* Revisitadas à Luz do Processo de Internacionalização e Globalização. In *Raça, Ciência e Sociedade,* ed. M. C. Maio and R. V. Santos. Rio de Janeiro: Editora Fiocruz.

Sherriff, R. 1994. *Woman/Slave/Saint: A Parable of Race, Resistance, and Resignation from Rio de Janeiro.* Unpublished manuscript. Nucleo da Cor, IFCS, UFRJ.

Silva, N. d. V. 1985. Updating the Cost of Not Being White in Brazil. In *Race, Class, and Power in Brazil,* ed. P.-M. Fontaine. Los Angeles: University of California, Los Angeles, Center for Afro-American Studies.

Skidmore, T. E. 1985. Race and Class in Brazil: Historical Perspectives. In *Race, Class, and Power in Brazil,* ed. P.-M. Fontaine. Los Angeles: University of California, Los Angeles, Center for Afro-American Studies.

———. 1993. Race Relations in Brazil. *Camões Center Quarterly* 4, no. 3–4: 49–61.

Stepan, A., ed. 1989. *Democratizing Brazil: Problems of Transition and Consolidation.* New York: Oxford University Press.

Stepan, N. L. 1991. *The Hour of Eugenics.* Ithaca, N.Y.: Cornell University Press.

Tavares, R. 1992. Black Candidate, White Fear: The Rio Mayoral Election and the Media. *Network Contato* 5 (Washington, D.C.: Brazil Network), nos. 7–8 (30 November): 1–4.

Telles, E. 1995. Who are the Morenas? *Social Forces* 73, no. 4: 1609.

Tocqueville, A. d. 1990. *Democracy in America*. New York: Vintage Books.

Twine, F. W. 1996. O Hiato de Género nas Perçepcões de Racismo: O Caso Dos Afro-Brasileiros Socialmente Ascendentes. *Estudos Afro-Asiáticos* (Rio de Janeiro: Conjunto Universitario Candido Mendes), no. 29 (March): 37–56.

Viotti de Costa, E. 1985. *The Brazilian Empire: Myths and Histories*. Chicago, Ill.: University of Chicago Press.

Virilio, P. 1977. *Speed and Politics*. New York: Semio(text).

Wade, P. 1993. *Blackness and Race Mixture: The Dynamics of Racial Identity in Colombia*. Baltimore, Md.: Johns Hopkins University Press.

Winant, H. 1994. *Racial Conditions: Theories, Politics, and Comparisons*. Minneapolis: University of Minnesota Press.

Wood, C. 1991. Categorias censitarias é classificaçãos subjectivas de paca no Brasil. In *Desigualdade Racial no Brasil Contemporãneo*, ed. P. A. Lovell. Horizonte, Brazil: MGSP Editores.

Wright, W. R. 1990. *Café con Leche: Race, Class, and National Image in Venezuela*. Austin: University of Texas Press.

Young, C. 1976. *The Politics of Cultural Pluralism*. Madison: University of Wisconsin Press.

Richard Graham

FREE AFRICAN BRAZILIANS

AND THE STATE IN SLAVERY TIMES

Most African Brazilians today are poor and most of the poor in
Brazil are African Brazilians (Hasenbalg 1985; Soares and Silva 1987;
Lovell Webster 1987).[1] There is an active debate in Brazil over how
to explain this situation. On the one side are those who say that
the plight of African Brazilians does not derive from racial prejudice but from poverty. They point to the fact that slavery existed
in Brazil until just over 100 years ago and that there are still people
alive who knew former slaves; they conclude that a century is too
short a time for the descendants of slaves to have emerged from
poverty, no matter how accepting or racially unprejudiced the rest
of society may be. The contrary view is that a century is long
enough for much more social mobility to have occurred than is
evident and that racial discrimination is the only persuasive explanation. Discrimination does not result from poverty, it is argued;
rather, poverty stems from discrimination. There are also some defenders of Brazilian exceptionalism who agree with this last position, but insist that at least in Brazil, the state does not share in the
blame for the plight of African Brazilians; that although it maintained slavery far too long, the Brazilian state has not, unlike government institutions in the United States, formally discriminated
against free African Brazilians.[2]

What all sides in this debate forget is that African Brazilians have
been free for much longer than one century. Attitudes and behavior patterns toward free men and women of color were built up
over centuries and had sunk deep roots well before the abolition
of slavery. Moreover, in preserving and building prejudice toward

free African Brazilians, the state always played an important and pervasive role. Present-day cultural responses and practices must be understood in relationship to this past, and we should be skeptical of any suggestions that they may be significantly altered merely through the recent process of democratization and the end of authoritarian rule. This essay, then, focuses on the period from the mid–eighteenth century to the abolition of slavery in 1888, and on the role of the state in maintaining free African Brazilians in subservient positions.

How many free persons of color were there in Brazil before the end of slavery? By 1872, there were 4.25 million free blacks and mulattos, and they accounted for at least three-quarters of all African Brazilians (as compared to a mere 262,000 or 6 percent of all African Americans in the U.S. South on the eve of emancipation).[3] Furthermore, at that same time, free blacks and mulattos made up more than two-fifths of the total Brazilian population (Cohen and Greene 1972, 314, 339). Nearly a century before that, in 1775, over a third of all African Brazilians in the city of Salvador (Bahia) were free, in this, the largest entrepôt of the slave trade in the Americas. In the province of Minas Gerais, a region of gold and diamond mining that had imported thousands of Africans in the eighteenth century, 41 percent of African Brazilians were free in 1786. And evidently, free blacks had been present in Brazil long before that. Even in the mid–sixteenth century, when the slave trade to Brazil was just beginning, over 7 percent of all blacks in Portugal were already free (Russell-Wood 1982, 48–49; Saunders 1982, 60).

These demographic features resulted from frequent manumission practiced over many years, and not just of the old and infirm, but of the newborn and the prized as well. Both cultural understandings and legal provisions made the granting of freedom to children and adults normal; such acts were regarded as praiseworthy, and foreign visitors were invariably startled to discover its frequency (Koster 1817, 2: 191–96, 215; Walsh 1831, 2: 342, 350–51, 365–66; Kidder 1857, 133; Williams 1930, 328–34). Lest we get carried away with admiration for the Brazilian slave owner, it is essential to note that between two-fifths and one-half of the adult slaves who were freed paid for their freedom in cash or with the promise of cash. Thus, many masters, while granting some slaves the opportunity to accumulate savings of their own, also demanded as payment for granting freedom the rough equivalent of the price of a new slave. And not just any slave could purchase his or her freedom; even when paid for in cash, manumission was still considered a concession on the part of the master, granted to the obedient and loyal, from whom gratitude was expected (Schwartz 1974, 623; Nishida 1993, 361–91; Mattoso 1972, 23–52).[4] Furthermore, the relatively openhanded freeing of children can be partly explained by the high cost of credit, which made the investment in childrearing too high in comparison to the low cost of buying a slave just off the boat from relatively nearby Africa (J. Reis n.d., 11, 16; Mello n.d.). As well, far fewer Europeans went to Brazil than to North America, so there were insufficient numbers of whites or at least too few who were willing to perform those innumerable tasks that could not be properly carried out by bondsmen (Harris 1964, 79–94).

Still, the rate of manumission was impressive. During the first half of the eighteenth century, women were freed twice as often as men, despite an overall predominance of males in the slave population as a whole. The bulk of these women were of childbearing age. Approximately 45 percent of all those freed in Bahia were under age thirteen, and relatively few were freed after age forty-five. Whereas mulattos accounted for only 10 to 20 percent of the slaves, they were freed in equal numbers to blacks (Schwartz 1974, 603–35). In the city of Rio de Janeiro in the early nineteenth century we find the same patterns. Two-thirds of the freed persons in the period 1807–1831 were women and, whereas African-born men there outnumbered women almost two to one, freedwomen somewhat outnumbered freedmen even among Africans (Karasch 1987, 349).[5] Remembering that the free-or-slave status of a child depended on that of the mother, it is no wonder that free African Brazilians came to account for such a large proportion of the population.

In considering the position of free persons of color in Brazil from the eighteenth to the late–nineteenth century, it is essential to examine the general structure of that society and the changes it was undergoing. Colonial Brazil, as was true for most ancien régime societies, was conceptually divided up into estates, reflecting the then general view that society was not formed by individuals equally protected in their rights and mobile in relationship to one another, but by castes, ranks, corporations, guilds, and brotherhoods, layered one atop another or arranged side by side.

Under this system, the individual had multiple identities and multiple loyalties without a single, truly all-encompassing one, except as a Christian (and only marginally, as a subject of a king)—never as a citizen of a nation. It was what Roland Mousnier (1973) would have described as a "society of orders," and what Brazilian historians refer to as a *sociedade estamental.*[6] Yet interfering with that conceptual construction was the reality of slavery driven by a profit-oriented mentality. The New World had provided to a few the opportunity to accumulate wealth, form classes, and gain power measured by their financial resources, not their status; the tragedy of the slave trade had introduced a group who had to be controlled by violence more than custom. So even in colonial times, Brazil does not entirely fit the *estamental* model.

By 1822, at the very end of the colonial period, and even more so in the ensuing years, a new philosophy emerged. Nineteenth-century elite Brazilians, at least in the cities, were not immune to the changes sweeping Europe since the mid–eighteenth century, and keenly felt the pull of a new system of ideas emanating from the world centers of political and economic power. With the overwhelming impact of the "Age of Revolution" came the tenets of liberalism and individualism. A new paradigm of the individual and society informed new political practices. Every free person was now to be a citizen—at least in theory. A constitutional monarchy was instituted with a parliament as well as an emperor, and a long list of individual rights were enshrined in the Brazilian constitution. The new understanding contrasted sharply with the older corporate one.

The intermingling of these two contradictory views of society, always in tension, had direct repercussions on the fate of free persons of color. On the whole and in practice, despite the new ideology, the acceptance of a multilayered social hierarchy continued to be a characteristic of the Brazilian polity throughout the nineteenth century. The hierarchical paradigm provided a means of assuring social order, for it diffused social tension, allowing almost everyone to be (and feel) superior to someone else. There is no equivalent word in current English usage for the Brazilian concept of *condição* (literally, condition), a term used to indicate social quality and precise social place. The nuanced distinctions of social ranking restrained the threat that freedmen might otherwise pose, and this partially explains why the manumission of slaves could be encouraged: freed blacks would easily fit into one of many possible social niches. Nor were all of them deemed equal to each other. Those born in Africa and those born in Brazil were clearly distinguishable. Attention to variations of skin color further contributed to locating people along a continuum of status, some being either darker or lighter than others. Brazilians took it for granted that people could generally be distinguished, as one writer put it, "according to the order, scale, or category into which [they were] placed within society" (Werneck 1855, 28).[7] This view meant that no one—black or white—thought himself equal to anyone else; all met within a hierarchy and found themselves either above or below everybody else.

One proof of the continuity between colonial and national periods is found in the variations in sentencing for criminal convictions. In colonial times, there was no presumption of equality. An identical crime would by law be punished differently if committed by a black or mulatto, even a free one, than if committed by a white person. The same was true for "New Christians" (descendants of forcibly converted Jews), and commoners were treated differently from nobles. Still today in Brazil, a university graduate is legally entitled to better quarters and preferential treatment in jail than the rest of the population.

Nor did national independence end the authority that the male head of household held over everyone within his domain. It is important to note that a father could, legally at least, imprison even his own sons, no matter their age, if they lived with him and if he did it to "punish or correct bad habits or behavior." The law also treated the property of unmarried sons, again regardless of age, as belonging to their father.[8] Moreover, a freedman remained in relationship to his or her former master as if in that household and, thus, under his authority. The law did not consider these two parties as equal; far from it.

As we look at the legal status of freed and free persons of African descent, we have to bear in mind this seeming ambiguity that juxtaposed the practices of hierarchy with the philosophy of legal equality. Historians can draw some initial and general conclusions, but they will not be clear-cut ones, for the dominant groups in Brazilian society have always dealt with racial issues through a complex mixture of force and co-optation.

Take, for instance, the issue of arming free blacks and mulattos. In colonial times, there were two simultaneous policies on this matter. On the one hand, laws were passed forbidding them from carrying any weapon. On the other, separate militia units—bearing arms—were organized for free blacks and mulattos, commanded by officers of their own color (Mott 1973, 129; Morton 1975, 263–68). In short, it was believed that some could loyally serve in this corporate body, one so typical of the system of estates, but that individuals outside such corporations were a threat. After independence, militia units segregated by race were abolished in the name of egalitarianism, while in practice, men of color were all relegated to the lowest army ranks. This change was one of the stimuli to a virtual race war that broke out in Bahia in 1837 (Kraay 1992, 501–27), to be discussed below. While one institution characteristic of the corporate society had been abolished, equality did not take its place.

For, regardless of any law, state officials now acted discriminatorily toward free African Brazilians in carrying out the military draft. Conscription was used throughout the nineteenth century (and well before) as a means of disciplining the poor. Although under nineteenth-century Brazilian law all men of a certain age were legally subject to forcible recruitment, the list of exempt occupations was long and left only the poor as truly subject to it. It was common practice both before and after independence for a judge or chief administrative officer of any locality (*capitães mores* in colonial times; *delegados* after 1841) to round up allegedly unsavory characters and send them to the army or navy. So it would be significant if the army's rank and file were predominantly made up of African Brazilians early on. We do not yet have direct evidence on this point, but in an 1827 list of 271 captured deserters, 222 (82 percent) were free men of color (Morton 1975, 258). Even though a judge who sent in three recruits in 1840 described each one in terms of his malfeasance, he casually noted that two were mulattos and the other a black.[9] Such examples could be multiplied at length. An Englishman in Rio de Janeiro in the late 1880s could still report that "the greater part of the privates in the army are Negroes or mulattoes" (Dent 1886, 287).

The fate of the draftee was a sorry one. Conditions in the army and navy remained so deplorable that the minister of war had to tell a provincial president in 1856 that recruits should march to

Rio de Janeiro "with all security, but not in irons."[10] Food was inadequate and lodging crowded; floggings were common (Morton 1975, 258). Desertion, therefore, can better be understood as a jailbreak, and the fact that African Brazilians were disproportionately represented in the ranks can only be seen as the result of prejudice and a state policy based on racism. Still, the state relied on blacks to fight its wars, even as it feared them. During the war with Paraguay (1865–1870), for instance, many slaves were purchased by the government and promised their freedom if they fought loyally. Since the bulk of the ordinary recruits were also black and mulatto, one can conclude that color determined who would be used as cannon fodder in that long and bloody struggle. This was the prize offered to free men of color; this was the benefit of citizenship.

If liberalism undid the color-specific militia units and demoted their officers, it also weakened one of the principal institutions that built black community in the old society of estates: the *irmandades*. These lay brotherhoods and sisterhoods had, since the sixteenth century, provided a means for people of color, often from particular language groups in Africa, to maintain solidarity. Like their white counterparts, these organizations were formed to venerate a specific saint and perform charitable acts, but they also functioned as mutual aid societies. In Portugal, they often grew up around individual guilds; in Brazil, even without a strong guild system, they continued to project the notion of a corporate society. Many were organized exclusively for blacks or mulattos, some excluded slaves, and some did not allow the African-born; others were open to all comers, provided they were of "good character." African Brazilian *irmandades* tended especially to honor Our Lady of the Rosary. They received state recognition through royal charters and their leaders were seen as spokesmen for the black community before government agencies. Members elected their own officers from their ranks. Frequently, they created funds to purchase the freedom of enslaved members. *Irmandades* usually had their seat in an established church where a side chapel was dedicated to "their" saint; sometimes, however, they acquired enough funds to build their own church, as happened in Salvador with Our Lady of the Rosary brotherhood. Religious processions were occasions to demonstrate the ranked order of society, with each *irmandade* in its predetermined social place, and each brother or sister ranked ahead or behind someone else according to the same principle (Mulvey 1976; Russell-Wood 1982, 128–60; Saunders 1982, 150–56).

In the nineteenth century, the *irmandades* gradually lost their place as central organizing institutions of society (to be superseded by political parties or, later, trade unions), although some of them retained considerable prestige (Oliveira 1988, 84). While the exclusion of potential members by overt criteria of race or place of birth also seems to have ended, to be replaced by financial ones, being of color may tend to exclude one from the most prestigious confraternities even today.[11] The principles of equality and individualism undermined the appeal of the *irmandades*. With their decline, the opportunity to have a voice and be consulted by authorities disappeared. *Irmandades* had never spoke for all blacks before the state, but in the nineteenth century, they now spoke for no one.

One of the most striking innovations of the liberal era was the introduction of national elections. Elections embody the idea of equal weight in political decisions, the concept of citizenship, and the belief in the individual. The Constitution of 1824 set up a system of indirect elections that specifically allowed freedmen to vote, although they could not be chosen as the electors who would then choose the members of parliament.[12] Other than this requirement, it made no distinction by race or color, and did not limit the suffrage to those who were literate. There was only a small income requirement for voting and, in practice, it was frequently ignored since the local panjandrums sought to gather as large a following as possible around the ballot box. With reference to the suffrage, the Brazilian state was far more liberal than contemporary European or North American ones. Yet the distinction between voters and electors was itself important since elections seem to have had as one purpose the visible demonstration of social hierarchies: the provision allowing freedmen to vote, but not to be voted for, publicly affirmed the differentiation between their rank and that of others (Graham 1990, 101–21).

An important component of the voting public in rural areas was made up of *agregados,* that is, farmers who worked the land of others. It was a common practice for landowners to grant poverty-stricken agricultural workers the right to raise subsistence crops on some outlying patch of their large estate, in exchange for which these *agregados* worked occasionally for the landowner, and proffered allegiance at times of armed struggle against neighboring landowners as well as loyalty in electoral disputes.[13] As one engineer described the situation on coffee plantations in 1879, much land was not used by the planter or his slaves, yet on the "large remaining area, . . . one notes a great number of people who settle there with the permission of the landowner or planter and who are called *agregados.* These *agregados,* far outnumbering the slaves, are impoverished citizens. . . . By their dependence on the owners these *agregados* constitute an enslaved class, which, although not subject to any tribute in money or labor, . . . are so, nevertheless, by the electoral tax [i.e., their vote], which they pay at the right moment at the ballot box, or else risk eviction."[14] Direct evidence on the color of these men and women is almost totally lacking. But we know that they were poor, that the poor were likely black or mulatto, and that most nonwhites were poor, so we can reasonably conclude that most *agregados* were black or mulatto. Outside the few Brazilian cities, voters in the first stage of the electoral process were generally *agregados.*

If we can see nonwhites participating in politics in this limited way, it should also be noted that within a patronage system such as this one, the state delegated to local potentates control over free blacks and other poor. Local judges, police commissioners, officers in the National Guard, and other vicinal authorities dealt with them and watched for signs of unrest. It was with these officials—mostly planters or ranchers, probably slave owners—that nonwhites negotiated on a daily basis and it was through them that free blacks encountered the state. Since there was no secret ballot, and the protection of a patron was crucial to an individual's success and even safety, it is not surprising that only the wealthy or well-born were chosen as electors. Thus, the bulk of free African Brazilians were pretty much excluded from participation in politics at a higher level, although as we shall see, a few exceptional men of color did manage to enter the political arena.

The actions of African Brazilians were circumscribed in more specific ways as well. In 1835, a famous revolt of Africans broke out in Salvador (J. J. Reis 1993). It has mostly been portrayed as a rebellion against slavery, but a large proportion of the participants were freedmen. Indeed, it was precisely that it was led by men without masters that particularly frightened the white elites. It is, therefore, not surprising to discover that once the revolt had been put down, stringent new laws were passed in that province that overtly relegated freedmen and free blacks and mulattos to a legally inferior status, albeit recognizing subtle differences between them and the slaves.

With the principle of liberalism on one side and the heritage of hierarchical social order on the other, Brazilian elites were often puzzled as to the right course of action. One example of this is a provincial law in Bahia regarding *ganhadores*—porters and stevedores—a group that had been prominent in the 1835 revolt. The legislators took it for granted that these men were people of color, for the first article of the regulation specified that it would apply to all "whether slave, free, or freed" (the fact that *ganhadores* were almost always African-born—that is, either slave or freed but never free—does not invalidate the significance of this legislative expression). All *ganhadores* were henceforth to be registered on a single list and were required to wear on their right wrist a copper bracelet with their registry number engraved on it. The overseer of each gang, mandated to be a free *ganhador,* would also wear diagonally across his chest a black leather belt with a tin badge bearing the number of his group. If any *ganhador* failed to comply with these rules, his masters, if he were a slave, would be fined; if free, he would be forcibly employed at public works for a period deemed equivalent to that fine.[15] No similar legislation applied to occupations in which whites predominated. Yet it is true that *ganhadores* ostensibly were singled out because of their occupation, not because of their color.

As long as slavery endured, the distinction between enslaved and free blacks remained. Even then, however, there was a tendency to see free African Brazilians, especially those of darker color, as if they were slaves. It was not uncommon for people of low status, regardless of color, to be flogged or kept in stocks; still, it is symptomatic that, in 1802, when an official was accused of torturing a freed black man (*preto forro*), he dismissed the accusation by saying that all he had done was to keep him in wooden stocks from Thursday until Sunday morning and then have him join some slaves in sweeping the *praça* in front of the jail.[16] He saw no contradiction between the free status of the subject and his treatment as if a slave, since their color was the same.

Reenslavement was a constant fear among the freed and even for those born free. To be sure, sometimes the state played the role of defender. For instance, one sixty-year-old woman and all her children and grandchildren were threatened with enslavement when someone claimed that she had never been free, but rather, had simply declared herself so when her mother's mistress died without heirs or an executor. In this case, a judge ruled in her favor, for she could show a baptismal record in which she had been labeled free.[17] Others may not have been so lucky. The effects of their fear were apparent. When the government announced plans in 1851—the year after the end of the slave trade—to carry out a census, many African Brazilians concluded reenslavement was its true purpose. In various parts of the northeast, "free mulattos, blacks, and half-breeds [*pardos, pretos, e cabras*]" formed groups of 400, 200, or 80, "all armed" to resist.[18] Plans for the census had to be abandoned. Leaving aside whether any such program of reenslavement was actually contemplated, it is significant that people of color believed this a likely action. They can only have come to that conclusion by their reading of official attitudes toward themselves.

As well, if they acted violently to avoid reenslavement, it means they saw a real difference between their own status and that of slaves. This point may seem obvious, but it is often overlooked by those who wish to portray the sad fate of free people of color by equating it to that of slaves. The historical actors themselves knew better. And historians may also find objective data to verify that they were right. For example, table 1 reveals how the dependency ratio in Bahia parishes in 1788 differed by race and status. The lower this figure, the greater was the likelihood of infant mortality and/or a short life expectancy. In the population of free people of color, there were nearly twice as many dependents (under fifteen years of age or over forty-four) than among the slaves.[19] The free could and did legally buy and sell real property and bequeath it to others, even in colonial times, when one might imagine otherwise. Whereas sumptuary laws were sometimes passed to prevent those of lower status from displaying their wealth too ostentatiously, no law prohibited them from holding it. (Poverty, of course, did prevent most of the freed or free of color from acquiring such property.) As well, the free could legally testify in court and often did so. Most of all, they could move from place to place. Their status was markedly different from that of the slave, even if lowly.

TABLE 1

Dependency Ratios[1] in Salvador, Bahia,
1788, by Color and Status

Free whites	143
Free pardos	125
Free blacks	173
All free colored	133
Pardo slaves	85
Black slaves	67
All slaves	69

Source: Schwartz 1985, 359.
[1] The number of those under fifteen or over forty-five years of age per 100 persons aged fifteen to forty-five.

Occasionally a white man could even be made subordinate to a free man of color. In one case, a *preto* (black) muleteer was placed in charge of a royal mule train. The viceroy found it essential to stress that, despite his color, he should be "treated with manners . . . making sure he is content and satisfied, providing him with food for himself and the slaves who accompany him, since this is the only way that the service can be completed in time with necessary regularity."[20] In other words, the viceroy recognized that other officials were likely to mistreat the muleteer if not forewarned. In another instance, when a white soldier refused to take orders from a mulatto sergeant, saying that "he could not stand to serve in a company under a black [*negro*]," an officer spoke up for the sergeant: "although he is a light-skinned mulatto [*pardo disfarçado*], he is a man of exemplary conduct," while the complaining soldier was a bad lot.[21] Presumably, if the sergeant were darker and the soldier better behaved, the complaint would have been taken more seriously; the defense was not that race was irrelevant.

The fate of the mulatto who aspired to better himself was not easy. In one district, men refused to serve as *juizes ordinarios* (a kind of justice of the peace) where the notary scribe was a light-skinned mulatto. He was so light-skinned that it had to be explained that he was a "*pardo* and so understood and reputed by his own people and his parents [*homen pardo e por tal tido e reputado pellos delle e das sua ascendencia*]."[22] Another man who sought the position of scribe and notary for a town council was denied the appointment on the grounds that "he is a *pardo*, . . . son of a woman who was born a slave; this circumstance alone seems enough to produce some intrigues between him and the officers of the council . . . who have some vanity respecting genealogy and know that all the scribes of other towns in this district are white men."[23]

So we see that although the state sometimes played the role of protector, most of the time, it reinforced the prejudices of white Brazilians, acquiesced in maintaining a hierarchy based on color, and acted to prevent the absorption of free African Brazilians into society on an equal basis with whites.

But another side of the question has to be considered, for there were some men of "color" who rose within the political system.[24] Many observers have commented on the well-known Brazilian technique of co-optation in which some African Brazilians are allowed to succeed, thus "proving" that Brazil is a racial democracy (Degler 1971, esp. chap. 5). As one politician maintained in 1880, "We enjoy full democracy in Brazil. . . . We live with everyone; we sit the freedman at our table and rely more on the trustworthy freedman than on many Brazilian citizens."[25] Trustworthiness was the key. To those who demonstrated loyalty and commitment to the general contours of that society, much could be given—but only to them. This same phenomenon can be looked at differently, that is, from the point of view of the upwardly mobile individual who took advantage of every opportunity offered by the ideology of the dominant class, without necessarily buying into that ideology. His actions may not spring from the success of the dominant group's attempt to impose a cultural hegemony, but from a clear-eyed weighing of alternatives on the part of the subaltern.

In either case, there are several examples of free-born mulattos (as distinct from freedmen or free-born blacks), especially light-skinned ones, who succeeded in nineteenth-century Brazil. While these are exceptions to the rule, they display the outer boundaries of the possible; some of them not only made it into politics, but even into high positions. Perhaps the best-known was Antonio Pereira Rebouças (1798–1880). He was born in the province of Bahia, the legitimate son of a Portuguese tailor and a mulatta ex-slave. With only an elementary formal education, he taught himself Greek, Latin, and French, and read voraciously. A man of unflagging energy, he became clerk to a lawyer and eventually learned so much law that his employer recommended he be allowed to take the bar exam—which he easily passed. When Brazil's political fate lay in the balance, with the Portuguese army in the capital city of Salvador hoping to reassert colonial rule, Rebouças astutely sided with the planter elite plotting independence and not with the Portuguese officials who were then offering freedom to those slaves who joined the loyalists. Rebouças was named a member and secretary of the planter-led insurgent council meeting in an interior town, and when the Portuguese were finally driven out, he was rewarded with the prestigious Order of the Cruzeiro and appointed acting president of the neighboring province of Sergipe; that is, he became the preeminent authority there, directly representing the emperor. When in 1837 radical elements in Salvador declared a republic, he decisively sided with the forces of order and the emperor, even though the war had quickly become a racial one, pitting the white planters against the free blacks and mulattoes of the city. Once the legalist forces regained control of the city, they slaughtered over 1,000 men, mostly those of color, impressing another 1,500 into the regular army to serve in other provinces and sending a shipload of free Africans (together with one mulatto and a Brazilian-born black) to Africa (Kraay 1992, 520–21). There is no record that Rebouças regretted his choice or saw those black and mulatto victims of repression as his fellows. He went on to serve in both the provincial and national legislatures, taking an active part in politics until his death. Although late in life he advocated the abolition of slavery, he had himself at one time or another owned several slaves (Spitzer 1989, 113–25). In these ways, he acted as did others of his class, and for us to expect race solidarity to predominate must surely be a form of racism itself.

An even more egregious example of a person of African descent—although remote—who made it in the white world and defended slavery is the Baron of Cotegipe (1815–1889). His grandson and biographer alleges an Indian great-grandmother and other sixteenth-century Indian ancestors (Pinho 1937, passim), but contemporary abolitionist newspapers accused him of turning his back on his own kind.[26] The son of a prominent landowning family, he came, through marriage, to own several more sugar plantations with numerous slaves.[27] He entered local politics soon after finishing law school and was elected to the national congress at the age of twenty-seven. By 1853, he had joined the cabinet and was named a senator (a lifelong post) in 1856. Other cabinet appointments followed, culminating in the prime ministership in 1885. In this post, Cotegipe successfully defeated the effort to include more liberal provisions in a bill designed to free slaves once they turned sixty-five. When, in the last months of 1887, slaves took matters into their own hands by fleeing the plantations en masse, he advocated harsh punitive measures. Cotegipe accused the abolitionists of being anarchists and got the police in the city of Rio de Janeiro to disrupt one of their meetings. After the resulting riot led to his dismissal as prime minister, he continued to argue vehemently against any move to end slavery and, after its abolition in May 1888, he proposed that the slave owners be compensated (Toplin 1972, 219, 235, 236, 251). If he ever acknowledged his color, he certainly showed no solidarity with the slaves. And in this he was not alone. It is generally believed that most mulattos preferred to assert their European background whenever possible and to identify with whites insofar as they were allowed to do so (Bergstresser 1973, 156).

Francisco Salles Torres Homem (1812–1876), a politician and newspaper editor, was less conservative. He is best known for his early virulent attacks on the monarchy and his later abrupt switch, when he became its staunchest defender. For such a somersault, he was rewarded with a place in the cabinet as finance minister in 1858, a post he occupied again in 1870, and the title of *visconde* de Inhomirim. According to one author, writing in 1894, his mother was a black street vendor; but another contemporary limited himself to saying that he came from "a family of modest means" (Carvalho 1894, 91; Dória 1908, 383). He was particularly known for his conservative fiscal principles, which endeared him to the planter elite and offended the emerging group of industrialists. Unlike Cotegipe, however, this mulatto, though far from an abolitionist, did argue for emancipation and supported the "Free Womb" law of 1871, which declared free the children born thenceforward to slave mothers.

A more critical stand was taken by the mulatto Francisco Otaviano de Almeida Rosa (1826–1889), a prominent publicist and reform politician. The son of a Rio de Janeiro physician, he graduated from the São Paulo law school, and was named secretary to the governor of the province of Rio de Janeiro at the age of twenty-two. Five years later, he was elected to the Chamber of Deputies, a position he secured again on various occasions, after which he then entered the life-tenured Senate. As a vehicle for his liberal ideas, he used the *Correio Mercantil,* a daily newspaper that he edited. He was sometimes called on to head difficult diplomatic missions abroad. He had a hand in almost every liberal advance of the era, forcefully contributing to the passage in 1871 of the "Free Womb" law. Later, he became an outright abolitionist (Serpa 1952).

None of these men offended the powers that be. Some, like Cotegipe, allied themselves unequivocally with the forces of conservatism, while others advocated reform. All of them participated in government and were allowed to do so because they did not threaten its fundamental principles.

Yet a distinct group, especially as the empire itself began to stumble and alienate some powerful people, took more radical stands. In doing so, they often found an outlet in the press, thus helping to form a civil society that debated public issues outside the administration.[28] Editorial offices became virtual political clubs, where men gathered to discuss issues and policies. These institutions emerged from the growing urban middle class trained at law and medical schools, the pharmaceutical college, the engineering school, or the military academy, and not so much from the planter class. Such men could make a career through talent, hard work, and luck. Among them were several mulattos who took up the cause of abolition, and their role merits attention. What characterizes them as a group was that they did not enter the apparatus of the state, but remained outside it as critics. Although outside government, they were successful in working to secure a change in the law and, in doing so, moved skillfully not only to occupy the space the state allowed them but to amplify it. Neither repression nor co-optation would silence them.

Three examples can be cited. One of them was José Carlos do Patrocínio (1853–1905). The son of a slave-owning priest-planter and a free-black fruit vendor, he began work in a charity hospital at age fifteen and eventually got a pharmacy degree. Since he could not secure a position as a pharmacist, probably because of his color,

Patrocínio sought employment as a tutor in the families of well-off whites. In one of these households he was well received and ended up marrying the daughter of his employers. Meanwhile, he had begun writing for the newspapers and, when he quit one such job because of his disgust at the editor's conservatism, his father-in-law bought him a paper of his own, *A Gazeta da Tarde*. Patrocínio transformed it into the premier abolitionist newspaper of the time, using as his motto, "Slavery Is Theft!" (Machado 1991).

Another mulatto abolitionist, André Rebouças (1838–1898), was the son of the Rebouças mentioned earlier. The younger Rebouças heard his father's tales of how he had suffered racial discrimination but kept his peace in order not to acknowledge the slight (Spitzer 1989, 121). André had entered the military academy and was a student there when it was transformed into Brazil's first engineering school in 1858. After graduation, he traveled to Europe to complete his professional training. He examined bridges, canals, tunnels, railroads, dock works, and factory buildings, seeking out the leading engineers of his day. Back in Brazil, he founded or directed a number of enterprises, ranging from railways to harbor works, and was employed as an engineer in the construction of wharves and waterworks. He also taught at the engineering school. André Rebouças believed Brazil should export nothing but manufactured goods, instead of remaining a supplier of foodstuffs and raw materials. He joined an abolitionist society early on and helped organize an abolitionist group among the engineering students (Graham 1968, 190–95, 209; Bergstresser 1973, 102–3). One of the few abolitionists to look beyond the end of slavery, he proposed a vast land reform, calling simultaneously for the "emancipation of the slave and his regeneration through land ownership" (Rebouças, 1883, 125).

A final and even more radical example is that of Luís Gama (1830–1882). His mother was an African-born freed woman who participated in the revolt of 1837 in Bahia that Antonio Rebouças had helped quell. She was deported to Africa as punishment (Conrad 1972, 154–55). When his Portuguese father fell on hard times, he sold Gama into slavery, and the boy was taken to Rio de Janeiro and then to São Paulo city, where he worked as a house servant at a boarding house. Befriended by a boarder, he learned to read. At age seventeen, he ran away, enlisted in the army, rebelled at its discipline—which reminded him of slavery—and was dishonorably discharged. He then found employment as a typesetter and soon began to write articles himself, signing his column, "Afro." Eventually he became a newspaper editor, joining those who advocated the complete abolition of slavery. Gama also proved in court that he had been born free. In doing this, he began to learn the lineaments of lawyering and soon put his knowledge to work for other African Brazilians. In the 1880s, he was especially successful in getting the courts to acknowledge that all Africans imported to Brazil after 1831 (when the slave trade was first declared illegal) were legally free along with their descendants (Menucci 1938, 165–86).

Although these men were exceptional, they demonstrate the complex way in which the Brazilian elite dealt with people of color. The state was deeply involved, as we have seen, in maintaining and perpetuating racial discrimination. At the same time—and even, it might be said, as one way of doing so—it admitted into the ranks of the powerful some light-skinned mulattos. This practice helped in the effort to construct the myth of a racial democracy in which a person's color was allegedly not held against him or her. The reality was quite different. The bulk of the free blacks and mulattos were discriminated against at every turn, and this was even truer once slavery was finally abolished in 1888.

The declaration of a republic the following year culminated the process of instituting a liberal state in Brazil. The new constitution was modeled on that of the United States, and Rui Barbosa, the champion of liberalism, was in its first cabinet. Already in 1881, liberals had instituted a new electoral system with direct elections for congress, but restricted the suffrage so as to exclude the poor and even the lower middle class and imposed a literacy requirement on those who would subsequently register to vote for the first time. As only 21 percent of the free could read and write (1872), this exclusion bore even deeper. Even in the capital city, where education was most advanced, only 60 percent could read and write as late as 1906.[29] Thus, African Brazilians were effectively denied citizenship, all in the name of liberal reform.

Even beyond legal provisions, the fate of African Brazilians worsened. Now that all were legally equal, the elite felt it imperative to search for other means to maintain inequality. They found the answer in racist doctrine. Before the abolition of slavery, there had been relatively little overt and systematic racist thought expressed in Brazil. Slavery was seen as a necessary evil, not a positive good. Hardly any writer argued that slavery was good for the blacks or that it was the only fate to which they were suited (Skidmore 1993, 21–27).[30] On the other hand, there was already an implied racism even in the positions of those many abolitionists who argued that slavery should be ended because it kept away white European immigrants from whom Brazilians could gain so much—especially their genes.

After abolition, however, "scientific" racism came into full vogue. This doctrine had already become a predominant one among European and North American scientists, and Brazilians now hoped to imitate Europe and North America in all aspects of their "progress." The spread of European colonialism and the rapid growth of the United States in the latter half of the nineteenth century brought supposedly irrefutable proof of the validity of a scheme that placed the so-called primitive African at the bottom of the scale and the "civilized" white European at its top. As a successful propagandist of the new truth, no one exceeded Herbert Spencer, who transformed Darwinism into a doctrine applicable to society. Human societies, he said, developed according to the same rules of differentiation and organization as did living organisms. It followed that natural selection and the survival of the fittest were inevitably the guiding principles both within particular societies and between nations. Just as "the struggle for existence has been an indispensable means to evolution" in the animal world, so too with "social organisms." He argued that since differing races exhibited differential abilities to survive and dominate, some were destined to triumph over others (Spencer 1891, 1:10; Spencer 1889, 1:462; 2:240, 241). Spencer was immensely influential in Brazil.

Brazilian intellectuals tended to ignore the Europeans' condemnation of race mixture and spoke instead of how Brazil would move toward progress through a steady "whitening" of its population. They simply ignored the fact that such a process must inevitably imply a "darkening" of some. Race, for them, was not immutable, and Brazil, far from being condemned to subservience, was destined for a bright future—only a bit later, after the continuous process of race mixture along with immigration from Europe and the alleged reproductive weakness of blacks had had time to work their magic. Raimundo Nina Rodrigues (1862–1906), possibly a mulatto himself, adopted the ideas of Cesare Lombroso to argue that blacks had innate criminal tendencies. In the 1920s and beyond—even as scientific racism was waning in Europe and North America, and several Brazilian thinkers had begun to denounce it—we find that F. J. Oliveira Vianna (1883–1951), a prolific writer, was propagating the gospel of "whitening." He tried to show with census data that there were increasingly fewer blacks and contended from a racist basis that this was all for the good (Skidmore 1993, 64–69, 200–205).

With racism as the accepted and acceptable ideology of the republican elites, ex-slaves and African Brazilians generally faced heightened discrimination in the late nineteenth and early twentieth centuries. Perhaps the clearest evidence was the use of state funds to subsidize massive immigration of Europeans to take the slaves' place in field and factory. The government paid for the passage of the immigrants, housed and fed them and their families on arrival in Santos or São Paulo, and managed a placement office to find them employment. Nothing was spent, meanwhile, on the education or placement of the ex-slaves, not to mention their transport or food and lodging. As well, the ex-slaves demanded too much in exchange for their labor: they desired to be independent and especially insisted that their women and children should not labor for someone else. On both counts the immigrant underbid them. As a planter-politician observed in 1888: "It is evident that we need laborers . . . in order to increase the competition among them so that salaries will be lowered by means of the law of supply and demand" (Andrews 1988, 494). Supply and demand would now substitute for the stocks and the whip. The result was that on the coffee plantations of west-central São Paulo by 1905, two-thirds of the agricultural workers were European.[31] The ex-slave was relegated to agricultural labor in less prosperous areas in the states of Rio de Janeiro or Minas Gerais. Frequently they became *agregados*. A coffee planter admitted in 1896 that European immigrants "contributed greatly to rescue our fazendeiros from their dependence on the freedmen" (Andrews 1988, 518). Meanwhile, in the cities, black workers found it hard going for the same reason: the state had financed the importation of cheap laborers from Europe. By 1902, 90 percent of industrial workers in São Paulo city were European (although this was hardly the case in Rio de Janeiro, which at that time, was the major industrial center) (Andrews 1991, 55–71).

Eventually these immigrants began to follow the example of the ex-slaves and demand more for their labor. Strikes broke out. Sometimes, as in 1891, African Brazilians were brought in as strikebreakers and then dismissed soon after. Not surprisingly, the labor movement in São Paulo was principally led by immigrants, although in Rio de Janeiro some mulatto leaders emerged. By the 1920s, labor leaders in São Paulo were at last beginning to recognize blacks and mulattoes as fellow workers to be recruited into union ranks. The state itself began to see the immigrant as a threat, while the Brazilian "national," that is, man of color, was now increasingly described as loyal and hardworking. Finally, in 1927, the program of subsidized immigration was suspended (Andrews 1991, 85–88).

In 1930, a new political regime was instituted in Brazil. When Getúlio Vargas seized power in that year, he turned his back on liberalism, which he saw as a bankrupt ideology that had made Brazil the maidservant of the industrialized nations. Although done for entirely nationalistic reasons, one of his measures powerfully aided African Brazilians: he decreed that two-thirds of all employees in the growing industrial establishments of the country should be Brazilians. While often evaded, this law greatly helped to open the way for blacks and mulattoes into the urban workforce. By the 1940s, more than half a century after the abolition of slavery, the urban proletariat fully included people of color.[32]

This could not be said for middle-class professionals, not to mention the elite, who continued to be overwhelmingly white. A few African Brazilians who had made it out of the working class organized the Frente Negra Brasileira in 1931. It set as its goal the election of black candidates to the Constituent Congress convened in 1934. But its attempts to mobilize black voters fell on deaf ears; the class division between its leaders and the mass of blacks was too large. And the literacy requirement for voting excluded most African Brazilians from the ballot box. In 1937, Vargas tore up the new constitution, openly declared a corporatist state, and outlawed all political parties and political activity generally. Caught up in his prohibition was the fledgling effort to organize blacks politically. Then as later, it was argued that any political movement that focused on the plight of blacks was racist and, therefore, incompatible with the principles of a racial democracy that allegedly sustained the Brazilian state (Andrews 1991, 139–56).

During the democratization period that succeeded the Vargas dictatorship (that is, 1945–1964), black leaders concentrated on building racial pride through cultural projects, particularly the theater, and made little progress toward enlisting the state in any effort to rectify past wrongs, despite the passage in 1951 of a law specifically prohibiting racial discrimination in education, employment, and public accommodations. The ensuing military dictatorship (1964–1985) usually considered protests against racial discrimination as subversive of the established order, defined again as one of racial harmony. The end result is that most nonwhites have been excluded from full participation as citizens in the Brazilian polity. Little has changed in this regard since colonial times.

Looking back over the last two centuries, several points are clear. Free men and women of color have been present in large numbers for a very long time, not just since the end of slavery. The state played an active part in discriminating against African Brazilians both before and after abolition, albeit occasionally co-opting the most loyal and agreeable among them; this practice did enable a handful of light-skinned mulattos to rise socially or politically. But far from ever being the land of racial democracy, Brazil has always been a racially divided nation, a heavy burden it still bears today.

NOTES

1 By African Brazilians, I mean all those descended from African ancestors, although most of them are also descended from Europeans. In making this choice, I am following a recent practice of specialists on racial categories in Brazil (such as those just cited) who refer to the nonwhites as a single category. To some degree, this may reflect a North American bias. The validity of such a classification for Brazil depends on what one wishes to find out; surely, the standard deviation from the mean social position is much greater for mulattos than it is for blacks.

2 These stances are rarely voiced in scholarly publications, but are frequently encountered in the discourse of the general population.

3 I say "at least" since the census categories "*pardo*" and "*preto*" probably

do not include all persons "of color"; census taker Haddock Lobo noted in 1849 that such data were imprecise because of the "inaccuracy with which each person reported on him or herself" (Holloway n.d.).

4   For more on how manumission for cash was treated as a favor, see, for example, Inventario of Antonio da Cruz Velloso. 1811. Arquivo Público do Estado da Bahia, Seção Judiciária, 04/1709/2179/02, fols. 50–52.

5   Women totaled 54 percent of the freed in 1849 (Holloway n.d., table 9).

6   No systematic study of the colonial judicial system or the society of orders in Portugal and colonial Brazil has been undertaken; starting points for such study would include Almeida 1870; Fernandes 1975; Aufderheide 1976; Russell-Wood 1968; and J. J. Reis 1991.

7   Hierarchy has served the same purpose elsewhere; see Dumont 1980, 18. On the hierarchy of color in Brazil, see Degler 1971, 88–112, although Degler fails to stress sufficiently the multiple ranks of color, simplifying the scheme into a tripartite one of whites, blacks, and mulattos. Contrast the Brazilian acceptance of complex social gradations with the contention of Oakes (1982) that the majority of slaveholders in the United States embraced an ideology of equality—for the free. As long as they maintained that view, freeing slaves would inevitably have threatened white rule.

8   See Almeida (1870), Liv. IV, tit. LXXXI, par. 3, and tit. XCVII, pars. 17, 19; Liv. V, tit. XXXVI, par. 1, and tit. XCV, par. 4. The Philippine Code issued in 1603 remained, with some emendations, the civil law of Brazil until 1916.

9   Juiz Municipal de Cachoeira to Presidente da Província da Bahia, Cachoeira, 1 June 1840, Arquivo Público do Estado da Bahia, M. 2273.

10 Ministro da Guerra to Presidente de Minas Gerais, Rio de Janeiro, 27 September 1856, in Brazil, *Colleção das leis do Imperio do Brasil,* aviso 317 (Guerra).

11 Nineteenth-century brotherhoods still remain to be researched. Prestige depends on the reference group; the most talked about *irmandades* today are black ones, but the Santa Casa de Misericórida is run by elite whites.

12 Brazil, *Constituição política do Império do Brasil,* art. 94 in combination with arts. 6 and 91.

13 For bits and pieces of information on *agregados,* see Werneck (1855, 36); Imperial Instituto Bahiano de Agricultura, "Relatorio," in Brazil, Ministerio da Agricultura, *Relatorio,* 1871, appenso C: 7; speech of Joaquim José Alvares dos Santos Silva, in Congresso Agricola (1878, 156); speech of Barbosa Torres, in Rio de Janeiro (province), Assembleia Legislativa, *Anais,* 1880, 593, quoted in Santos (1984, 126); Laerne (1885, 309n);

Wells (1886, 168); Smith (1879, 402–3); Schwartz (1975, 144–54); Stein (1957, 32n, 57n, 58); Andrade (1963, 93–95); Franco (1974, 94–107).

14 João da Rocha Fragoso, report, 31 March 1879, quoted in Brazil, Ministério da Fazenda, *Relatório*, 1891, vol. 2, anexo C, 4–5.

15 Regulamento, art. 1, lei de 2 de junho de 1835, *Collecção das leis e resoluções da Assemblea Legislativa da Bahia . . . 1835 a 1838* (Salvador: Typ. de Antonio Olavo da França Guerra, 1862), 40.

16 Deposition of Angelo de Sá Tenorio, Ilha Grande, 4 September 1802, enclosed in João Pimenta de Carvalho to Viceroy, Angra dos Reis, 8 June 1803, Arquivo Nacional, cx. 484, pac. 1 (1220).

17 Ouvidor to Governador, Jacobina, 16 March 1820, Arquivo Público do Estado da Bahia, m. 239 (Cartas ao Governo, 1819–1820).

18 Arquivo Público do Estado de Pernambuco, Polícia Civil, 1852, 39; Arquivo Nacional, Seção do Poder Executivo, IJ1824. I owe these references to Joan Meznar.

19 Much has been made of the fact that the death rate of slaves in Brazil exceeded their birthrate, in contrast to the situation in the United States, but little attention has been paid to the birthrate among freed blacks. The birthrate of all African Brazilians may even have exceeded the birthrate among Brazilian whites.

20 Viceroy quoted in Joaquim José da [?] to Viceroy, Villa de S. Antonio de Saã, 13 December 1786, Arquivo Nacional, cx. 484, pac. 2.

21 Pedro Alvares de Andrade to Viceroy, Angra dos Reis, 23 June 1794, Arquivo Nacional, cx. 484, pac. 1.

22 Camara de Jaguaripe to Governador, Jaguaripe, 27 September 1783, Arquivo Público do Estado da Bahia, m. 199 (Câmaras do Interior, 1766–1799).

23 Ouvidor da Comarca de Ilhéus to Governador, Barcellos, 26 September 1806, Arquivo Público do Estado da Bahia, M. 206 (Cartas ao Governo, 1803–1806).

24 Another essay could be written about the ambivalent position of the state-sponsored established church toward free men and women of color. We have mentioned the *irmandades,* which were invariably connected to church institutions. There were also men of color in the priesthood ever since the son of the king of the Kongo became a bishop in 1518. In 1808, the newly arrived king of Portugal named a mulatto priest as his royal chapel master in Rio de Janeiro (see Saunders 1982, 157; Macaulay 1986, 37).

25 Speech of Saraiva, 4 June 1880, Brazil, Congresso, Câmara dos Deputados, *Anais,* 1880, 2, 43.

26 *Gazeta da Tarde,* 1 September 1880, quoted in Bergstresser (1973, 161);

"Mulatos e negros escravocratas," *A Redemção,* 25 September 1887, quoted in Azevedo (1987, 224).

27 Inventário da Baronesa de Cotegipe, 4 April 1877, AIHGB–CC, L92, D7.

28 Another important group, still to be studied, would be the mulattos who succeeded in the world of art, music, and belles lettres (Haberly 1983).

29 The first figure refers to the percentage of total literates among the total of free persons over six years of age, calculated from Brazil, Directoria Geral de Estatistica (1873–1876); the second figure also refers to those over six (Brazil, Officina da Estatistica 1907, 110).

30 Even before abolition, frankly racist arguments were used in the São Paulo provincial legislature to favor immigration and forbid the transport of more slaves from other provinces into São Paulo (Azevedo 1987, 154–57).

31 Rebecca Baird Bergstresser (1973) cites evidence on how planters were pleased to have "thrown Africans [i.e., blacks] onto the road." See also Hall (1969, 165–66). Then as now, the police were far harsher in their treatment of African Brazilians than of others; see, for example, Azevedo (1987, 245).

32 In 1950, the proportion of African Brazilians in the industrial labor force was equivalent to that of African Brazilians in the general population (Andrews 1991, 101).

REFERENCES

Almeida, C. M. de, ed. 1870. *Codigo Philippino; ou, Ordenações e leis do reino de Portugal recopiladas por mandado d'el rei D. Philippe I . . .* Rio de Janeiro: Instituto Philomathico.

Andrade, M. C. de. 1963. *A terra e o homen no Nordeste.* São Paulo: Brasiliense.

Andrews, G. R. 1988. Black and White Workers: São Paulo, Brazil, 1888–1928. *Hispanic American Historical Review* 68, no. 3 (August): 491–524.

———. 1991. *Blacks and Whites in São Paulo, Brazil, 1888–1988.* Madison: University of Wisconsin Press.

Aufderheide, P. A. 1976. Order and Violence: Social Deviance and Social Control in Brazil, 1780–1840. Ph.D. diss., University of Minnesota.

Azevedo, C. M. M. de. 1987. *Onda negra, medo branco: O negro no imaginário das elites—Século XIX.* Rio de Janeiro: Paz e Terra.

Bergstresser, R. B. 1973. The Movement for the Abolition of Slavery in Rio de Janeiro, Brazil, 1880–1889. Ph.D. diss., Stanford University.

Brazil, Directoria Geral de Estatistica. 1873–1876. *Recenseamento . . . 1872.* Rio de Janeiro: Leuzinger.

Brazil, Officina da Estatistica. 1907. *Recenseamento do Rio de Janeiro (Districto Federal) realizado em 20 de setembro de 1906.* Rio de Janeiro: Officina da Estatistica.

Carvalho, J. M. de. 1894. *Reminiscencias sobre vultos e factos do imperio e da republica.* Amparo, Brazil: Typ. do "Correio."

Cohen, D. W., and J. P. Greene, eds. 1972. *Neither Slave nor Free: The Freedman of African Descent in the Slave Societies of the New World.* Baltimore, Md.: Johns Hopkins University Press.

Congresso Agricola. 1878. *Congresso agricola: Coleção de documentos.* Rio de Janeiro: Typographia Nacional.

Conrad, R. 1972. *The Destruction of Brazilian Slavery.* Berkeley: University of California Press.

Degler, C. N. 1971. *Neither Black nor White: Slavery and Race Relations in Brazil and the United States.* New York: Macmillan.

Dent, H. C. 1886. *A Year in Brazil.* London: Kegan, Paul, Trench.

Dória, L. G. d'E. 1908. Cousas do passado. *Revista do Instituto Histórico e Geográfico Brasileiro* 71, no. 2: 383.

Dumont, L. 1980. *Homo Hierarchicus: The Caste System and Its Implications,* trans. M. Sainsbury, L. Dumont, and B. Gulati. Rev. ed. Chicago, Ill.: University of Chicago Press.

Fernandes, F. 1975. *A revolução burguesa no Brasil: Ensaio de interpretação sociológica.* Rio de Janeiro: Zahar.

Franco, M. S. de C. 1974. *Homens livres na ordem escravocrata.* 2d ed. Ensaios no. 3. São Paulo: Ática.

Graham, R. 1968. *Britain and the Onset of Modernization in Brazil, 1850–1914.* Latin American Studies no. 4. Cambridge, England: Cambridge University Press.

———. 1990. *Patronage and Politics in Nineteenth-Century Brazil.* Stanford, Calif.: Stanford University Press.

Haberly, D. T. 1983. *Three Sad Races: Racial Identity and National Consciousness in Brazilian Literature.* Cambridge, England: Cambridge University Press.

Hall, M. M. 1969. The Origins of Mass Immigration in Brazil, 1871–1914. Ph.D. diss., Columbia University.

Harris, M. 1964. *Patterns of Race in the Americas.* New York: Walker.

Hasenbalg, C. A. 1985. Race and Socioeconomic Inequalities in Brazil. In *Race, Class, and Power in Brazil,* ed. P.-M. Fontaine. Los Angeles: University of California, Los Angeles, Center for Afro-American Studies.

Holloway, T. H. n.d. Haddock Lobo e o recenseamento do Rio de Janeiro de 1849. Unpublished paper.

Karasch, M. C. 1987. *Slave Life in Rio de Janeiro, 1808–1850*. Princeton, N.J.: Princeton University Press.

Kidder, D. P., and J. C. Fletcher. 1857. *Brazil and the Brazilians Portrayed in Historical and Descriptive Sketches*. Philadelphia, Pa.: Childs and Peterson.

Koster, H. 1817. *Travels in Brazil in the Years from 1809 to 1815*. Philadelphia, Pa.: Carey and Sons.

Kraay, H. 1992. "As Terrifying as Unexpected": The Bahian Sabinada, 1837–1838. *Hispanic American Historical Review* 72, no. 4 (November): 501–27.

Laerne, C. F. van D. 1885. *Brazil and Java: Report on Coffee-Culture in America, Asia, and Africa to H. E., the Minister of the Colonies*. London: Allen.

Lovell Webster, P. 1987. The Myth of Racial Equality: A Study of Race and Mortality in Northeast Brazil. *South-Eastern Latin Americanist* 22, no. 2 (May): 1–6.

Macaulay, N. 1986. *Dom Pedro: The Struggle for Liberty in Brazil and Portugal, 1798–1834*. Durham, N.C.: Duke University Press.

Machado, H. F. 1991. Palavras e brados: A imprensa abolicionista do Rio de Janeiro, 1880–1888. Ph.D. diss., University of São Paulo.

Mattoso, K. M. de Q. 1972. A propósito de cartas de alforria na Bahia, 1779–1850. *Anais de História*, no. 4: 23–52.

Mello, P. C. de. n.d. Estimating Slave Longevity in Nineteenth-Century Brazil. Report no. 7475-21, University of Chicago, Department of Economics, Chicago, Ill.

Menucci, S. 1938. *O precursor do abolicionismo no Brasil (Luiz Gama)*. São Paulo: n.p.

Morton, F. W. O. 1975. The Military and Society in Bahia, 1800–1821. *Journal of Latin American Studies* 7, no. 2 (November): 249–69.

Mott, L. 1973. A escravatura: A propósito de uma representação a El-Rei sobre a escravatura no Brasil. *Revista do Instituto de Estudos Brasileiros* 14:127–36.

Mousnier, R. 1973. *Social Hierarchies 1450 to the Present*, trans. P. Evans. New York: Schocken.

Mulvey, P. A. 1976. The Black Lay Brotherhoods of Colonial Brazil: A History. Ph.D. diss., City University of New York.

Nishida, M. 1993. Manumission and Ethnicity in Urban Slavery: Salvador, Brazil, 1808–1888. *Hispanic American Historical Review* 73, no. 3 (August): 361–91.

Oakes, J. 1982. *The Ruling Race: A History of American Slaveholders*. New York: Alfred A. Knopf.

Oliveira, M. I. C. de. 1988. *O liberto: O seu mundo e os outros. Salvador, 1790–1890*. São Paulo: Corrupio.

Pinho, J. W. [de A.]. 1937. *Cotegipe e seu tempo: Primeira phase, 1815–1867.* Brasiliana no. 85. São Paulo: Editora Nacional.

Rebouças, A. 1883. *Agricultura nacional, estudos economicos: Propaganda abolicionista e democratica.* Rio de Janeiro: Lamoureux.

Reis, J. n.d. Abolition and the Economics of Slave-holding in North East Brazil. Occasional paper, Glasgow Institute of Latin American Studies, Glasgow, Scotland. Mimeographed.

Reis, J. J. 1991. *A morte é uma festa. Ritos fúnebres e revolta popular no Brasil do século XIX.* São Paulo: Companhia das Letras.

———. 1993. *Slave Rebellion in Brazil: The Muslim Uprising of 1835 in Bahia,* trans. A. Brakel. Baltimore, Md.: Johns Hopkins University Press.

Russell-Wood, A. J. R. 1968. *Fidalgos and Philanthropists: The Santa Casa de Misericórdia of Bahia, 1550–1755.* Berkeley: University of California Press.

———. 1982. *The Black Man in Slavery and Freedom in Colonial Brazil.* New York: St. Martin's Press.

Santos, A. M. dos. 1984. Agricultural Reform and the Idea of "Decadence" in the State of Rio de Janeiro, 1870–1910. Ph.D. diss., University of Texas at Austin.

Saunders, A. C. d. C. M. 1982. *A Social History of Black Slaves and Freedmen in Portugal, 1441–1555.* Cambridge, England: Cambridge University Press.

Schwartz, S. B. 1974. The Manumission of Slaves in Colonial Brazil: Bahia, 1684–1745. *Hispanic American Historical Review* 54, no. 3 (August): 603–35.

———. 1975. Elite Politics and the Growth of a Peasantry in Late Colonial Brazil. In *From Colony to Nation: Essays on the Independence of Brazil,* ed. A. J. R. Russell-Wood. Baltimore, Md.: Johns Hopkins University Press.

———. 1985. *Sugar Plantations in the Formation of Brazilian Society.* Latin American Studies no. 52. Cambridge, England: Cambridge University Press.

Serpa, P. 1952. *Francisco Otaviano: Ensaio biográfico.* Rio de Janeiro: Publicações da Academia Brasileira.

Skidmore, T. E. 1993. *Black into White: Race and Nationality in Brazilian Thought.* 2d ed. Durham, N.C.: Duke University Press.

Smith, H. H. 1879. *Brazil— The Amazons and the Coast.* New York: Scribners'.

Soares, G. A. D., and N. do Valle Silva. 1987. Urbanization, Race, and Class in Brazilian Politics. *Latin American Research Review,* 22, no. 2: 155–76.

Spencer, H. 1889. *The Principles of Sociology.* 3 vols. New York: Appleton.

———. 1891. *Essays: Scientific, Political, and Speculative.* 3 vols. New York: Appleton.

Spitzer, L. 1989. *Lives in between: Assimilation and Marginality in Austria,*

Brazil, West Africa, 1780–1945. Cambridge, England: Cambridge University Press.

Stein, S. J. 1957. *Vassouras: A Brazilian Coffee County*. Cambridge, Mass.: Harvard University Press.

Toplin, R. B. 1972. *The Abolition of Slavery in Brazil*. New York: Atheneum.

Walsh, R. 1831. *Notices of Brazil in 1828 and 1829*. 2 vols. London: Richardson, Lord, and Holbrook and Carvill.

Wells, J. W. 1886. *Exploring and Travelling Three Thousand Miles through Brazil from Rio de Janeiro to Maranhão*. London: Low, Searle, and Rivington.

Werneck, L. P. de L. 1855. *Idéias sobre colonização precedidas de uma sucinta exposição dos princípios que regem a população*. Rio de Janeiro: Laemmert.

Williams, M. W. 1930. The Treatment of Negro Slaves in the Brazilian Empire: A Comparison with the United States of America. *Journal of Negro History* 15, no. 3 (July): 313–36.

Michael Hanchard

BLACK CINDERELLA?

Race and the Public Sphere in Brazil

On 26 June 1993, an incident in Vitória, the capital city of Espírito Santo, Brazil, drove another nail into the coffin of the ideology of Brazilian racial democracy. Ana Flávia Peçanha de Azeredo, a nineteen-year-old college student, was accosted and punched in the face by a forty-year-old woman and her eighteen-year-old son in the service elevator of an apartment building where Peçanha was visiting a friend. The physical assault was the result of an argument between the three over Peçanha's use of the elevator. The mother and son disliked the fact that this young black woman not only entered their building and held up the public elevator to talk to a friend, forcing them to use the service elevator, but also that she dared tell them to respect her after they informed her that "black and poor don't have a place here" in the building where they lived (Cinderela Negra 1993).

This incident, like so many other acts of racist violence in Brazil, would have gone unnoticed if Peçanha's father, Albuino Azeredo, was not the governor of the state of Espírito Santo. With the resources available to him, Governor Azeredo employed lawyers and physicians to examine his daughter's situation, and filed suit against Teresina and Rodrigo Stange, the alleged assailants. If convicted of racial discrimination under Article Five of the federal constitution, both mother and son could be sent to prison for one to five years. Ironically, the Brazilian press referred to Peçanha as the black Cinderella, with her father the governor playing the role of prince. One may wonder, however, which Cinderella they were referring to: the one who is fitted with the errant glass slipper and lives with the prince happily ever after, or the one who wears worn-out clothing and spends her days performing domestic labor? In fact, as a woman of African descent, Peçanha is neither. She is closer to a composite of status-filled and status-less roles in Brazilian society: considered a member of Brazil's elite when identified by birth; treated as a lowly, powerless member of society when identified by race.

The tale of black Cinderella is resonant with many of the constitutional, legal, cultural, and societal issues of Afro-Brazilians within the Brazilian public sphere. It encapsulates the intersection of race, citizenship, and modernity in a society that in theory is committed to liberal-democratic principles, but in practice still struggles with the legacies of patron-clientelism, racial slavery, and oppression. The above incident might seem commonsensical enough from a comparative perspective, but within the context of Brazilian racial politics, it further confirms the denial of full citizenship to people of African descent during this most recent period of democratization. It also attests to the pervasiveness of black subjectivity in societies under the template of modernity, both inside and outside the West. The public sphere, far from being simply the location of bourgeois culture's prized subject—the individual—has also been the place where the West's others have been displaced and marginalized, inside and outside its borders. Indeed, as I will argue in this explication and critique of notions of the public sphere put forth by several social and political theorists, it has been upheld as the benchmark of modernity, the principal indicator of political and socioeconomic development.

People of African descent, however, have been granted contingent and partial citizenship within these spheres, and only as a consequence of their own political struggles that have gone beyond the boundaries of liberal discourse. What I would like to demonstrate in this essay is the symbolic function of Afro-Brazilians within Brazilian society as bearers of noncitizenship, in accordance with racist ideologies and practices by the Brazilian state, as well as in civil society during the nineteenth and twentieth centuries. In short, Afro-Brazilians—like many other Afro-diasporic populations—have been depicted as embodying the antithesis of modernity.

Yet this depiction has two specific implications for scholarly intervention. First, it points to modernity's limitations in terms of racial politics and the manner in which its ideals have been intrinsically racialized. Second, it highlights the abstractness of the theorizing on citizenship and the public sphere by scholars like Charles Taylor and Jürgen Habermas, as well as the radical disjuncture between ideals of the public sphere and their historical embodiments.

While many theorists have considered racism within the public sphere as a mere aberration along the road to modernity, I suggest that the distinctly oppressive conditions under which people of African descent have lived partially constitute modernity and the public sphere. Racial difference is but one of modernity's internal contradictions and disjunctures; it has been a criteria of both citizenship and noncitizenship.

Through a brief analysis of the Afro-Brazilian public sphere, I examine how the dialectics of race and modernity are embodied in Brazilian racial politics. This, in turn, suggests first that Afro-Brazilians have been accorded partial and contingent access to the public sphere, a domain that has been defined explicitly and implicitly as white. While this in itself is no innovative conclusion, it can be utilized to interrogate the notion of the bourgeois public sphere as the sole arena or possibility for cultural articulation. This then leads to my second point: through segregation and other forms of racial alienation, alternative public spheres operate within a broadly defined public sphere. Marginalized groups create territorial and epistemological communities for themselves as a consequence of their subordinate location within the bourgeois public sphere. Along these lines, Afro-Brazilians have constructed public spheres of their own that critique Brazil's societal and political norms.

MAKING PRIVATE: THE PUBLIC SPHERE
AND RACIAL EXCLUSIONS

In his pathbreaking work, *The Structural Transformation of the Public Sphere,* Jürgen Habermas (1991) defines the bourgeois public sphere as "the sphere of private people come together as a public; they soon claimed the public sphere regulated from above against the public authorities themselves, to engage them in a debate over the general rules governing relations in the basically privatized but publicly relevant sphere of commodity exchange and social labor." The important historical precedent, within Habermas's interpretation, lies in the confrontation between "public authority"—namely, depersonalized state power—and individual, propertied subjects over the "private sphere of society that has become publicly relevant." With the advent of capitalism, commerce, and the related growth of mass news and information, propertied subjects came to use reason in ways formerly reserved for private concerns, such as the domestic economy, household management, and private business interests. This interface would radically shift the locus of power from feudal landlords to state institutions and socially engaged, private citizens who had become public.

Rather than engage in an extended discussion of Habermas's explication of the public sphere, for which there is already an extensive literature,[1] I shall point out several contradictions that emerged from this historical precedent, and that have been commented on by public sphere specialists and social theorists more generally. While the creation of this new public sphere did supplant the old—becoming the dominant, most logical social forum and institution in countries like France, Germany (Brubaker 1992), Britain, and Denmark—it did not automatically sever the formerly dominant modes of economic and political relations (Robinson 1983). Members of unpropertied social groups, who were never *private* citizens under the previous socioeconomic order, still remained outside the category of citizen within the new public sphere. The mark of difference—education, religious affiliations, dress, habits, speech, language, an entire way of life—haunted these unpropertied social groups as they were reinscribed into newly subordinate social relationships.

Thus, the bourgeois public sphere was simultaneously expansive and exclusive. It burgeoned with new forms of social inequality to parallel new forms of public authority and financial organization. Yet the working classes were neither entirely nor permanently outside the new social order, since universal suffrage, along with freedom of assembly and association, provided certain sectors of working-class groups with the opportunity to contest the inequalities of the new order and, in the process, construct what I shall call micropublic spheres, that is, spheres of public articulation that were not limited to, but dominated by the idioms, norms, and desires of working-class women and men.[2]

The bourgeois public sphere's ability to be perceived not as one space among several, but as the only forum for all social groups to engage in normative debate—either among themselves, or between two or more groups—was the crowning ideological achievement of bourgeois culture. Another way to view this (mis)perception relates to the evolving presumption that the bourgeois public sphere superseded private/public relations of the feudal order, and that all previously subordinate subjects and groups henceforth operated as social and political equals. The reality, however, was that "the oligarchy of capital was replacing the oligarchy of birth" (Viotti 1985, 55). Habermas clearly recognized this contradiction within the remaking of civil society. Yet other social theorists, particularly liberal ones, and architects of modernity in the New World did not, and in some cases, neglected it completely. This misconception has led *the* public sphere to become reified by most analysts of it and its virtues and problems. The most serious consequence of this reification is the equation of an ideal-type public sphere with Western polities, thus ignoring the internal contradictions within Western polities themselves concerning the realities of racial and ethnic difference.

RACE, MODERNITY, AND THE PUBLIC SPHERE
IN THE NEW WORLD

Habermas has suggested that the philosophical discourses of modernity are distinguished by their orientation toward the future, and their need to negate previous conceptions of time and history. In *The Philosophical Discourses of Modernity,* Habermas (1987) applies Hegel's understanding: "Modernity can and will no longer borrow the criteria by which it takes its orientation from the models supplied by another epoch; *it has to create its normativity out of itself.* Modernity sees itself cast back upon itself without any possibility of escape."

Yet modernity cannot efface history entirely. It needs history for points of reference from which to distinguish itself. A much greater impediment to complete historical denial was the discovery of the New World and the slave trade. This led to the presence of New

World and African people and/or their artifacts and other forms of production in the West, as well as in emergent New World nations. By the end of the nineteenth century, elites in most American nations decided to appropriate French or U.S. models of republicanism and liberal democracy in the transition from colony to free nation-state (Davis 1961). The fundamental contradiction in cultural terms that emerged from this was the presence of non-Western peoples amid projects of modernity and the public sphere in the New World. Latin American elites and intellectuals had less difficulty reconciling European modernity's break with the past in nation-states with no previous *national*-state history (Cuba, Brazil, Colombia, and Argentina, for example), than in accounting for the presence of sizable populations of "premodern people." Such populations were regarded as being without reason and rationality; they were treated as the ant colonies of Latin American modernity—excavating mines, constructing cities, harvesting crops, tending to children. They enabled those very same elites to become modern like their Western models.

In Brazil and many other Latin American countries, the shift from slave to wage labor was not as momentous an event as the shift from feudalism to capitalism in Europe. The repercussions of this shift, however, profoundly affected the dynamics of social interaction between landed and landless groups, as well as among white, indigenous, and African-derived populations. This signaled the inauguration of the *modern moment* in Latin America, in which various nations in this region of the world attempted to pattern themselves after the nation-states and civilizations of western Europe. Yet the modern moment in Latin America differed from its western European model due to the relatively late growth of industry, mass communications networks, and centralized state power. Furthermore, the landowning classes were not rendered obsolete, but rather, transformed their mode of social dominance. These historical differences complicated the evolution of an ideal-type public sphere, for the slave owners and landowners occupied the sociological location of the bourgeoisie without actually constituting a bourgeoisie themselves. Thus, the collision between feudal and slave labor, on the one hand, and capitalist wage labor, on the other, was not as radical as it may have appeared. The dominant ideological amalgam in Brazil came to be known as conservative liberalism. Viotti (1985, 55) characterizes conservative liberalism as a contradiction between liberal discourse and liberal practice: the expressed interest in the bourgeoisie's economic project without its attendant political and "valuative" responsibilities, like respect for the rights of individuals. Slavery and patron-clientelism, then, fused with liberal rhetoric to create a much more ambiguous setting for civil society than in European nation-states.

The specific consequence for the various African slave populations in Brazil was that they were the last in the New World to be granted emancipation (Conrad 1983). Elites justified the long delay in unchaining the enslaved on the grounds that Brazilian slavery was actually less harsh than the working conditions of peasants and wage laborers in southern Europe, and that slaves were spared the horrors of savage Africa by being transported to the more civilized and enlightened Brazil. These rationales, buttressed by the purported cultural differences between Portuguese and other European civilizations, underpinned the now-well-known myth of racial democracy (Freyre 1946). The realities of Afro-Brazilian life by 1888, when slavery was abolished, were quite different. In 1871, slavery was clearly on the wane, and planters in the province of São Paulo decided to subsidize southern European immigration to Brazil in order to develop a European proletariat, even though there were already more free Afro-Brazilians than slaves in the region (Andrews 1991). It was a simultaneous expression of racial and economic interests through state implementation of racially and economically specific policies.

These policies basically disqualified freedpersons from objective competition in the emergent capitalist marketplace, thus limiting their prospects regardless of occupational differentiation within Afro-Brazilian communities. Large landowners in most cases refused to hire former slaves, in part on the grounds that they were recalcitrant and demanded specific conditions under which they would labor, but largely due to the landowners' desire to engage in economic relationships with those whom they most resembled, even in subordinate roles. European immigrant labor was preferred, despite the fact that many Afro-Brazilians were skilled laborers at the time of abolition, already possessing the skills that Italian and other immigrants were just developing (Dean 1976). Previously freed Afro-Brazilians did not fare much better, even though by

1872, 74 percent of all Afro-Brazilians were free (as compared to 6 percent in the U.S. South on the eve of emancipation) (Klein 1972, 319).

The employment practices were consistent with the marginalization of enslaved and free blacks during the period of national formation that culminated in Brazil's independence from Portugal. The first national elections, in 1821, for a centralized government—one year before independence—created the electoral conditions for the Brazilian elite to participate in public debate about Brazil's transformation into an independent monarchy, but excluded those who remained enslaved until 1888 (Bastos 1994). Lùcia Maria Bastos suggests that the 1821 election was a defining moment in Brazilian political culture, for the new constitutional order helped integrate previously marginalized groups—such as small merchants, artisans, salespeople, and others—by elevating them to the status of citizens. These groups were similar to those who made up the petit bourgeoisie in revolutionary France by the late eighteenth century. The Constitution of 1824 defined Brazil as a constitutional monarchy; it gave black freedmen the right to vote, but they could not be chosen as electors.[3]

The slave population was well aware of the struggles between monarchal nationalists and loyalists to the Portuguese crown. In fact, slaves and mulattoes were key participants on both sides. Moreover, Africans in Bahia, like their counterparts in other slave societies in the New World, used moments of elite crisis in Brazil to their own advantage, fomenting revolts and rebellions at critical instances of disunity among these elites who were largely rural landholders that had maintained their power after independence in 1822 (Kraay 1992). Revolts in 1835 and 1837 in Bahia led to waves of repression not only against blacks, but also against the poor and other urban elements who remained politically excluded after independence. In Salvador, Bahia, local officials responded to the 1835 rebellion by African Brazilians by imposing stringent laws that monitored the movement of freed and enslaved blacks. Porters and stevedores, who were predominantly black, had to be registered on a single list and were required to wear a copper bracelet engraved with their registry number (Reis 1993).

These and other acts suggest that by the 1830s in Brazil, the status of African and Afro-Brazilian slaves and *libertos* (freed slaves) held marginal distinctions, even though there were considerable social tensions between Brazilian- and African-born slaves (Graham 1993). The free and the enslaved often worked side by side (Flory 1977). By this time, the Brazilian empire relied on the discourse of the social problem to refer to free and nonfree blacks as vagrants and idlers (*vadios e ociosos*) to avoid the complexities of distinguishing the *escravo* from the *liberto* (Flory 1977). As in the United States, blackness overrode the constitutional or legal mandate of citizenship for Afro-Brazilians. Republican institutions, despite their status as impartial purveyors of law and merit, actually institutionalized racist discourses and practices, and empowered many individuals who believed that African presences in Brazil doomed their nation to second-class status. Laws and policies specifically prohibited nonwhite immigration to Brazil, and there were congressional debates over the alleged racial inferiority of Africans, Chinese, and southern Europeans (Mitchell 1977). When coupled with the powerful albeit contradictory ideology of whitening, which asserted that miscegenation would eventually eliminate people of African descent, Afro-Brazilians were remarginalized in the shift from slave to wage labor in a manner that implied far more than a desire to exclude these people from choice labor markets.

The politics of racial exclusion were even more comprehensive. The uneven but continuous oppression and marginalization of Afro-Brazilians in the late–nineteenth and early–twentieth centuries was an effort by Brazilian elites to expunge Afro-Brazilians and their cultural practices from their portrait of modernity. Modernity, in short, did not include Afro-Brazilians. They were the antithesis of a modern nation. This effort contrasted with those of Brazilian modernists such as Mário and Oswaldo de Andrade, the anthropologist Gilberto Freyre, and even some politicians, who sought to refute the positivist legacy in Brazil by suggesting that African and indigenous elements in their nation were uniquely Brazilian. It was also at odds with Afro-Brazilian modernism in dance, religious practice, drama, and the plastic arts. Yet the landholding elites, Catholic Church, and culturally conservative politicians carried the day, setting the tone for any future discussion of Afro-Brazilian and national identity.

The irony of such maneuvers, which took place well into the 1930s, was the proliferation and expansion of African cultural presences within modern Brazil, presences that were stronger than in any other nation-state in the New World. These presences, at once residual and dominant in the sense that Raymond Williams (1977) uses these terms, are evidenced by national, transracial participation in Afro-Brazilian religions like Candomblé and Umbanda, and in the importance of an African-derived corporal aesthetics for a national standard of beauty.[4] In popular culture, samba was appropriated by the emergent middle classes in the 1940s. They were seeking a popular form of recreation and selected samba, despite the disdain it evoked among elites, who detected an expression of sensuality not found in the fox-trot or other European imports. By the 1940s, African elements of Brazilian culture were selectively integrated into the discourses of national identity. With the ascendance of the ideologies of racial democracy and whitening, Afro-Brazilians came to be considered part of the cultural economy, in which their women and men embodied sexual desire and lascivious pleasure. At the same time, Afro-Brazilians were denied access to virtually all institutions of civil society that would have given them equal footing with the middle classes of modernizing Brazil. Prestigious schools, neighborhoods, clubs, and professions were closed off to Afro-Brazilians, much in the same way that they were to African Americans in the United States, Afro-Cubans, and other New World blacks during this period, only in more ambiguous, coded ways (Fernandes 1969; Andrews 1991). Thus, in both eighteenth-century Europe and twentieth-century Latin America, the bourgeois public sphere was a contradictory, politically bifurcated domain, open to some groups and closed to others. The extent of marginality was, and is, determined by the degree and conditions of otherness on each continent.

Claims to citizenship and equality of opportunity in labor and ancillary markets could not be the hallmarks of Afro-Brazilians' modern identities. Instead, the denial of participatory citizenship in the bourgeois public sphere for Afro-Brazilians marked their existence as subaltern elements of modern life. Yet they lived within this sphere nonetheless, so that any characterization of their lives as premodern or archaic (Fernandes 1969) ignores the discontinuity of modern time and the multiplicity of spheres within bourgeois civil society.

A common characteristic that Afro-Brazilians shared with their counterparts of the African diaspora in the New World was the constant attacks on their dignity. Charles Taylor (1989, 15) identifies dignity as a crucial element in the constitution of the modern, individual self: it reflects "our power, our sense of dominating public space; or our invulnerability to power; or our self-sufficiency, our life having its own centre, or our being like and looked to by others, a centre of attention." The keywords and phrases relevant to my critique of Taylor's passage are "public space," "invulnerability to power," "self-sufficiency," and "centre." Taylor appears to use the phrase "public space" in a manner indistinguishable from the contemporary usage of "public sphere." This usage has come to be equated with civil society itself, in which a diverse array of interests, institutions, and individuals are intertwined to constitute the modern moment. An important, if subtle, distinction could be made here that relates to a point I raised earlier about the totalizing quality implicit in the notion of the public sphere. This particular sphere could be a dimension of public space but not its totality, despite its representation as such. Yet for Taylor, this form of dignity is seemingly universal and not limited to a particular sphere.

What happens to this notion of dignity when the role of racial or gendered inequality in Taylor's public space is viewed from theoretical and historical perspectives? In theoretical terms, is it possible for people who are denied the constitutional and normative rudiments of modern citizenship to operate in public space with such a *general* sense of dignity, a presumption of citizenship? In light of the previous discussion of Afro-Brazilians and the emergent public sphere in Brazil, would it not have been impossible for those porters and stevedores in Salvador, Bahia, to have imagined that they could "dominate public space," even in the mild form that Taylor suggests? For Peçanha, the governor's daughter, her inability to dominate public space as an individual stemmed from the lowly status accorded to those who resemble her, regardless of their differences as individual, private citizens. Thus, the public and private distinctions so neatly laid out by Taylor collapse at the intersection of reason and coercion, power and powerlessness. Considering the legacy of the civil rights movement in the United States, the anti-apartheid movement in South Africa, and other social movements engineered by people of African descent in distinct parts of the world, there clearly has not been "invulnerability to power" in pub-

lic space for them in modern times.[5] A sense of self-sufficiency—
which Taylor defines as the ability to provide for oneself and one's
family, and to command respect—is structurally inaccessible to the
African American communities of the New World.

Despite Taylor's lofty standards and claims, his universalizing
principles for the moral sources of dignity presuppose a subject
who is male, property owning, Western, and white. His characterization is informed by what feminist psychoanalytic critics call the
male gaze, a projection of his particular "subject position" onto the
rest of the world, with the desire that others conform to the image
he has of himself, and of others as a wished-for extension of himself (Mulvey 1989). In racial and gendered terms, being a "centre
of attention" has distinct connotations for different racialized and
gendered subjects.

As a communitarian, Taylor could respond to this critique on
theoretical and historical grounds. The claim might be made that
the Brazilian polity is not the West that Taylor had in mind; this
is a legitimate point since Brazilian society is pervaded by a con-
fluence of feudalism and dependent capitalist culture. It could be
further argued that both Habermas and Taylor have laid the economic, administrative, and normative foundations for the public
sphere/space, and cannot be critiqued for the less-than-ideal functioning of these domains in the real world. After all, the histories of
racial oppression shared among peoples of African descent in the
West, which Habermas and Taylor briefly note and deplore, also
disclose the malfunctioning of the public sphere according to its
own principles. The eventual, if uneasy, inclusion of previously disenfranchised groups could be perceived as another triumph of reason and rationalization, a pit stop along the tortuous track toward
liberal pluralism (Taylor) or democratic socialism (Habermas).

Such neat distinctions between Western and non-Western, ideal
and practical public spheres have a flimsy ontological basis. They
ignore the fact that the geographic distinctions of West and non-
West are not only arbitrary, but also neglectful of the role of Western *influences* globally in hundreds of societies built on variations
of parliamentary, republican models. Moreover, such distinctions
ignore the reaction within Western polities to the others, and the
chasm between liberal theory and liberal history (Mehta 1990). Recent events in both western and eastern Europe demonstrate the

intensity of reactions to otherness—anti-immigration violence, neo-Nazism, and other fascist movements—and how strongly the public sphere is *racialized*. This refutes positions supporting notions of abstract, individual propriety in the public sphere, and emphasizes the ways that citizenship is differentially embodied by race and gender. Modernity requires some sense of the past in order to distinguish itself and it uses people of African descent in predominantly white nation-states as contrasting symbols of noncitizenship in the public sphere, just as colonial rulers have used "Third World" peoples in the same manner (Chatterjee 1986). Afro-Brazilians, like so many other people of African descent in the New World, are used for the same purpose.

BLACKNESS THEN AND NOW

It is not really race in a narrow, phenotypical sense that links Peçanha, the governor's daughter, to the seemingly disparate incidents of the slave revolt in 1835 or the marginalization of Afro-Brazilians in the shift from slave to wage labor between 1880 and 1920. More precisely, the *meanings* attached to purported racial groups are markers that convey the alleged disparities in intellect, industriousness, wealth, beauty, and aesthetics—as well as the capacity to alter them. As long as Brazilian society in general, whites and nonwhites alike, share a commonsense basis for negative stereotypes of blacks and positive stereotypes of whites, then the apparent fluidity historically associated with racial categorization in Brazil needs to be qualified. The preoccupation with color categories belies the other dimension of racial "common sense" in Brazil: the widespread belief held by many whites and nonwhites that Brazil is a racial democracy.

The equation of blackness with sloth, deceit, hypersexuality, and waste of all kinds is confirmed by the relative infrequency with which the terms *preto* or *Negro* (black) are used in daily life. Brazilians reluctantly use these terms in describing others; they rarely describe friends this way, for fear of insulting them (Maggie 1988). This underscores the paradox of racial politics in Brazil and in much of the hemisphere. While racial identification is more contextual in Brazil than in other multiracial polities, certain limits also obtain. One person's mulatto is another's Negro; yet Negro remains a racial category many people do not want ascribed to them. If *preto* or Negro only meant dark skin color, then why would the usage of these terms be any different from, say, referring to someone as white? Part of the reason for a multiplicity of descriptions for nonwhite Brazilians, particularly for those whose African descent is visible in the texture of their hair or the shape of their nose or buttocks, is because such categorizations attempt to avoid the mark of blackness. Why is it more likely that a "colored" person would be described as "brown" or "mulatto" than as half-white, nearly white, or quasi-white? Focusing on the numerous color categories in Brazilian racial politics can obscure the broader racialized social totality in which these categories operate, and the racial meanings that *structure* social interactions and limit individuals' ability to simply choose their own racial category.

When considered comparatively, these examples illustrate the limits of blackness over historical/racial time. In the case of the 1835 revolt in Bahia, African Brazilians responded to their mistreatment through rebellion, regardless of occupational distinctions among them. The animosity between Brazilian-born slaves, mulattoes, and whites on the one hand, and African Brazilians on the other, suggests at the least that blackness, laden with negative connotations, pertained to African Brazilians and not necessarily to those who looked black. Peçanha, the daughter of a black man and a white woman, could easily be considered a mulatta in both contemporary and historical Brazil. Her blackness in the eyes of her assailants implies a broadening of the category of Negro/a in Brazil and, more important, an increasing polarization of racial categories. Her beating may signal that the mark of blackness has come to include Brazilians who are perceived as people of African descent, whether from Brazil or not. Unlike the distinctions between African- and Brazilian-born slaves in the previous century, Africanness—the parent symbol for blackness—no longer marks a place; it now marks a people.

The seemingly arbitrary manner in which Peçanha the mulatta could become Peçanha the Negra, affirms the greater importance of the interpretive, as opposed to the phenotypical, criterion of racial differentiation. Like McCarthyism in the United States and the military dictatorship from 1964 to 1985 in Brazil, the enemy is continually invented. Thus, in the absence of "real" blacks, Peçanha becomes black, much in the same way that liberals and other moderates were transformed into communists during the era of anticommunist hysteria. Once identified the enemy, the actual ideological or racial position of the signified has secondary importance. The meaning of racial or ideological difference attached to the individual or group is paramount for understanding the politics of polarization, of distancing the marginal or soon-to-be marginal subject from the center of the body politic.

This gives credence to Thomas Skidmore's (1993) assertion that Brazil's racial politics are becoming more and more like the relatively dichotomous patterns of racial interaction in the United States. With the emergence of groups calling themselves skinheads and Black Muslims in São Paulo, the existence of organizations that reflect the most obvious forms of and responses to racial animus affirms racially discriminatory practices in Brazil that are longstanding and embedded in the ideology of racial democracy. As far as I know, such organizations are new to Brazil, yet such sentiments must have been in place for some time in order for them to assume organizational, collective form.

The meanings attached to blackness, whiteness, and positions in between constitute the public aspect of the racial dimension of public spheres: these meanings are located in specific social contexts. Habermas's etymological and genealogical considerations of the terms *publicity* and *public opinion* are relevant here. Tracing the meaning and conceptualization of these terms in philosophers as diverse as Locke, Rousseau, Kant, and Hegel, Habermas notes how public opinion was often meant to infer a normative matrix of the good, right, and just in emergent civil societies of the West. Though Hegel would disparage public opinion as unmediated mass knowledge, each aforementioned philosopher acknowledged public opinion's power to convey a popular authority—what Foucault refers to as a regime of truth. Racist ideologies are facets of publicity and public opinion, insofar as they mark bodies to inform others of the meanings of those bodies in racial terms.

It is not, therefore, only discursive formations and processes of reason and rationalization that shape publicity and public opinion about race. *Nondiscursive* formations also define people's location and degrees of participation in public realms. In short, it is the *structures* of race, racial difference, and racism that often go unsaid that provide the parameters of racial dynamics and the range of possibilities of discourse itself. This is why the Brazilian historian João Reis suggests that the Bahia slave revolt of 1835 was not, as previous historical accounts imply, merely a Muslim revolt of a certain category of slaves. Both slaves and *libertos* participated in the revolt, along with a high percentage of non-Muslim Africans. Reis regards the revolt as principally the result of an "embryonic Pan-African identity," an emergent ethnic consciousness among *liberto* and *escravo* participants that was forged by the similarity of racial and economic exploitation (Reis and Silva 1989, 109). Religious affiliation was the vehicle through which the revolt's leadership emerged, but was certainly not the sole reason for the revolt itself.[6]

Moreover, the distinctions between *escravo* and *liberto* were principally *occupational* distinctions, which by themselves, tell us little about the respective treatment accorded individuals from either category in the public sphere. As noted earlier, *libertos* were not given the same status or rights of whites, and could only vote in primary elections. Therefore, while the degree of racial/civic exclusion might have been less for the *liberto,* the nature and kind of exclusion was more similar than dissimilar to that of the *escravo.* Reis and Silva (1989, 106; translation mine) describe the broader context in which these occupational distinctions operated:

If the freed black stopped being a slave, he did not exactly become a free man. He did not possess any political right and, even though considered a foreigner, was not granted the privileges of a citizen from another country. The stigma of slavery was irreducibly associated with the color of his skin and above all, his origin. The free Africans were treated by whites, blacks, browns and even by creoles as slaves. They were not second or third class citizens. They were simply not citizens.

At the level of resistance, however, the 1835 revolt is a historical example of an activity that emerged from a micropublic sphere, one that operated outside the purview of the liberal-minded but ultimately oligarchic elite within the dominant public sphere. The participants in the revolt were aware of the activities and crises of their masters and employers, and fashioned modes of racial and ethnic consciousness in response to them. The simultaneity of these two spheres suggests that an elite public sphere, such as in the case of nineteenth-century Brazil or eighteenth-century Europe, is also an essentially *privatized* domain. This privatization is also apparent in twentieth-century Brazil, as Peçanha was rudely reminded; public space is not necessarily a democratic space. It is not democratic precisely because of the manner in which it is privatized for members of a certain race and/or class. While the old Brazilian adage that "money whitens" is true in certain cases, it is equally true that blackness taints.

This leads us to another understanding of how the public sphere and public space is privatized by the manner in which its privileged subjects or citizens publicly discriminate against the less privileged. Even in circumstances where citizenship is a given, as in contemporary Brazil, some people are considered lesser citizens than others. Racial prejudice is not only privately held, but invariably, publicly articulated and at some level sanctioned. Thus, the liberal presumption of reason in Habermas's formulation is often rebuffed at the lived conjunctures of white and black, as in the case of Peçanha. It was precisely at this moment that ideology and coercive power outstripped reason as the bordering, structuring parameters of the elite public sphere. Moreover, contrary to the liberal—and often communitarian—notion that citizens are abstract bearers of rights, black Cinderella highlights the need to conceive of citizenship as that which should inhere in concrete persons. Along with property, gender, age, and reason, race and racial difference imbue individuals with their concreteness, a material and symbolic grounding of their existence.

AFRO-BRAZILIAN CULTURE AND THE PUBLIC SPHERE

As Wade (1993) has noted in his study of Afro-Colombians, one of the comparative peculiarities of Latin American racial politics has been its rhetorical collapse of racial difference under the banner of national identity. In Brazil, Mexico, Cuba, Venezuela, Colombia, and other nations of the region, Afro–Latino Americans are supposedly without a racially specific identity, unlike their Afro–North American, Afro-European, or English-speaking counterparts in the Caribbean. Some allege that this has been due to the absence of legislated racial discrimination and segregation. Such forms of racial apartheid have led to the development of parallel institutions in other multiracial polities, such as the United States. Therefore, music, cuisine, dress, and artifacts that would be representative of a particular racial, or more accurately cultural, group elsewhere appear as national commodities in Latin American polities (Fry 1983).

Afro-Brazilian cultural production fit this model until the 1970s, when Afro-Brazilian cultural and political activists affiliated with the *movimento negro* began to explore symbolic linkages with other communities of the African diaspora. These explorations led to the formation of organizations and cultural expressions that were neither Brazilian nor national but Afro-diasporic. Ironically, racially specific Afro-Brazilian cultural practices—namely, forms of expression produced and directed toward Afro-Brazilians—emerged during the height of the military dictatorship in Brazil. Black soul, the dance hall phenomena of the 1970s that first appeared in Rio de Janeiro but later spread to other cities in the country, was the precursor to the African blocs (*blocos Afros*) such as Olodum and Illê-Aiyê. Such organizations have a specifically Afro-Brazilian leadership and constituency; they produce lyrics and music that utilize Afro-Brazilian identity and racial discrimination as principal themes.[7] These organizations are quite distinct from samba schools, Candomblé, Umbanda, and other Brazilian cultural artifacts that are perceived and manipulated as national symbols. In the realm of cultural and religious practice, *terreiros de candomblé,* samba schools, ethnic brotherhoods, and the emergent *blocos Afros*—like Agbara Dudu, Olodum, and Illê-Aiyê—represent the expanding racialization of Afro-Brazilian cultural practice. Afro-Brazilians increasingly recognize the need to use cultural practice and production as organizing principles against racial oppression, and as tools for constructing and enacting Afro-Brazilian identities. In many instances, these organizations are successful attempts at creating both spaces for and values of Afro-Brazilian identity and community that are related to, but distinct from the Catholic Church, mass culture, and markets. The emphasis on space within the *terreiro* provides the articulation of an alternative public sphere (Braga 1992; Elbein dos Santos and dos Santos 1984).

Organizations such as Olodum and Illê-Aiyê do not necessarily affirm a growing polarization along clearly demarcated racial lines, but rather, an increasing awareness among Afro-Brazilians and white Brazilians that Afro-Brazilians *can* use racial identity as a principle to organize collective action. It is not a sign of greater racism among Afro-Brazilians, though at some level, it is surely a response to racism in the land of racial democracy. The Afro-Brazilian public sphere shares a paradox with its white, more dominant counterpart: it is at once public and private.[8] Brazilian national culture has always translated and transformed Afro-Brazilian cultural practices into national cultural practices, thereby rendering them as commodities of popular culture to be consumed by all (Hanchard 1993, 1994). The question, Just what is Afro-Brazilian culture? is much more complicated than in the United States, South Africa, or Britain, where residential and other forms of racial segregation make distinct histories more obvious. It appears, however, that with the increasing racial polarization in Brazilian society, African blocs and other organizations are using music, dance, and religion as explicit organizing principles to create schools, childcare facilities, political groups, and other organizations specifically for Afro-Brazilians. In turn, this heightens tensions between a Brazilian elite that has historically claimed Afro-Brazilian cultural practices as simply Brazilian cultural practices, and Afro-Brazilian activists and intellectuals who seek to claim some form of autonomy within their own public sphere.

The struggles between dominant and subordinate racial groups, the politics of race, help constitute modernity and modernizing projects across the globe. They use racial phenotypes to assess, categorize, and judge persons as citizens and noncitizens. Racial politics operate not only in a polity's defining moments, but in the ongoing process of its re-creation. They permeate the minutiae of daily life: nervous, furtive glances are exchanged in elevators, men and women are rendered suspects without ever having committed a crime; not yet socialized by racist practices, white children run gleefully into the arms of their parents' racial others as their parents watch uncomfortably. This is racial politics between whites and blacks in the late–twentieth century, and Brazil is no exception. For Peçanha—the black Cinderella—the clock struck midnight the moment she was born.

NOTES

1 For critiques of the exclusionary character of Habermas's public sphere, or rather, considerations of the evolution of micropublic spheres for groups and subjects excluded from participatory roles within the bourgeois version, see Fraser 1991, 109–42 and Ryan 1991, 259–88.
2 The works of E. P. Thompson (1966), Paul Willis (1981), Raymond Williams (1975), and George Orwell (1958) provide evidence of a public sphere of the working class that is quite distinct from its more affluent counterparts.
3 Brazil, Constituicao politica do Imperio do Brasil, art. 94, in combination with arts. 6 and 91; quoted in Graham 1993.
4 It may seem contradictory to suggest that the presence of Afro-Brazilian cultural practices and productions is at once residual and dominant, but it is the closest I can come at the present time to characterizing the pervasiveness of the "Africanisms" in Brazilian daily life, and the powerlessness of Afro-Brazilian religious, cultural, and political institutions relative to both the state and civic institutions of the Brazilian polity. They are residual in a more explicitly political sense. Afro-Brazilian cultural practices are considered *national* practices and are manipulated for their symbolic resonance by Brazilian elites to display the heterogenic cohesiveness of Brazilians; they are dominant in that they are suffused in an almost transracial way throughout the norms and values of civil society. An example of this in Brazil—found also in Latin nations like Cuba and Venezuela— is a corporeal aesthetic of the female body that emphasizes distinctly African considerations of physical attractiveness—large hips and buttocks, and a narrow waist, with little attention to breast size—as opposed to the more Western standards of feminine beauty, which in the twentieth century, favor small hips, a narrow waist, large breasts, and thin thighs. For a U.S. audience—or more broadly, those familiar with contemporary U.S. popular culture and rap music in particular—one would have to imagine Sir Mix-A-Lot's hit, "Baby's Got Back," not merely as a popular song, but as an expression of a *national* disposition toward a particular standard of beauty to appreciate the extent to which the fetishization of the *bunda* (buttocks) in Brazil is as much evidence of an African presence as it is a specifically national cultural norm. The "Africanization" of the female bodily aesthetic is one of Brazil's distinctive features as a nation with the largest population of people of African descent outside of Nigeria.
5 Unless, of course, one considers Gandhi's or King's nonviolent resistance as movements, which given their appeals to a higher moral order,

projected a sense of invulnerability to the power of the state, colonial authority, or dominant ethnic group. Yet one is still struck by the reality of their respective struggles; they made appeals based on the moral authority of reason and were answered with coercion, the highest form of unreason.

6 Reis notes that the males decided on Ramadan as the moment for revolt because it is a time when Allah is said to "control malignant spirits and reorder the affairs of the world." See Reis and Silva 1989, 122.

7 For more information on Afro-Brazilian cultural practices, especially Black soul, see Hanchard 1994, Brown and Bick 1987, and Rodrigues da Silva 1983.

8 The diaphanous nature of the barrier between black private and public spheres is also evident in other national contexts. Consider the following autobiographical observations of Wahneema Lubiano, a U.S. African American theorist, on her childhood experiences as a preacher's daughter whose father's church was next door to a brothel. "Our church and our apartment were both private and public: the two constituted a space that described both the destitution and constellation of the neighborhood, and what black people in that neighborhood and town meant to themselves and to the larger social, economic and political space of the town. It marked us, we marked it." See Lubiano 1993, 56.

REFERENCES

Andrews, G. R. 1991. *Blacks and Whites in São Paulo, Brazil, 1888–1988.* Madison: University of Wisconsin Press.

Bastos P. Neves, L. M. 1994. As eleiçoes na construção do emperio Brasileiro: Os limites de uma nova practica da cultura politica Luso-Brasileira (1820–1823). Paper presented at the workshop on Political Representation and Nation Building in Nineteenth-Century Latin America, 7–9 March, University of Texas, Austin.

Braga, J. 1992. Candomblé: Força e Resistência. *Afro-Asia* 15: 13–17.

Brown, D. D. G., and M. Bick. 1987. Religion, Class, and Context: Continuities and Discontinuities in Brazilian Umbanda. *American Ethnologist* 14, no. 1:73–93.

Brubaker, R. 1992. *Citizenship and Nationhood in France and Germany.* Cambridge, Mass.: Harvard University Press.

Chatterjee, P. 1986. *Nationalist Thought and the Colonial World.* London: Zed.

A Cinderela Negra. 1993. *Veja* (7 July): 66–73.

Conrad, R. 1983. *Children of God's Fire*. Princeton, N.J.: Princeton University Press.

Davis, H. 1961. *Latin American Social Thought*. Washington, D.C.: University Press of Washington.

Dean, W. 1976. *Rio Claro: A Brazilian Plantation System, 1820–1920*. Palo Alto, Calif.: Stanford University Press.

Elbein dos Santos, J., and D. M. Dos Santos. 1984. Religion and Black Culture. In *Africa in Latin America*, ed. M. M. Fraginals. New York: Holmes and Meir.

Fernandes, F. 1969. *The Negro in Brazilian Society*. New York: Columbia University Press.

Flory, T. 1977. Race and Social Control in Independent Bahia. *Latin American Studies*, no. 2: 199–224.

Fraser, N. 1991. Rethinking the Public Sphere: A Contribution to the Critique of Actually Existing Democracy. In *Jürgen Habermas and the Public Sphere*, ed. C. Calhoun. Cambridge, Mass.: MIT Press.

Freyre, G. 1946. *The Masters and the Slaves*. New York: Alfred A. Knopf.

Graham, R. 1993. Free African Brazilians and the State in Slavery Times. Paper presented at the conference, Racial Politics in Contemporary Brazil, 8–10 April, University of Texas, Austin.

Habermas, J. 1987. *The Philosophical Discourses of Modernity*. Cambridge, Mass.: MIT Press.

————. 1991. *The Structural Transformation of the Public Sphere*. Cambridge, Mass.: MIT Press.

Hanchard, M. G. 1993. Culturalism versus Cultural Politics: Movimento Negro in Rio de Janeiro and São Paulo, Brazil. In *The Violence Within*, ed. K. B. Warren, 57–86. Boulder, Colo.: Westview Press.

————. 1994. *Orpheus and Power: The Movimento Negro of Rio de Janeiro and São Paulo, Brazil, 1945–1988*. Princeton, N.J.: Princeton University Press.

Klein, H. 1972. Nineteenth Century Brazil. In *Neither Slave nor Free: The Freedmen of African Descent in the New World*, eds. D. Cohen and J. Green, 309–34. Baltimore, Md.: Johns Hopkins University Press.

Kraay, H. 1992. "As Terrifying as Expected": The Bahian Sabinada, 1837–1838. *Hispanic American Historical Review* 72, no. 4 (November): 501–27.

Lubiano, W. 1993. If I Could Talk about It, This Is Not What I Would Say. *Assemblage* 20 (April): 56–57.

Maggie, Y. 1988. O que se cala quando se fala do negro no Brazil. Photocopy.

Mehta, U. S. 1990. Liberal Strategies of Exclusion. *Politics and Society*. 18, no. 4:427–54.

Mitchell, M. 1977. Racial Consciousness and the Political Attitudes and Behavior of Blacks in São Paulo, Brazil. Ph.D. diss., University of Michigan.

Mulvey, L. 1989. *Visual and Other Pleasures.* Bloomington: Indiana University Press.

Nishida, M. 1993. Manumission and Ethnicity in Brazil, 1808–1888. *Hispanic American Historical Review* 73, no. 3:361–91.

Orwell, G. 1958. *The Road to Wigan Pier.* San Diego, Calif.: Harcourt Brace Jovanovich.

Reis, J. J. 1993. *Slave Rebellion in Brazil: The Muslim Uprising of 1835 in Bahia.* Trans. A. Brakel. Baltimore, Md.: Johns Hopkins University Press.

Reis, J. J., and E. Silva. 1989. *Negociação e Conflito: A Resistência Negra No Brasil Escravista.* São Paulo: Editora Schwarz.

Robinson, C. 1983. *Black Marxism.* London: Zed.

Rodrigues da Silva, C. B. 1983. Black Soul: Aglutinação Espontanea ou Identidade Etnica. In *Movimentos Sociais, Urbanos, Minorias Etnicas e Outros Estudos,* eds. L. A. Silva et al., 245–62. Brasília: ANPOCS.

Ryan, M. 1991. Gender and Public Access: Women and Politics in Nineteenth Century America. In *Jürgen Habermas and the Public Sphere,* ed. C. Calhoun. Cambridge, Mass.: MIT Press.

Skidmore, T. E. 1993. Race Relations in Brazil. *Camões Center Quarterly* 4, nos. 3–4:49–61.

Taylor, C. 1989. *Sources of the Self: The Making of Modern Identity.* Cambridge, Mass.: Harvard University Press.

Thompson, E. P. 1966. *The Making of the English Working Class.* New York: Vintage Books.

Viotti da Costa, E. 1985. *The Brazilian Empire: Myths and Histories.* Chicago, Ill.: University of Chicago Press.

Williams, R. 1975. *The Country and the City.* New York: Oxford University Press.

———. 1977. Dominant, Residual, and Emergent Cultures. In *Marxism and Literature.* London: Oxford University Press.

Willis, P. 1981. *Learning to Labor: How Working Class Kids Get Working Class Jobs.* New York: Columbia University Press.

Edward E. Telles

ETHNIC BOUNDARIES AND

POLITICAL MOBILIZATION AMONG

AFRICAN BRAZILIANS

Comparisons with the U.S. Case

The low levels of political mobilization among Afro-Brazilians are often attributed, at least in part, to the role of the Brazilian state. Analysts have pointed to the effective management of racial tensions and inequality by the Brazilian elite (Nascimento 1982; Hasenbalg 1979), or to the failure of the state to enact democracy, through which participation would enable the clarification of racial identities for Afro-Brazilians as well as whites (Winant 1992). Others have focused on cultural issues in which racial identity is made ambiguous by a continuous rather than categorical system of racial classification (Degler 1985; Souza 1971). While these arguments may have their merits, I believe that social structural issues are fundamental and have been overlooked. In this chapter, I focus on a series of structural constraints that impair the formation of an Afro-Brazilian identity and, thus, political mobilization on a large scale. I also compare this case to that of African Americans, as an example of successful political mobilization that grew out of a distinct structural context.

Research on ethnic movements in a wide range of situations has shown that the major prerequisite for organizing and mobilizing enough people to sustain prolonged resistance is a clear sense of shared ethnic identity (Zimmerman 1980; Olzak 1983). Some marker of ethnic identity—whether it be language, religion, skin color, or nationality—must be used so that a group can define its boundaries to pursue its collective ends. The more markers there are, and the sharper they distinguish groups, the stronger ethnic identity tends to be.

Comparisons of the African-origin populations in Brazil and the United States offer clear examples of peoples who were stripped of much of their original ethnic cultures through slavery, although some cultural remnants of Africa remain to different degrees in the two countries. Interestingly, direct and continuous links to African culture in general are greater in Brazil (for instance, Yoruba language, syncretic religion, and West African musical rhythms) than in the United States, suggesting at first that these cultural markers are stronger bases of ethnic identification in Brazil. I argue, however, that despite the closer ties to African culture found in Brazil, there is a far deeper sense of a separate ethnic identity for the African American population due to clear boundaries from the dominant culture; such boundaries are much less distinct in Brazil. Whether or not black cultures in the Americas can be linked to Africa, in the United States, there is a tenacious African American ethnic identity based on cultural distinctiveness, while the formation of an analogous identity in Brazil has been much more ambiguous for most of the Afro-Brazilian population. Many of the surviving and transformed Africanisms in Brazil have become part of the national culture, rather than an Afro-Brazilian ethnic culture.

Institutions and social structures are essential in supporting or reinforcing ethnic identity, and those that support separate ethnic identities and cultures, particularly residential segregation, are stronger in the United States. This chapter explores what seems to be the key markers of Afro-Brazilian identity, especially as compared to markers of Afro-American identity. These include skin color, class, and residential concentration.

The data I present come from the 1980 Census of Brazil. Data by race are presented with the census categories of black (*preto*), brown (*pardo*), and white (*branco*). I refer to blacks and browns collectively as Afro-Brazilian, even though many browns may be of Indian or primarily Indian ancestry or identity. Thus, the combined brown and black categories form the closest proxy available for Afro-Brazilians in the 1980 Census. Occasionally, I use the term *mulatto* to refer to the white-black mixed-race category.

SKIN COLOR, INEQUALITY, AND IDENTITY

Skin color or ancestry might seem to be the main ethnic marker in countries having large populations of both European and African origin. A racial classification system, in which racial categories (such as *pardo,* brown, and mulatto) between white and black are used, and a whitening ideology, which places a higher value on lighter skin color, have been blamed for inhibiting the formation of an Afro-Brazilian identity (Skidmore 1974; Nascimento 1982). Brown persons perceive themselves and are perceived as intermediate to whites and blacks on a racial hierarchy, and therefore, superior to black Brazilians. Thus, it is in the interests of brown persons not to identify as black since their opportunities are obviously greater as such. Indeed, among browns and blacks, a whitening ideology proposes that marriage to persons of lighter skin tone will improve life chances for their children and possibly themselves (Degler 1986). Furthermore, the boundary line between white and brown is often blurred; there is a tendency to identify as white persons near the white-brown color boundary (Hasenbalg, Silva, and Barcelos 1989). In order for blacks and browns to be mobilized together or as a single group, ethnic markers must be that much crisper.

By contrast, ethnic distinctiveness based on ancestry, and increasingly on skin color (Daniel 1992), is greater in the United States because of a racial caste system that legally segregated whites and blacks in all of life's dimensions. For most of this century, to accomplish such segregation, definitions of white and black had to be adopted. The solution was to define anyone having one drop of African blood as "black." In Brazil, legal segregation did not occur for reasons that continue to be highly debated (Harris 1964), and one's skin color on a racial continuum became the dominant means for classification. Moreover, these sharp categorical distinctions between black and white became the basic ethnic distinctions between the so-constructed white and black races in the United States, whereas skin color distinctions among blacks received little attention, at least among whites. Persons of any African origin in the United States have been defined, for the most part, as black, although there are many cases of communities that sought to define themselves as multiracial (Daniel 1992).

Despite much ado about the privileged status of the mulatto compared to blacks in Brazil (Degler 1985), evidence based on human-capital models shows that blacks and browns experience similar levels of racial discrimination in the labor market (Silva 1985; Lovell 1989), and that the gap between brown and black earnings is much greater than that between white and brown earnings. The top part of table 1 supports this argument, showing that black families earn about 40 percent and brown families about 45 percent of what white families earn. Not only do both blacks and browns have lower incomes than whites, but black family income is fully 90 percent of brown family income. Thus, there is a huge white-Afro-Brazilian gap and a relatively tiny gap between blacks and browns. Although blacks may suffer a bit more discrimination than browns, it is not unreasonable to expect that blacks and browns are aware that being of African origin as opposed to being white is the fundamental cleavage determining life chances along Brazil's racial continuum.

This might suggest, then, that the relation between skin tone and income among the black and brown populations is similar to that in the United States. That is, that light-brown African Americans might earn more than dark-brown or black African Americans, but that the differences would be slight when compared to the much higher earnings of whites. Data from the *National Survey of Black Americans,* however, shows that family incomes of African Americans range from 53 percent of mean white incomes for the darkest subgroup to 80 percent of white income for the lightest. Not only does the African-origin population in the United States have average incomes that are nearer to those of whites than in Brazil, but there is a substantially wider variation by skin color. When the five reported skin color groups in the United States are aggregated to form a brown and black group for comparison with Brazil, the results show that there are greater differences between dark- and light-skinned Africans in the United States than in Brazil, contrary to what the continuum versus caste hypothesis would suggest. U.S. "black" families earn 81.7 percent of what U.S. "brown" families earn, compared to 90 percent in Brazil. Furthermore, the gap between white and brown in Brazil is much greater. "Brown" families earn 67.8 percent of what white families earn in the United States and only 44.7 percent in Brazil. In terms of income, blacks and browns are structurally very similar, and both are quite distinct

TABLE 1

Mean Annual Family Income in Brazil and the United States by Skin Color among African-Origin Populations

Country and Skin Color	Distribution of African Origin[1] by Skin Color	Annual Family Income (Dollars)	Percent of White Income[2]	Black as Percent of Brown Income
BRAZIL:				
Black	13.2	2,154	40.2	90.0
Brown	86.8	2,393	44.7	—
African origin[1]				
(nonwhite)	100.0	2,362	44.1	—
UNITED STATES:				
Black equivalent	38.4	11,759	55.4	81.7
Very dark	8.5	11,303	53.2	—
Dark brown	29.9	11,888	56.0	—
Brown equivalent	59.0	14,390	67.8	—
Medium brown	44.6	13,900	65.5	—
Light brown	14.4	15,907	74.9	—
Very light	2.6	16,977	79.9	—
African Origin	100.0	13,447	63.3	—

Source: Data for Brazil are from a 25 percent microdata sample of the 1980 Brazilian Census; data for the United States are from the *1979–1980 National Survey of Black Americans,* as reported by Keith and Herring (1991).

[1] For Brazil, "African origin" is assumed to be roughly equivalent to the nonwhite (black and brown) population.

[2] In 1980, mean annual family income for whites in Brazil was $5,351 and $21,235 for non-Hispanic whites in the United States.

from whites in Brazil, implying *more of* a caste for the African-origin population in Brazil, while racial differences in the United States better resemble a color continuum.

This actual color continuum, albeit an often unrecognized one, has not impeded the formation of strong black identities in the United States. Nor has an economic caste for African Brazilians

TABLE 2

Indexes of Residential Dissimilarity by Skin Color in the Ten Largest
Brazilian and Select U.S. Metropolitan Areas, 1980

Metropolitan Area	White versus African	White versus Black	White versus Brown	Brown versus Black
São Paulo	37	40	38	36
Rio de Janeiro	37	43	38	31
Belo Horizonte	41	41	43	34
Porto Alegre	37	43	41	42
Recife	38	50	39	42
Salvador	48	53	49	35
Fortaleza	40	56	41	56
Curitiba	39	48	42	47
Brasília	39	42	41	42
Belem	37	49	38	43
New York	—	73	—	—
Los Angeles	—	86	—	—
Chicago	—	76	—	—
Detroit	—	87	—	—
Philadelphia	—	77	—	—
Washington, D.C.	—	69	—	—

Source: Indexes for Brazil are based on *setor censitario* (mean population of 1,150)
and calculated from a 25 percent microdata sample of the 1980 Brazilian Census;
indexes for the United States are based on census tract data (mean population of
4,000), and taken from Massey and Denton 1993.

strengthened a common racial identity. Indeed, the U.S. black
middle class, comprised largely of relatively light-skin-tone persons, identifies as black and provides important leadership for the
movement. Yet this black identity does not arise merely out of inequality, since the status of light-skinned blacks is closer to that of
whites than to dark-skinned blacks. It is rather segregation, legal
in the past and extreme residential segregation in the present, that
primarily shapes such racial identity. In Brazil, by contrast, where

TABLE 3

White Versus Nonwhite Residential Dissimilarity by Family Income
for Three Metropolitan Areas in Brazil

Number of Minimum Salaries	Rio de Janeiro	Belo Horizonte	Salvador
1–1.99	35	38	49
2–2.99	36	39	50
3–4.99	36	39	49
5–9.99	40	43	49
10–19.99	53	54	50
20 and more	—	—	50

there was no legal segregation and racial residential segregation is
relatively moderate, lighter-skinned African Brazilians have a much
lower status than white Brazilians.

One might contend that Brazilian racial definitions miss the real
extent of brown-white inequality because higher-class brown persons might identify as white, thus deflating actual mean income for
the brown population. Such an argument comes out of the work of
social anthropologists, who have discussed how racial definitions
are not strict, as in the United States, but flexible and negotiated,
especially among persons of high social status (see, for instance,
Harris 1964). For example, the middle-class status of persons who
appear to be black or brown allows them to be treated and even
identified as white. Evidence based on a recent DataFolha survey of
5,081 persons in 121 municipalities in Brazil, however, reveals that
white-nonwhite income differences are greater when race is evalu-
ated by interviewers rather than by self-identification, as in the census (Telles and Lim 1997). Class does not affect racial identification.

Table 2 shows the distribution of persons by race and income
under both forms of racial identification. The three income categories are less than ten minimum salaries, ten to twenty minimum
salaries, and twenty-plus minimum salaries, which refer roughly
to monthly incomes of less than $1,000, $1,000 to $2,000, and
more than $2,000. Table 3 concludes that the income distribution

among those self-identifying in these three racial categories is similar to the income distribution for those placed in the categories by an interviewer. In other words, income seems to make little or no difference to one's racial self-identification in urban areas of Brazil, suggesting that data based on racial self-identification in Brazil is fairly close to social classification. The inconsistency between self-reporting and subjective classifications in earlier studies by social anthropologists may reflect that time period's culture of racial classification. These studies were mostly conducted in the 1960s or before, and in isolated small towns or rural areas.

CLASS AND ETHNIC IDENTITY

Relatedly, income inequality between whites and Afro-Brazilians, and a more similar status between blacks and browns, in most of Brazil might suggest that social class could be an important ethnic marker. Most notably, blacks and browns are nearly absent from the Brazilian middle class and are likely to remain so even with economic development. Whites are 5.3 times as likely as blacks to be in professional occupations in Brazil compared to only 2.2 times as likely in the United States. In fact, industrialization and educational expansion has tended to increase the racial gap in access to professional and managerial positions, although it has improved access to skilled blue-collar jobs (Telles 1994).

Yet the political mobilization that might be expected from a high level of inequality may actually be constrained by such structural inequalities. In particular, race may be too correlated, although far from perfectly correlated, with class in Brazil. While the process of group formation—that is, skin color as determinant of class position—may be firmly grounded in economics, there is confusion over which of the two boundaries is operative in creating inequalities and determining collective action. An emphasis on class divisions, as a basis for political organization and the focal point for Brazilian social problems, and the general disavowal given to racial divisions, guide mobilization around collective interests based on class commonalties, which cut across racial lines. The Brazilian labor movement's failure to acknowledge race has been beneficial for generally preventing racial fragmentation among the working class, but has also denied the importance that race could have in organizing workers, and that race plays in channeling Brazilians into the poor and working classes as well as in shaping middle-class perceptions about the Brazilian working class.

RESIDENTIAL CONCENTRATION AND IDENTITY

Residential concentration or segregation may directly reinforce ethnic distinction, or a long history of it may create the conditions for the establishment of other markers, such as language and religion. The case of African Americans illustrates this. A high level of residential segregation since about 1930 has led to a high degree of ethnic consciousness and corporate organization among African Americans. While it has had devastating effects on the psyches and life chances of African Americans, as well as on U.S. race relations in general, it has at the same time afforded opportunities for the large-scale mobilization of African Americans.

First of all, segregation neatly separated the worlds of whites and blacks, allowing the formation of separate black and white cultures, including religion and language, and thus facilitating the development of ethnic identities. Awareness of blacks by whites and vice versa has been low because of segregation. Extremely limited exposure between races due to segregation also severely hindered intermarriage and interracial friendships, so that ethnic boundaries have become sharply demarcated. Further, for these separate communities to function, parallel institutions emerged. Universities, banks, churches, newspapers, and other institutions were established, entirely owned and managed by blacks. From these, African Americans learned the mechanics of resistance and drew resources for such resistance. A black leadership evolved and, more important, formed under a politicized ethnic identification. Separate black communities offered blacks opportunities for entrepreneurship with a strictly black clientele and the strength of black electoral power was ensured with the concentration of black votes in electoral districts. At the same time, the mobilization of the black community is mostly due to the reinforcement of a separate identity through all-black neighborhoods. Paradoxically, the extreme spatial distance between whites and blacks in the United

States has aided blacks in mounting challenges to white dominance.

On the negative side, the persistence of black-white segregation for the past sixty years has been largely responsible for the creation of a black underclass today (Massey and Denton 1993). The institutional outcome of segregation is the black ghetto, in which high levels of unemployment, single-parent households, and unusually high concentrations of poverty have created an environment of hopelessness and despair that further handicaps the life chances of African Americans.

Legal segregation has not existed in Brazil since at least abolition in 1888. Additionally, residential segregation, by race, was believed to exist only to the extent that it was correlated with class (Pierson 1942). My research demonstrates that urban residential segregation in Brazil exists, but at levels lower than in the United States (Telles 1992). Also, only moderate segregation occurs between whites, browns, and blacks of similar incomes. When compared to the separate and unequal black-white relations in the United States, black-white relations in Brazil are less separate but more unequal.

Table 2 shows this dissimilarity between racial groups in the ten largest metropolitan areas of Brazil and in select U.S. cities. Dissimilarity measures the extent to which two populations are unevenly distributed across residential space vis-à-vis each other. Indexes range from zero to one hundred, where zero is absolutely no segregation and one hundred is complete segregation. These indexes are plainly higher in the United States. The highest index of white versus Afro-Brazilian dissimilarity in Brazil is forty-eight for Salvador, which indicates that forty-eight percent of the nonwhite population would have to move out of their neighborhood (*setor censitario*) so that they would be evenly distributed with whites across neighborhoods. By contrast, residential segregation as measured by dissimilarity is very high in the United States, with values ranging from sixty-nine in Washington, D.C., to eighty-seven in Detroit (Massey and Denton 1993).

The moderate segregation that does exist in Brazil is generally dismissed as an effect of class, rather than due to ethnicity or racism. To explore whether this is true, I computed segregation indexes for six income groups in three metropolitan areas where

TABLE 4

Residential Isolation of African-Origin Populations in the Ten
Largest Brazilian and Select U.S. Metropolitan Areas, 1980

Metropolitan Percent Area African Origin	Extent of African-Origin[1] Isolation					Percent African Origin
	Brown + Black[1]	Browns	Blacks	Brown Isolation	Black Isolation	
São Paulo	37	38	34	33	9	26
Rio de Janeiro	50	51	49	39	16	39
Belo Horizonte	58	59	53	50	14	46
Porto Alegre	23	24	23	16	12	14
Recife	70	70	67	65	13	67
Salvador	82	82	81	67	27	76
Fortaleza	75	76	69	73	12	69
Curitiba	25	26	21	24	5	15
Brasília	57	57	49	54	7	46
Belem	77	77	73	74	7	72
New York	—	63	—	—	—	21
Los Angeles	—	60	—	—	—	13
Chicago	—	83	—	—	—	20
Detroit	—	77	—	—	—	21
Philadelphia	—	70	—	—	—	19
Washington, D.C.	—	68	—	—	—	28

Source: Indexes for Brazil are based on *setor censitario* (mean population of 1,150)
and calculated from a 25 percent microdata sample of the 1980 Brazilian Census;
indexes for the United States are based on census tract data (mean population of
4,000), and taken from Massey and Denton (1993), and the U.S. Bureau of the
Census (1982).
[1] For Brazil, "African-origin" is assumed to be roughly equivalent to the nonwhite
(black + brown) population.

whites and nonwhites are both well represented. Table 3 reveals
that segregation is moderate even among persons in the same income bracket. Thus, either ethnicity plays an important role in the
choice of a place to live for Afro-Brazilians or white racism has kept
them out of certain neighborhoods, or both. Segregation tends to
increase with income in Rio de Janeiro and Belo Horizonte, sug-

gesting that racism may be greater for the middle class or that ethnicity becomes especially salient at this level, as Afro-Brazilians must make a greater effort to find a neighborhood with a significant number of coethnics. In the case of Salvador, segregation remains the same for all income brackets, perhaps because middle-class Afro-Brazilians there more easily find housing near coethnics. Segregation holds at about fifty even in the highest income category (twenty and more minimum salaries), a category that contains significant numbers of nonwhites only in Salvador (Telles 1992).

Because Afro-Brazilians often constitute the numerical majority in some regions of Brazil, however, extreme segregation is not needed to isolate them from whites in certain areas, like Salvador. Segregation experiences for individuals may depend more on the extent to which they are isolated from members of other racial groups, than to the evenness (dissimilarity) of distribution of the entire group. Such experiences would be vital to the question of identity formation. To capture this effect, I calculated isolation indexes that measure the proportion of neighbors that are coethnics for the average Afro-Brazilian. These are listed in table 4. Like dissimilarity, these indexes range from zero to one hundred, where one hundred means that Afro-Brazilians are completely isolated in neighborhoods separate from whites. The second column of table 4 shows that the isolation of nonwhites varies widely among the ten largest metropolitan areas of Brazil. In Salvador, an index of eighty-two indicates that the average Afro-Brazilian will live in a neighborhood where 82 percent of the residents are also nonwhite. At the other end, indexes with values less than fifty demonstrate that the average nonwhite in São Paulo, Porto Alegre, and Curitiba lives in a predominately white neighborhood. For the United States, the average African American in all six metropolitan areas lives in a predominately black neighborhood, with ranges from sixty in Los Angeles to eighty-three in Chicago (Massey and Denton 1993).

SALVADOR, BAHIA, AS AN EXCEPTION

The work of ethnographers at the Federal University of Bahia demonstrates that there is a clear sense of Afro-Brazilian ethnic identity among a large part of the African-origin population in Salvador, more so than that found in other Brazilian metropolitan areas

(Agier 1992; Morales 1991). For example, *blocos afros* began and are especially important in Salvador. There, the racism that has set the Afro-Brazilian community apart has been transformed into a positive sense of ethnic identification among members of the group. The creation of a distinctive ethnic identity in Bahia is often seen to be a result of the maintenance of diverse tribal cultural elements from Africa (Bastide 1978). The question still remains as to why these have been maintained to date, fully 140 years since the end of the slave trade, and particularly in Bahia. I argue that the racial isolation of the Afro-Brazilian population of Salvador has been the major determinant for the maintenance and construction of this identity. Distinct cultural elements, whether "African" or Afro-Brazilian, are reinforced in a ghetto environment that isolates the worlds of Afro-Brazilians in Salvador from those of whites. Additionally, such isolation produces other conditions that fuel identification, such as the generation of Afro-Brazilian institutions and a professional class.

The average nonwhite in Salvador lives in a neighborhood that is 82 percent nonwhite. Because of moderate rather than high dissimilarity, and due to the smaller census tracts, an isolation index of eighty is probably analogous to an index of some level over sixty-five or seventy in the United States, which generally means that some blacks live in integrated neighborhoods while the majority live in neighborhoods that are all black (Massey and Denton 1993). While isolation is due partly to some unevenness in the spatial distribution of race groups, it mostly owes its emergence to the large black and brown component of the population. In fact, both blacks and browns share this extremely high level of isolation, which is roughly the same as that as of the most segregated major metropolitan area in the United States. The creation of such high residential isolation in Salvador has also been largely responsible for the emergence of a significant Afro-Brazilian middle class, unique for Brazil, which provides service functions to ghetto residents and can take advantage of ethnic markets that provide opportunities for entrepreneurship, including entrepreneurship in the culture industry (for example, Olodum). A separate Afro-Brazilian community in Bahia favors the formation and maintenance of a truly Afro-Brazilian culture and the construction of a separate identity that is reinforced through daily (endogamous) interaction.

Therefore, although residential isolation for the African-origin population in Brazil develops from very different causes than in the United States, its consequences for identity formation may be similar. It does not appear that this strong sense of identity has yet been channeled into large-scale political mobilization, but the potential is great. A culturalist political orientation (Hanchard 1992), arising primarily out of residential concentration, would seem to be a stimulus to ethnic mobilization for Salvador, but not necessarily for other large metropolitan areas.

FUTURE PROSPECTS

Despite these structural constraints, Afro-Brazilian leaders seeking to mobilize the masses of blacks and browns may succeed by appealing to their common history of oppression and their similar socioeconomic status, at least in Brazil's more developed regions. Efforts to build a common ethnicity that focus only on cultural differences such as religion are not likely to succeed, as past experience has shown.

While Afro-Brazilian leaders value a society in which relations with whites are often fluid at a social level and in which whites share in the celebration of a hybrid African culture, they justly decry the oppression and even brutalization of African-origin peoples. The existence of such contrasts, they feel, has led to a system of racial oppression that is extremely effective; the glorification of African culture and the appearance of racial universalism reinforce the idea of Brazil as a racial democracy, despite the actual position of Afro-Brazilians.

By no means am I holding a structurally determinist position. Institutions like segregation do not determine outcomes like identity and mobilization, but they are powerful conditioning forces that facilitate or constrain the construction of distinctive identities or mobilization by ethnic groups, particularly for those whose original markers of ethnicity have been destroyed or severely damaged. Even in "desegregated" settings in the United States, political mobilization by African Americans occurs, although it is in the context of segregation that a distinct African American culture has formed. My point is that segregation is a powerful structural element that ultimately contributes to differences in comparative political mobilization among the African-origin populations of Brazil and the United States.

Such constraints that restrict the formation of ethnic identities might be overcome through the efforts of individuals, especially in an era of increasing, though still quite limited, democracy. Inroads to diminishing and raising consciousness about racism have been made without the mobilization of the masses of blacks and browns. In the case of Brazil, the struggle by Afro-Brazilian activists has already gained nationwide attention through the media and various organizing efforts. Even in the past, newspapers and community-based organizations helped bring the problem of racism to Brazilians of all colors, even though they have not necessarily succeeded in affecting state policy. Education about racism and the causes of racial inequalities since the *centenario* has been critical to raising racial/ethnic consciousness as well.

REFERENCES

Agier, M. 1992. Ethnopolitics: Racism, Culture, and Black Movement in Bahia, Brazil. Paper presented at the Seventeenth International Congress of the Latin American Studies Association, September, Los Angeles, California.

Bastide, R. 1978. *The African Religions of Brazil: Toward a Sociology of the Interpenetration of Civilizations.* Baltimore, Md.: Johns Hopkins University Press.

Daniel, R. 1992. Passers and Pluralists: Subverting the Racial Divide. In *Racially Mixed People in America,* ed. M. P. P. Root, 91–107. Newbury Park, Calif.: Sage Publications.

Degler, C. N. 1971. *Neither Black nor White: Slavery and Race Relations in Brazil and the United States.* New York: Macmillan.

Hanchard, M. G. 1992. Culturalism versus Cultural Politics: The Movimento Negro in Rio de Janeiro and São Paulo, Brazil, 1970–1988. Paper presented at the Seventeenth International Congress of the Latin American Studies Association, September, Los Angeles, California.

Harris, M. 1964. *Patterns of Race in the Americas.* New York: Walker.

Hasenbalg, C. A. 1979. *Discriminação e Desigualdades Raciais no Brasil.* Rio de Janeiro: Graal.

Hasenbalg, C. A., N. d. V. Silva, and L. C. Barcelos. 1989. Notas Sobre Miscegenação Racial no Brasil. *Estudos Afro-Asiáticos* 16:188–97.

Keith, V. M., and C. Herring. 1991. Skin Tone and Stratification in the Black Community. *American Journal of Sociology* 97:760–78.

Lovell, P. A. 1989. *Income and Racial Inequality in Brazil.* Ph.D. diss., University of Florida.

Massey, D. S., and N. A. Denton. 1993. *American Apartheid: Segregation and the Making of the Underclass.* Cambridge, Mass.: Harvard University Press.

Morales, A. 1991. Blocos Negros em Salvador: Reelaboração Cultural e Simbolos de Baianidade. In *Cantos e Toques: Etnografias do Espaço Negro na Bahia,* ed. M. Agier. Salvador, Bahia: Suplemento Caderno CRH.

Nascimento, A. d. 1982. *O Negro Revoltado.* Rio de Janeiro: Nova Fronteira.

Olzak, S. 1983. Contemporary Ethnic Mobilization. *Annual Review of Sociology* 9:355–74.

Pierson, D. 1942. *Negroes in Brazil: A Study of Race Contact at Bahia.* Chicago, Ill.: University of Chicago Press.

Silva, N. d. V. 1985. Updating the Cost of Not Being White in Brazil. In *Race, Class, and Power in Brazil,* ed. P.-M. Fontaine. Los Angeles: University of California, Los Angeles, Center for Afro-American Studies.

Skidmore, T. E. 1974. *Black into White: Race and Nationality in Brazilian Thought.* New York: Oxford University Press.

Souza, A. d. 1971. Raça e Política no Brasil Urbano. *Revista de Administração de Empresas* 11, no. 4:61–70.

Telles, E. E. 1992. Residential Segregation by Skin Color in Brazil. *American Sociological Review* 57, no. 2 (April):186–98.

———. 1993. The Contextual Nature of Racial Inequality in Brazil. Unpublished manuscript.

———. 1994. Industrialization and Racial Inequality in Employment: The Brazilian Example. *American Sociological Review* 59:46–63.

Telles, E. E., and N. Lim. 1998. Does It Really Matter Who Answers the Race Question: Self vs. Interviewer Classification and Income Inequality in Brazil. *Demography* (November).

U.S. Bureau of the Census. 1982. *1980 Census of Population: General Population Characteristics.* Washington, D.C.: Government Printing Office.

Winant, H. 1992. The Fact of Blackness in Brazil. Paper presented at the Seventeenth International Congress of the Latin American Studies Association, September, Los Angeles, California.

Zimmerman, E. 1980. Macro-Comparative Research on Political Protest. In *Handbook of Political Conflict,* ed. T. R. Gurr. New York: Free Press.

Howard Winant

RACIAL DEMOCRACY AND RACIAL IDENTITY

Comparing the United States and Brazil

For a long time, the foundation of all comparative studies of race in the United States and Brazil was the *contrast* between the two countries. In the United States, so the argument went, a rigid color line divided white and black, and "hypodescent" or the "one-drop rule" made all gradations of racial difference insignificant. In Brazil, on the other hand, the gradations were of immense importance, since racial categories were organized along a "racial continuum" (Harris 1964; Davis 1991). In the United States, race was a matter of state policy, of politics. The state established and policed the color line, through slave codes and slave patrols under slavery, segregation in the pre–civil rights period, and equal opportunity and affirmative action policies in the post–civil rights era. In Brazil, by contrast, the state and the political system have been extremely reluctant—at least in the century since abolition—either to enforce or suppress racial boundaries; far more prevalent has been the blanket denial that racism exists there, and the assertion that it is, in fact, racist to denounce racism.[1]

As a consequence of these contrasts (so the argument goes), racial antagonisms have been polarized and politicized in the United States, and diffused and depoliticized in Brazil. At a certain point, before the emergence and consolidation of the U.S. black movement in the late 1950s and early 1960s, the contrast-based comparison seemed to extol the virtues of the Brazilian model. Against what was essentially a herrenvolk democracy in the United States,[2] and in sharp distinction to the U.S. hyperconsciousness of racial difference in every dimension of sociopolitical and cultural life, Brazil appeared a lot more relaxed and accepting of race. Miscegenation was not a big deal there, it seemed, and overt racial conflict hardly existed.

Later, however, after serious confrontations had taken place in the United States over racial issues, and after extensive though basically moderate reforms had been initiated, the contrast-based argument began to turn against Brazil (Skidmore 1985). Suddenly, Brazilian racial dynamics seemed ossified and anachronistic, plagued by something like a "false consciousness" and subject to manipulation by elites. Fueled by the publication of the UNESCO studies, which demonstrated what such writers as Thales de Azevedo (1966) and Florestan Fernandes (1978) labeled "the myth of racial democracy" in Brazil (see also, Bastide and Fernandes 1959), criticism of racial inequality in Brazil underwent a resurgence. The question of why a robust black movement did not exist was raised with greater intensity as well (Degler 1986). The contrast between the United States and Brazil now appeared as one of "progress" (however uneven and conflictual) versus "stasis" (however smooth and cordial). And although this synoptic account doesn't address the many subtle dimensions through which race is organized in the two countries, in general terms, it describes where matters rest even today.

But matters *don't* rest, especially racial ones. Race is constantly being transformed and recast as political, cultural, and indeed global developments affect our sense of who we are, and shape the demands we place on social institutions. At present, race takes new forms in both countries, as a result of new conflicts and new perceptions—about racial identity, racial politics, and the very meaning of race in everyday life. As a result, a new comparative examination may be in order.

Sociological and historical comparisons of the two countries' racial dynamics have long been recognized as useful, due to their similar development as settler states and slavocracies in the Americas, their subsequent abolition of slavery, and their acceptance of large waves of European (and Asian) immigration. While these parallels obviously have their limits, they have been sufficient to inspire a host of scholarly investigations. New developments in both countries, I want to suggest, invite a renewed comparative analysis of their racial politics.

What could we learn from such a reexamination? Simply as an effort to describe developing racial trends and communicate these views between the countries involved, I believe such work is valuable. But beyond that, the comparative analysis of race responds to a growing awareness of race as a global phenomenon whose importance, far from diminishing in the postindustrial, post–cold war, postmarxist, and incipient postapartheid world, is in fact increasing. Finally, at the most concrete level, as conditions change, they must be reevaluated, and theory must be developed or revised as appropriate. And racial conditions are changing dramatically in both the United States and Brazil.

In this essay, I examine these shifts from two related but distinct perspectives. I begin with the transformations in the political systems of the two countries that relate to race. This discussion focuses on a term that is highly charged (especially in Brazil): *racial democracy.*

Brazilian democracy overall remains fragile, and Brazil's "racial democracy" was, of course, a myth that played the authoritarian role of denying racial difference and suppressing racial mobilization. Yet, beginning in the *abertura* and continuing in the renewed democratic Brazil of today, blacks have been able to experiment with modes of racial organization and protest that surpass anything achieved since the 1930s. I do not think it is possible yet to speak of a general politicization of race in Brazil. But the increasing level of political awareness—itself a function of democratization, as well as of economic crisis, the impeachment of former president Fernando Collor de Mello, etc.—also has a stronger racial component than before. In such a context, the tendency exists, to be sure gradual but hopefully permanent, of turning the myth of racial democracy into a reality of racial politics and opposition.

The United States, by contrast, has been for most of its history a herrenvolk democracy in which basic political rights only extended to white men, and in some respects, it remains so today. Yet U.S. society has been significantly transformed as a result of the civil rights reforms achieved a quarter century ago. I analyze here the multiple consequences of these reforms in terms of racial mobility and stratification, fragmentation of racially defined communities, and finally, problematization of racial identities themselves.

I also suggest that each country is experiencing a deepening awareness of the complexity and permanence of *racial difference*. In the United States, race is becoming more complicated and nuanced, largely as a result of the struggles of the recent past, so that the color line and the traditionally bipolar, black-white foundation of racial politics and identity is eroding. In Brazil, race is becoming more politicized, so that the color continuum and the techniques available to elites to deny and diffuse racial difference, and to disrupt and suppress racially based politics, are breaking down. Yet because this politicization has thus far been expressed through collective action only to a limited extent, its chief impact has been to increase the sense of dualism experienced by Brazilian blacks. These developments have crucial consequences for the politics of racial identity in each country. The "double consciousness" in the United States once posited by W. E. B. DuBois is becoming much more variable in response to shifting demographic, political, and class-based factors. Something like a black "double consciousness" is developing in Brazil as well, as the realities of racism are increasingly exposed, but not yet challenged in a fundamental and organized way.

RACIAL DEMOCRACY

Comparative analysis of recent racial politics in the United States and Brazil points to the centrality of a "transition to democracy" in both cases. This is perhaps a controversial assertion. There were certainly substantial differences between the herrenvolk democracy of the United States, which was based on a formalized and legally constituted racial caste system with a nearly rigid color line, and the "racial democracy" of Brazil, which was based on a combination of factors:

a) the assumption, mainly by white elites, that . . . racism does not exist in Brazil or at least not on the level of countries such as South Africa and the United States; b) the continuing reproduction and dissemination of stereotypes denigrating blacks and valorizing whites which results in low, distorted self-images and an aversion to collective action among the former; and c) coercive sanctions and the pre-emption of dissent imposed by whites upon blacks who question or threaten the fundamentally asymmetrical patterns of racial interaction (Hanchard 1994, 103; see also, Azevedo 1975).

But there were significant similarities as well. Both systems—to begin with the obvious—were considered to be democracies, a fact that can only inspire either irony or dread. In both countries, it was whites who advocated the merits of the particular brand of "racial democracy" that operated. The effect of each system was to suppress (or even entirely avert) any demand for the extension of full rights to blacks. Thus, for a long period after abolition, inequalities or even the fundamental absence of citizenship rights, rights to equality before the law and in access to state institutions, and the right to participate equally with whites, all went unrecognized in both countries.[3] Finally, the particular racist practices employed in both systems bore more than a casual resemblance: for example, in terms of the content of stereotypes.

The similarities between the two systems should not be exaggerated. Their chief distinction—the presence of explicit and legally sanctioned racial difference in the postabolition United States, and its relative absence in postabolition Brazil—was of course extremely important. This disparity had a centuries-long gestation in the singular racial formation process that each country underwent. The contrast was further heightened by distinctive processes of abolition, which came in the United States as an aftermath (and afterthought) of the disruptive and bloody Civil War, and in Brazil, as a much-belated recognition by the state that perhaps 90 percent of Afro-Brazilians had already obtained their own emancipation. Nor should persistent racial violence in the United States—and its absence (until recently) in Brazil[4]—be ignored.

Overall, the comparison of U.S. herrenvolk democracy and Brazilian "racial democracy" is justified not because the two countries experienced overarching similarities in their developing racial politics, but rather, because in both countries the claim that the system was democratic served to deny racially defined groups their democratic rights. The low status ascribed to these groups, their availability for exploitation and abuse, and their sociocultural marginalization was thus assured. It is the deeply ideological—or more properly, hegemonic—character of these two racial regimes that ultimately justifies their comparison.

There can be little question that the Brazilian "myth" retained a greater grip on its black subjects (though by no means as great a grip as it did on white Brazilians) than white supremacist ideology did on U.S. blacks. The informality alone of the Brazilian system—in contrast with segregation in the United States—went a long way to mask its character. Indeed, it was precisely the formality of the U.S. racial order, its politicization and enforcement by the state, that provided the black movement with a suitable target for mobilization. But it should also be noted that even this contrast is not an absolute one. The Brazilian state *did* intervene in racial politics from time to time—witness Vargas's suppression of the Frente Negra Brasileira in the 1930s or the military's reaction to the Tiete Club incident of 1978 (Andrews 1991, 205–6). And the U.S. civil rights movement was to discover to its chagrin that the informal elements of white supremacy are a good deal more difficult to dismantle than the laws that enforce it.

The Brazilian transition to democracy was shaped by the prolonged *abertura* of 1974–1985 (Mitchell 1985). During the preceding six-year period, the dictatorship's most brutal and repressive years, the military adopted the "racial democracy" myth *tout court,* denouncing any antiracism activity as a species of leftist subversion. But from the mid-1970s onward, a general upsurge of democratic aspirations took place, nurtured in various sectors such as the church, unions, feminism, and the neighborhood movement. Blacks participated in all these activities, but qua blacks launched the most significant racial organization of the period, the Movimento Negro Unificado (MNU), in 1978. The appearance of the MNU signaled the greatest upswing in black political activity since the 1930s (Hanchard 1994, 221–40; Nascimento 1989; Gonzalez 1985). Not only did the MNU explicitly attempt to fight racial discrimination, but alongside it and in its wake, there appeared a wide variety of black political organizations, caucuses, study groups, journals, and such. Black cultural groups proliferated, including the *afoxes* and *blocos afros* (especially in the northeast).[5] Many of them had a specific political orientation to community organization and racial consciousness-raising. Important black feminist tendencies also gestated within the MNU, giving rise to black women's organizing projects and strategies that continue to the present (Carneiro and Santos 1985; Mills 1992, 15).

As the *abertura* gave way to greater civilian rule and finally to a full-fledged democracy (though not without warts), black movement organizations and activities multiplied. The 1982 elections saw the participation of numerous black candidates, although their performance was generally poor. By 1992, the leading Afro-Brazilian elected official, Partido dos Trabalhadores (PT) Federal Deputy Benedita da Silva, was able to mount (and nearly win) a campaign for the mayoralty of Rio de Janeiro. Mainstream cultural and political institutions began to address racial issues more directly: for example, racial themes appeared in party platforms, religious services (Andrews 1991, 202–4), and with increasing frequency, the mass media. Government agencies responded to problems of racism with greater openness, and the Constituent Assembly of 1987 debated the merits of a new constitutional prohibition on racial discrimination, though it ultimately adopted only a minimal provision.

Perhaps most revealing, the centenary of the *Lei Aurea,* the final decree of abolition, was celebrated in 1988 with a significant public debate on the continuities of racism in Brazil. Mainstream media demonstrated in numerous articles the persistence of racial discrimination; there were many obituaries for the "myth of racial democracy." Black organizations—by now plentiful—denounced the celebration as a farce and stated their intention to commemorate not 13 May the date of the 1888 decree of Princess Isabel, but 20 November, the date of the death in 1695 of Zumbi, the leader of the *quilombo* of Palmares (Maggie 1989).[6] The year saw numerous actions of opposition and protest, including the suppression by the military of a black march in Rio (Hanchard 1994, 265–85). In the last few years, black campaigns have continued: for example, in respect to the census, the murders of street children, and abusive sterilization practices.[7]

Something has definitely changed in Brazil—the Afro-Brazilian movement is now a firm presence. The movement still has major limitations: it is small and lacks a substantial base among the millions of Afro-Brazilians for whom daily survival is the only issue. There is no established national black organization—the MNU, though it continues to exist, has not been able to overcome various problems, chiefly a range of factionalisms. But the movement overall exhibits a certain robustness that argues against any claim of transience and places even its faults in a new light.

Brazilian racial politics—by the mere fact of their existence—now resemble their counterparts in the United States more than ever before. The appearance of the black movement in the 1970s could not have the same ruptural impact on the Brazilian political scene that the U.S. civil rights movement did; it was marked by its birth in an atmosphere of dictatorship and repression, and also by the greater effectivity of the "racial democracy" myth. Still, today it is possible to say that a transition to racial politics is underway; it will be lengthy and undoubtedly not as confrontational as in the United States. But it will take place.

In the United States, the logjam of white supremacist racial politics—which had been eroding steadily under legal pressure since the 1930s and political pressure since the 1950s—finally broke in the mid-1960s. At that time, a massive movement succeeded in overthrowing the legal underpinnings of the system of herrenvolk democracy and instituting moderate but nevertheless far-reaching racial reforms. Among the consequences were greater social mobility for some, though by no means all, members of racially defined minority groups; the reorganization of the political system to accommodate minority voters, interests, and officials; the increased politicization of race throughout U.S. society; the emergence of a range of related social movements, such as "second-wave" feminism, that drew inspiration from the black freedom struggle; and the eventual resurgence, in suitably modified form, of racial reaction. This upheaval had the overall effect of seriously damaging, but by no means destroying, white supremacy and of extending the possibility of democracy to racial minority (and other formerly disenfranchised) constituencies, without fully consolidating those gains (Omi and Winant 1986).

As a result, the United States is now experiencing a totally unprecedented racial situation, in which large-scale uncertainty exists as to the meaning of race or the proper orientation of state racial policies. On the one hand, race continues to structure everyday life, social practices of all types, and the personal—indeed even the unconscious—dimensions of everyone's identity. On the other hand, the susceptibility of race to further state intervention or political action—beyond that deriving from the moderate egalitarianism of the civil rights movement—is denied, not only on the racial Right, but also among many on the Left and in various nationalist currents. Prominent among such arguments is an assertion that would be familiar in Brazil: that at present, the issue confronting racially defined minorities is less centrally one of racism per se, but more crucially, one of class.[8] And prominent too is the idea, also quasi-Brazilian, that racial identity is becoming more flexible (Omi and Winant 1995). It is to the issue of the politics of racial identity that I now turn.

RACIAL IDENTITY

In both Brazil and the United States, contemporary racial politics have changed dramatically over the past few decades. The current racial situations in these two countries themselves may be understood in terms of "transition to democracy": in both countries, as a result of substantial movement activity, far more political freedom exists for racially defined minorities than in the past. Yet in neither country has the racial dimension of stratification and social inequality been seriously transformed. Rather, the more overt manifestations of racism have receded, as white supremacy in the United States and the blanket denial of racism in Brazil have been weakened, *without any fundamental reorganization of the racialized social structures of the two societies.*[9]

As reform has undermined the more overtly racist features of state institutions, and discredited the formerly established ideologies of "white supremacy" and "racial democracy," the political significance of the issue of racial identity has grown. In the two countries, however, the new racial politics of identity are taking very different forms. In the United States, racial identity is being transformed from dualistic to multipolar in the case of minorities, and is becoming more problematic (or dualistic, if you prefer) in the case of whites. In Brazil, black identities are becoming more dualistic (as opposed to continuous), while white identities remain largely unitary and unreflexive.

The characteristic that previously defined racial identity most centrally in the United States, the color line, has been deeply eroded. Yet this process has not taken place evenly or openly; rather, a moderate racial ideology whose focus is on the equality of individuals, the invidiousness of racial distinctions, and the equivalence of race and ethnicity, has become hegemonic. The official denial of the importance of race combines with constant, daily, practical reminders that race is as crucial a factor as ever in shaping life chances and experiences. As a result, both individuals and groups suffer from confusion and anxiety about the impact and significance of race in their lives. This situation bears some resemblance to that of Brazil.

In *The Souls of Black Folk,* DuBois (1989) argued that a "veil" divided the black psyche into "two warring souls." The veil had many manifestations, but at its core, it was a line drawn within black people. It was a survival mechanism that permitted one to see her/himself not only from within, as a black person with a particular identity, but also allowed for an externalized self-recognition: one could learn, out of necessity, to see oneself as the white sees him/her. The veil thus served, social psychologically, as a protection against racism, but also operated dialectically to limit and stifle the very identity, the very black self, that it preserved.[10]

This "double consciousness," I suggest, was a logical analysis of the dynamics of racial identity when it was written, and for a good while thereafter. But today it requires, if not rejection, at least updating. At the turn of the century, and indeed in important ways until the mid–twentieth century, the rule of the color line was all but absolute in the United States. Segregation was the norm in the residential, educational, social, cultural, military, and political mainstreams. Only in some industrial sectors, which since the late-1930s had undergone strenuous unionization drives led by the integrated CIO, was a modicum of race-mixing practiced, and even there internal labor markets were mostly segregated. If this remained largely true on the eve of World War II, it was just about absolutely true when DuBois first set it down in 1903.

The postwar political transformations wrought by the civil rights movement, however, dramatically altered racial identity, in ways that we are still discovering a quarter century later. The civil rights movement wrenched from the state a recognition of the realities of discrimination and forced the development of limited but real policies, such as affirmative action and minority set-asides, that were designed to counter it. It also succeeded in overcoming discriminatory immigration laws and in democratizing voting rights. Such changes created incentives for the consolidation of racial identities among "other" groups, that is, groups that were neither black nor white, groups that had substantial experience of racial discrimination, but that had previously been divided by ethnic, regional, or political differences and antagonisms. Vastly aided not only by the transformation of the U.S. racial landscape wrought by the civil rights reforms, but also by the realities of "racial lumping" — since many North Americans cannot distinguish between a Korean American and a Chinese American, or between Chicanos and Ecuadorans for that matter — this *pan-ethnicizing* or racializing experience generated the racial categories "Latino" (or "Hispanic") and "Asian American" (Espiritu 1992; Oboler 1995). It also consolidated the category "Native American" (Cornell 1988). The long-term result of this process was the transformation of the U.S. racial order from its earlier black-white bipolarity to a more multipolar system.

The shift to racial multipolarity also spelled changes in racial identity. For black people, it meant a new series of antagonisms with burgeoning Latino and Asian American groups. These "other" minorities competed for the resources of a welfare state that was under severe attack from the Right. In addition, they occupied "middleman" economic niches in the black community, thus giving rise to a host of familiar antagonisms and conflicts.

Furthermore, stratification *within* the black community was stimulated in the aftermath of the 1960s, as the black middle class discovered new opportunities and achieved greater mobility, abandoning the ghettos for the suburbs, entering the professional and corporate worlds, and so on. Meanwhile, the black working class was severely pressured by deindustrialization, and the poor were abandoned by the welfare state. The result was increasing division among blacks and a greater tendency in the society at large to correlate race with class. Although the color line was not superseded, its salience diminished for blacks; a situation emerged that in limited but real respects resembled the Brazilian one in which "o dinheiro embranquece" (money whitens).

Finally, the shifts brought on by the civil rights movement and the reforms it engendered also had an impact on white racial identity, which was rendered much more problematic than in the days of segregation. Whites had to change their attitudes toward minorities, which meant (since all identity implies difference) that they had to change their attitudes toward themselves. A desirable feature of this shift was the beginning—and this was obviously just a beginning—of racial dualism in whites: in other words, whites had to begin looking at themselves from the standpoint of *how they were being perceived by nonwhites.* On the negative side, whites were threatened by minority gains. They sensed a loss (actual or potential, real or imagined) of their majority status, their dominant position. They suddenly noted an *identity deficit:* their whiteness, since it constituted the norm, was formerly invisible, transparent; but now, in a more highly racially conscious atmosphere, they felt more visible and indeed threatened (Alba 1990; Waters 1990). The result was a rearticulation of the egalitarianism embodied in the civil rights agenda in a far more conservative and individualistic direction, a kind of "antiracist racism." This view, which denies the significance of race (espousing a "color-blind" approach), also claims that affirmative action and similar programs employ racism "in reverse." Such a perspective would certainly be recognizable in Brazil, where many whites claim that to focus attention on race or racism is itself racist.

In Brazil, the development of a black movement since the 1970s, while achieving tremendous successes in challenging the "myth of racial democracy," has not resulted in more than very limited reforms in the institutional structure of Brazilian racism. These should not be dismissed; the creation of various state entities specifically charged with addressing discrimination or Afro-Brazilian issues, the restoration to the 1990–1991 census of questions regarding race, the clear-cut (though brief) recognition of racism in the new constitution, and the various acknowledgments made by high state officials in recent years (and particularly in the 1988 centennial year) of the existence and severity of racism in Brazil, were all important departures from the traditional denial of racism that has characterized the Brazilian state in the past.

Yet all these actions and measures do not add up to much more than a symbolic shift. The major change in Brazilian racial dynamics has been the emergence of a viable movement, one that recognizes the political dimensions of race, and the necessity of naming and defending Afro-Brazilian interests as such. This movement has focused its attention on campaigns against discrimination, against the murder of street children, and on community organization in poor neighborhoods. Undoubtedly, the majority of the many black organizations founded since the 1970s are mostly cultural groups, which stress such issues as consciousness-raising, linkages with Africa, the role of Afro-Brazilians in Brazilian history, and the commemoration of the Palmares *quilombo*. And there remain significant debates between the primarily "Africanist" orientation of culturally based Afro-Brazilian groups and the primarily "Americanist" orientation of more explicitly political groups (Hanchard 1994).

This combination of limited reforms and greater black consciousness and organization spurred by democratization, suggests that blacks in Brazil will experience an increasingly contradictory situation. Indeed, as the number of racially conscious blacks grows, the Brazilian scene may in some respects come to resemble racial politics in the United States before the upsurge of the modern civil rights movement. In such circumstances, individuals and personal relationships must undertake much of the ideological "work" needed to manage the stresses and contradictions of a pervasive "practical" racism that social institutions, by and large, refuse to address. Meanwhile, viable black organizations will have to act as what Aldon Morris (1984) calls "movement halfway houses," preserving and slowly building the movement.

Such are the conditions, mutatis mutandis, that DuBois sought to address in his discussion of "double consciousness" or racial dualism. As race becomes more politicized in Brazil, as the state recognizes officially that Brazil is not and never has been a "racial democracy"—but neglects any effort to overcome the inequalities that exist—as a black movement builds slowly and painfully to challenge this situation—under conditions of extreme poverty—Afro-Brazilians can be expected to experience greater stress than ever before. Their awareness of themselves as both black and Brazilian, both discriminated against and expected to deny the significance of race, can only increase.

As a final note: there is little evidence that white racial attitudes are changing significantly in Brazil. Far more than blacks, whites continue to uphold the familiar positions: "No Brasil nao da racismo. O negro conhece o seu lugar" (Racism does not exist in Brazil. The Black knows his place). This suggests that a crucial indicator of the next turning point in Brazilian racial politics—one that still appears quite distant, unfortunately—will have been reached when white Brazilians begin to experience the "identity deficit," the sense of threat, that a powerful movement for racial justice tends to invoke, especially when it has gained some foothold within the state. Of course, before such a moment is reached, one would expect substantial numbers of whites to join the movement for racial equality in Brazil.

LIBERATION OF RACIAL IDENTITY

The battle for racial justice is fought not only in the open political arena of the state and social movements, in the struggle for adequate cultural representations, significations, and consciousness of difference; it is also fought on the interior terrain of the individual—her/his intrapsychic world and immediate relationships. As Norbert Lechner (1988) has argued, democracy has not only an outside but an inside, whose principal terrain is the construction of subjectivity. To be sure, these two "spaces" of democracy are deeply intertwined, so that developments in one area necessarily create changes in the other.

With respect to race, in both the United States and Brazil, the relationship between racial subjectivity—what I have called here the politics of racial identity—and the state has undergone enormous changes in the past few decades. These shifts have been more far-reaching in the United States, but this is no more than the whole comparative literature on racial politics in the two countries has led us to predict.

The surprising feature of this comparison, I think, is how much has changed in Brazil. I make this assertion in the full awareness that in terms of general racial inequality, as well as the stratification of education, employment, health, mortality, and so on, little has improved. In fact, the general economic crisis of the country, as always enacted most intensively in the lives of its poorest citizens, has almost certainly increased levels of inequality by nearly any measure. What, then, has changed?

The existence of a modern Afro-Brazilian movement, in my view, is the big change. This movement appears permanent, although such an assertion is inevitably speculative; it also appears to be linked to the consolidation and expansion of democracy in Brazil.

In both the United States and Brazil, the extension of democracy to address racial issues has generated a vast increase in racialized subjectivity. This ran counter to what most observers—both activists and pundits, politicians and academics—expected to happen. Most saw racism, whether white supremacy in the United States or the "myth of racial democracy" in Brazil, as anachronistic, something that would disappear when basic rights were extended and fundamental inequalities addressed. Of course, that has not happened, and not only because reform programs have been limited (as in the United States) or negligible (as in Brazil). It has not happened because racial difference, racialized subjectivity, is a permanent feature of both societies, and of much of the world.

The liberation of racial identity is as much a part of the struggle against racism as the elimination of racial discrimination and inequality. That liberation will involve a reenvisioning of racial politics and a transformation of racial difference, one that will render democracy itself much more radically pluralistic, and will make identity much more a matter of choice than of ascription. As the struggles to achieve these objectives unfold, we shall gradually recognize that the racialization of democracy is as important as the democratization of race.

NOTES

1 Some key works in this tradition are Degler 1986, Hasenbalg 1979, Skidmore 1972, and Wagley and Harris 1958.

2 The term *herrenvolk democracy* was coined, as far as I know, by Pierre L. van den Berghe (1967). It suggests, at a minimum, a situation in which democracy is profoundly limited, principally on race- and sex-based criteria.

3 The systematic nature of racial discrimination in the United States is often contrasted with the supposedly more benign and casual discrimination of Brazil. Recent historical research, however, has demonstrated the extent to which overt and systematic racial discrimination was practiced in postabolition Brazil. See Andrews 1991.

4 In a strict sense, racial violence has always existed in Brazil, especially in rural areas and in the northeast, where its primary logic has been the struggle over land (see, among a voluminous literature, Movimento dos Trabalhadores Sem Terra 1986). This type of violence, however, has been less explicitly racialized than the recent urban type. The prime ex-

ample of the latter is the proliferating "death squads" whose primary targets are black street children in the many favelas encircling Brazilian cities. This seems to be a new form of racial violence, symptomatic of changing patterns of racism in Brazil (see Centro de Articulacao de Populacoes Marginalizadas 1989).

5 Most prominently, the Olodum Cultural Group. A 1992 statement by Olodum, "In Freedom's Rhythm," is reprinted in translation in Mills 1992, 14.

6 *Quilombos* were Brazilian maroon communities, that is, settlements of runaway slaves and their allies (often indigenous people). The *quilombo* of Palmares, in the interior of the State of Bahia, was the most long-lived and legendary of these efforts at slave revolt and resistance, enduring for almost 100 years despite various expeditions sent against it.

7 In 1990, a group of nongovernmental organizations concerned with racism in Brazil formed Projeto Censo 90 with the aim of convincing Afro-Brazilians to identify themselves accurately, rather than to "lighten" themselves, in the upcoming census. The census itself was later postponed to 1991. The campaign, whose slogan was "*Nao deixe sua cor passar em branco: responda com bom c/senso*" ("Don't let your color pass for white: respond with good sense," punning on 'sense/census/consensus'), achieved significant attention through its strategy of using the mass media to get the message out. See Domingues 1992a.

8 The locus classicus of this position is William Julius Wilson (1980), but it is very widely argued today.

9 For a review of the continuing (and in some respects worsening) dynamics of racial stratification in the United States, see Hacker 1992. For a review of Brazilian conditions, see the various papers in Lovell 1991.

10 Such was the interiority of the veil, with which I am particularly concerned here. But the veil also partook of exteriority: it was the color line, the color bar, segregation, Jim Crow, the racialized social structure as a whole. It tantalized and tormented black people as a collectivity, permitting them to view—but not granting them the right to partake of—their social, political, and economic birthright. It constantly proffered and withdrew alternative strategies for dealing with racism: the possibility of separation, of return to Africa, of abandoning the hateful white world. DuBois continued his engagement with the metaphor of the veil throughout his work. See DuBois 1991, 130–32 for a treatment of the theme that focuses more extensively on segregation.

REFERENCES

Alba, R. D. 1990. *Ethnic Identity: The Transformation of White America.* New Haven, Conn.: Yale University Press.

Andrews, G. R. 1991. *Blacks and Whites in São Paulo, Brazil, 1888–1988.* Madison: University of Wisconsin Press.

Azevedo, T. d. 1966. *Cultura e Situacao Racial no Brasil.* Rio de Janeiro: Editora Civilizacao Brasileira.

———. 1975. *Democracia Racial: Ideología é Realidade.* Petropolis, Brazil: Editora Vozes.

Bastide, R., and F. Fernandes. 1959. *Brancos e Negros em São Paulo.* São Paulo: Companhia Editora Nacional.

Carneiro, S., and T. Santos. 1985. *Mulher Negra.* São Paulo: Nobel/Conselho Estadual da Condicao Feminina.

Centro de Articulacao de Populacoes Marginalizadas (CEAP). 1989. *Exterminio de Criancas e Adolescentes no Brasil.* Rio de Janeiro: CEAP.

Cornell, S. 1988. *The Return of the Native: American Indian Political Resurgence.* New York: Oxford University Press.

Davis, F. J. 1991. *Who Is Black? One Nation's Definition.* University Park: Pennsylvania State University Press.

Degler, C. N. 1986. *Neither Black nor White: Slavery and Race Relations in Brazil and the United States.* Madison: University of Wisconsin Press. First published in 1971.

Domingues, R. 1992a. The Color of a Majority without Citizenship. *Conexoes* 4, no. 2 (November). *Conexoes* is available from the African Diaspora Research Project, Urban Affairs Programs, Michigan State University, East Lansing, Mich. 48824–1109, U.S.A.

DuBois, W. E. B. 1989. *The Souls of Black Folk.* 1903. Reprint, New York: Penguin.

———. 1991. *Dusk of Dawn: An Essay toward and Autobiography of a Race Concept.* 1940. Reprint, New Brunswick, N.J.: Transaction Publishers.

Espiritu, Y. L. 1992. *Asian American Panethnicity: Bridging Institutions and Identities.* Philadelphia, Pa.: Temple University Press.

Fernandes, F. 1978. *A Integracão do Negro na Sociedade de Classes.* 3d ed. 2 vols. São Paulo: Editora Atica.

Gonzalez, L. 1985. The Unified Black Movement: A New Stage in Black Political Mobilization. In *Race, Class, and Power in Brazil,* ed. P.-M. Fontaine. Los Angeles: University of California, Los Angeles, Center for Afro-American Studies.

Hacker, A. 1992. *Two Nations, Black and White, Separate, Hostile, Unequal.* New York: Scribner's.

Hanchard, M. G. 1994. *Orpheus and Power: The Movimento Negro of Rio de Janeiro and São Paulo, Brazil, 1945–1988.* Princeton, N.J.: Princeton University Press.

Harris, M. 1964. *Patterns of Race in the Americas.* New York: Walker.

Hasenbalg, C. A. 1979. *Discriminação e Desigualdades Raciais no Brasil.* Rio de Janeiro: Graal.

Lechner, N. 1988. *Los Patios Interiores de la Democracia: Subjetividad y Politica.* Santiago de Chile: FLACSO.

Lovell, P. A., ed. 1991. *Desigualdade Racial no Brasil Contemporâneo.* Belo Horizonte, Brazil: MGSP Editores.

Maggie, Y., ed. 1989. *Catalogo: Centenario da Abolicao.* Rio de Janeiro: CIEC/UFRJ.

Mills, G., ed. 1992. The Black Movement Today. *Contato* 5, nos. 7–8 (30 November).

Mitchell, M. 1985. Blacks and the Abertura Democratica. In *Race, Class, and Power in Brazil,* ed. P.-M. Fontaine. Los Angeles: University of California, Los Angeles, Center for Afro-American Studies.

Morris, A. D. 1984. *The Origins of the Civil Rights Movement: Black Communities Organizing for Change.* New York: Free Press.

Movimento dos Trabalhadores Sem Terra. 1986. *Assassinato no Campo: Crime e Impunidade.* São Paulo: Sem Terra.

Nascimento, M. E. d. 1989. *A Estrategia da Desigualdade: O Movimento Negro dos Anos 70.* Master's thesis, University of São Paulo.

Oboler, S. 1995. *Ethnic Labels, Latino Lives: Identity and the Politics of (Re)presentation in the United States.* Minneapolis: University of Minnesota Press.

Omi, M., and H. Winant. 1986. *Racial Formation in the United States: From the 1960s to the 1980s.* New York: Routledge.

Skidmore, T. E. 1972. Toward a Comparative Analysis of Race Relations since Abolition in Brazil and the United States." *Journal of Latin American Studies* 4, no. 1 (May).

Skidmore, T. E. 1985. Race and Class in Brazil: Historical Perspectives. In *Race, Class, and Power in Brazil,* ed. P.-M. Fontaine. Los Angeles: University of California, Los Angeles, Center for Afro-American Studies.

van den Berghe, Pierre L. 1967. *Race and Racism.* New York: Wiley.

Wagley, C., and M. Harris. 1958. *Minorities in the New World: Six Case Studies.* New York: Columbia University Press.

Waters, M. C. 1990. *Ethnic Options: Choosing Identities in America.* Berkeley: University of California Press.

Wilson, W. J. 1980. *The Declining Significance of Race: Blacks and Changing American Institutions.* Chicago, Ill.: University of Chicago Press.

Michael Mitchell

MIGUEL REALE AND THE IMPACT OF

CONSERVATIVE MODERNIZATION ON

BRAZILIAN RACE RELATIONS

The politics pursued by Afro-Brazilians take place within a network of ideas and institutions that are social constructs created by others. If scholars are to understand the specific dynamics of Afro-Brazilian politics, they must come to terms with the ways in which a wider set of ideas and institutions shape the environment in which Afro-Brazilian political action occurs. Moreover, if Afro-Brazilians are to engage in politics successfully, they must devise strategies that take into account the peculiarities of the larger institutional and ideological system in which they are compelled to operate.

In this regard, this article argues, first, that the broad network of Brazilian politics works to delegitimize the political claims of Afro-Brazilians. Even while Afro-Brazilians have at certain times been highly successful at pressing claims within the larger arena of Brazilian politics, more often than not the expressions of these claims are met either with official silence or, at best, superficial recognition of the importance of the claims.[1] In effect, Brazilian elites have developed strategies that allow them to avoid engaging in any meaningful discourse about the politics of race.

Since our second argument draws on insights offered in the works of Michel Foucault,[2] it might be useful to sketch briefly those components of his thinking that have a bearing on this analysis. In Foucault's terms, the modern state emerged in Western history simultaneously with the appearance of new intellectual elites asserting their authority as the creators of new philosophical discourses. As Foucault provocatively suggests, these new discourses, which provided the philosophical bases for the new natural and social sciences, evolved to claim privileged positions in intellectual inquiry. Moreover, as the range of acceptable discourses on truth narrowed toward these new philosophical bases, so too, at the same time, did the strength of the state increase through the institutionalization and centralization of its powers.

For Foucault, the elites of Europe's Enlightenment devised new structures of discourse whose logic and premises inspired visions of society that, on the one hand, appeared to improve the human condition, but which, in actuality, strengthened the degree of state control over the lives of individuals. In other words, the purported progressive reforms of the Enlightenment turned out to be measures that served to alienate the individual from the state, and that compelled the individual to relinquish freedoms by deferring in matters of epistemology to the authority of the adepts in the seemingly unassailable truth discourses of therapy and science.[3]

Brazilian intellectual history appears to fall into this Foucauldian scheme in several respects. For instance, Brazilian intellectuals absorbed the prevailing trends in nineteenth-century European science and used their claims of possessing a superior epistemological discourse to thoroughly critique Brazilian society, as well as its politics. The intellectual elites of the late–nineteenth and early–twentieth centuries, furthermore, began articulating a new vision of politics and society under what loosely would be called modernization in contemporary terms. Nevertheless, the modernization project envisioned by Brazil's intellectual elites involved both an appeal to progress as well as a caution about the impediments to reform to be found in Brazilian society. From their earliest articulations, Brazilian intellectuals for the most part redefined the modernizing purpose so that it would alter the demographic, cultural, and racial contours of Brazilian society. Certain groups, specifically Afro-Brazilians, were to be recast as drags on modernization and made, consequently, the targets of social and political exclusion.

The pioneering Brazilian modernizers, in fact, incorporated heavy doses of scientific racism into their visions (Skidmore 1974; Stepan 1991). Eugenics became the concrete and political expression of this stance. Even a writer like Euclydes da Cunha, the founder of modern Brazilian sociology, who was otherwise sympathetic to the plight of Brazil's masses, could not escape the power of the racist doctrines in vogue in the last years of the nineteenth century. Ultimately, scientific racism and eugenics would reach their height of influence in the 1930s, as reflected in the several eugenics measures introduced into the Constituent Assembly of 1933–1934 (Stepan 1991, 165–66).

Our third argument suggests that a conservative vision of modernization—one in which elites encoded into Brazilian political culture racial prohibitions as well as other controls on social behavior—survived, reproduced itself, and has maintained its power within both modernization and race relations as the dominant discourse. Brazilian elites who have occupied strategic positions within the Brazilian state, or who command positions of influence as leaders of cultural and intellectual institutions, have continued to express this conservative vision.

This argument has one important implication with respect to the dynamics of Afro-Brazilian politics. Much of the difficulty that Afro-Brazilians have encountered in articulating what Florestan Fernandes has called a counter ideology of race is that the ideological claims of Afro-Brazilians enter into the dominant discourse on modernization in a way that compels a racial counter ideology to only implicitly challenge the vision of conservative modernization (Fernandes 1965, 70–95; 1972, 259–83; 1976, 75–84). Refining Fernandes's analysis a step further, Miriam Ferrara (1986, 195–203) has identified three components of this counter ideology that have captured almost the exclusive attention of those Afro-Brazilians who have attempted to shape black public opinion. According to Ferrara, efforts at formulating the semblance of a counter ideology have focused primarily on the issues of racial discrimination, racial uplift, and racial solidarity.

This restrictive strategy of ideological formulation leaves the capacity of Afro-Brazilians for ideological confrontation open to the designs of an apparently more embracing discourse, which can suffocate the claims of a genuine Afro-Brazilian discourse on Brazilian society. In effect, the ideological formulations of Afro-Brazilians, as Fernandes has argued, have become vulnerable to the charge that they create obstacles to a vision of Brazilian grandeur that includes rapid development and entry into the community of nations as a nation-state of the highest rank. To insist on racial justice where rapid modernization seems the greater imperative would both threaten the realization of a presumed larger national vision and challenge what would appear to be the indisputable tenets of a more powerful discourse.

The major portion of this chapter deals with this dynamic. It is an effort to demonstrate how closely the discourses of race and conservative modernization fit together. The article also illustrates how the discourse on modernization reproduces itself. To develop these themes, focus is placed on the figure of Miguel Reale, one of Brazil's leading jurists and philosophers.

MIGUEL REALE: A FIGURE OF BRAZIL'S INTELLECTUAL ELITE

Unquestionably, Miguel Reale (b. 1910) has exerted a pervasive influence over Brazilian intellectual life. As a scholar, teacher, and academic administrator, he has established an international reputation in several fields. He is particularly noted as an active philosopher, which is indicated by an excerpted inclusion of his work in an English-language anthology on Latin American philosophy (Garcia 1986, 197–205). Such is the extent of his renown that at a symposium organized at the Universidade de Brasília to discuss his works, he was described as a scholar of the first rank, comparable to figures like John Kenneth Gailbraith, Raymond Aron, Maurice Duverger, and Friedrich Hayeck (Azevedo 1981, 1). His published works include over twenty book-length monographs, principally in the fields of jurisprudence, theories of the state, and as mentioned, philosophy. He was instrumental, moreover, in founding the Brazilian Institute of Philosophy in 1949. And, on two occasions, he presided as rector over the University of São Paulo, Brazil's premier institution of higher learning.[4]

Reale's intellectual preeminence, which he had already acquired by the 1960s, provided him the platform from which to launch a series of attacks against the presidency of Joao Goulart during the regime crisis of 1963–64. His criticism became part of an arsenal of indictments leveled against Goulart by the military. Reale continued playing the role of national critic even after the installation of the military government in 1964, to which he initially gave his strong endorsement. In a series of essays collected in the volume *Da*

Revolucao a Democracia, Reale (1977) even admonished the regime for apparently abandoning a project of his architecture on the reform of national political institutions.

Nevertheless, Reale showed sympathy for the *dictablanda,* or the Sorbonne wing of the military establishment. For instance, he cautioned the regime to formulate clear principles for its legitimacy and recommended that the series of institutional acts that severely restricted civil liberties be codified as transitional measures to be rescinded after the promulgation of a constitution in 1969. Reale never strayed far outside of the regime's circle of influence, however. His second appointment as rector of the Universidade de São Paulo in 1970 attests to the confidence that regime leaders—particularly then Minister of Justice Luis Antonio Gama e Silva, who had suggested the appointment—had in him.

Reale also has actively pursued a political career. He maintained a long, but not always warm relationship with the populist leader, Adhemar de Barros of São Paulo. It was largely through Barros's initiative that Reale received his first appointment as rector of the University of São Paulo in 1949. Prior to this, Reale served for two years in Barros's gubernatorial cabinet in the capacity of minister of justice. Relations between the two became strained in the early 1950s, however, when Reale decided on a run for the governorship under Barros's own party banner, the Partido Social Progressita (PSP).

The early years of the democratic regime established in 1945 allowed Reale to rehabilitate his political career of sorts. During the 1930s, he had participated openly in the right-wing Integralist movement led by Plinio Salgado. Participation in this movement also occasioned uneasy alliances. His association with the Vargas revolution mirrored the fluctuations of support and opposition that characterized the relationship between Vargas and the Integralistas. Reale (1986, 128–36), in fact, decided on a self-imposed exile to Italy, fearing that he had been marked for Vargas's retaliation after an abortive Integralist putsch in 1938. This was not the first time that Reale might have been charged with complicity in an armed rebellion; he was also a combatant in São Paulo's secessionist revolt in 1932.

Reale came to these insurgencies as a student critic of the First Republic. Along with many other students at São Paulo's faculty of law, he shared a bitter enmity for the rural oligarchy that had served as the main prop of the First Republic. He was an opponent of the oligarchy's Partido Republicano Paulista and enlisted in the ranks of the dissident Partido Democratico, which included a wide assortment of the First Republic's critics. One of Reale's (1983a) earliest published works, *A Formacao Politica da Burguesia Brasileira,* was in fact a broadside attack against Brazil's rural oligarchy.

Early on, Reale apparently decided that he would assume intellectual leadership in the political circles that emerged in Brazil after the collapse of the First Republic. He started on this path by associating himself with the conservative critics of the old regime. One of his first significant intellectual contacts during the heady and confusing days of the Vargas revolution was with the prominent jurist Francisco Jose Oliveira Vianna. Besides being an acerbic critic of the First Republic, Oliveira Vianna was also openly sympathetic with scientific racism.[5] Reale's ambitions went further than this. While still a law student, he published his first book, *O Estado Moderno. O Estado Moderno* was an effort to sketch out the basic properties of three regime models. In this analysis, Reale (1934) found fault with the regime types of liberal democracy and socialism, and concluded that a third model was more appropriate for a modernizing nation. Taking stock of this work in his memoirs, Reale (1986, 90–91) describes *O Estado Moderno* as an attempt to provide an analytical rationale for the Integralist movement.

Reale's embrace of criticisms of the old regime stemmed largely from his experiences in his hometown of São Bento de Sapucai, near Campos de Jordao in the state of São Paulo. Reale (1986, 7–8) mentions having realized there the tacit cultural prohibitions that separated the region's rural oligarchy from the families of Italian immigrants, the community to which Reale belonged. Reale notes that the segregation of the Italian community from the families of the *quatrocentistas* was readily apparent. No doubt this figured into his engaging in the dissident activity of the revolution of 1930.

The occasional references in Reale's memoirs regarding race and ethnicity deserve some comment. When he approaches this subject, he reflects a certain unresolved tension about the matter. For instance, his recording of the patterns of segregation in São Bento de Sapucai is prefaced by a somewhat formulaic statement about the existence of racial democracy. The juxtaposition of the two discordant descriptions, racial democracy against the segregation of Italian families, suggests a certain myopia induced by a strongly held ideological position. His belief in the doctrine of racial democracy had apparently clouded an otherwise rigorously analytical mind to the personal experiences that influenced his later outlooks, particularly his antipathy to the oligarchs of the First Republic.

There are a couple of points that warrant underscoring in this narrative of Reale's career. The first is the resilience of his position in Brazil's intellectual and political life. Through prodigious scholarship as well as his leadership in the fields of philosophy and jurisprudence, Reale established the credentials that allowed him to reenter Brazil's political and intellectual elites in light of his controversial association with integralism, a movement of right-wing ideological outlook that had been discredited pretty much after its failed attempt to come to power in 1938. Reale has successfully navigated a career through the kinds of political crises that would have ended the careers of individuals of less daunting energies.

Moreover, the positions in politics and intellectual life that Reale would assume enabled him to shape the discourse on the major issues facing Brazil. His professional life, in other words, suggests the ways in which a member of an intellectual elite engenders the reproduction of ideas, even when the movements with which they are associated disappear from the scene. If Reale was able to survive professionally, he succeeded as well in enlarging the arena of his own intellectual influence.

The second point that deserves highlighting is the partisan political position Reale would adopt under the democratic regime of the 1940s and 1950s. His preference for the ideologically ambiguous and leader-dominated populist politics of the era reflects his own more sophisticated vision of the modernizing project. Just as populism promised benefits for the masses while holding a firm grip on politics through a strong leader, so Reale's vision was of a process that distributed the fruits of modernization widely, but in which political and intellectual elites retained control.

Reale's ideas reflect these assertions more clearly. Before turning to an exposition of these ideas, however, it is useful to situate them more directly in the tradition of conservative thinking on race and modernization.

THE CONSERVATIVE INTELLECTUAL TRADITION
ON MODERNIZATION AND RACE

Brazilian elites' preoccupation with the matter of race can be traced back to the latter days of the empire at the end of the nineteenth century, particularly to the national debates over the issue of slavery. For Brazilian abolitionists, race and slavery became an emblem that defined national culture and identity, as well as Brazil's place in the world. As Thomas Skidmore (1974, 11–26; 1990) has pointed out, slavery also became intertwined in elite thinking with their program of modernizing reforms.

Making the link between slavery, on the one hand, and race as an impediment to modernization, on the other, took on a particular urgency after slavery's abolition in 1888. Elites maintained their long-standing and commonly held assumptions about race in order to devise ways out of a perceived irrecusable state of backwardness and underdevelopment. One of these assumptions postulated that Brazilian elites could control both the process of modernization and the impact that race would have on it. This belief hinged on the doctrine of *branqueamento,* a theory that claimed that the presence of Afro-Brazilians would gradually disappear through miscegenation, hence removing the racial barrier to modernization. Some intellectuals came to this conclusion from reasoning based on the premises of scientific racism.

Brazilian elites expressed sympathy for scientific racism and found it compatible with their notions of modernization for several reasons. Many would discover in it a logical extension of the positivist doctrines that had entered into Brazilian intellectual life toward the end of the imperial era. Scientific racism appeared to hold out an equally powerful intellectual source for articulating critiques of Brazil's First Republic.

At the beginning of the twentieth century, Raimundo Nina Rodrigues, professor of legal medicine at the University of Bahia, based his studies of Afro-Brazilian culture and history on the assumptions of scientific racism. He carried out his pioneering research in an effort to better clarify for the modernizing elites of the time the presumed natural tendency of blacks toward various forms of criminality and other manifestations of antisocial behavior. With the weight of scientific authority, and a seemingly impeachable and daunting volume of evidence, Nina Rodrigues set out to offer some measure of guidance for formulating social policy and modernizing reforms in the early years of the First Republic.

In any event, during the First Republic, modernizing elites tended to view race as a drag on Brazilian development. Race became linked with the servile labor that constituted the economic foundation of the old empire. These elites embraced the pseudoscience of eugenics as the modernizing response to the racial question. The scientific racists, through the eugenics movement, reached their height of influence during the Vargas revolution of the 1930s. In the Constituent Assembly of the mid-1930s, the eugenists persuaded the assembly to pass a number of measures that would establish quotas on the immigration of Asians and blacks, as well as extend to the state the power and discretion to regulate marriages. In a curious twist of the theory, the eugenists based most of their policies on the doctrine of *branqueamento*. Their supposition was that *branqueamento* was contributing directly to the disappearance of blacks from Brazil's population. Their aim was to invest the state with the means of steering the process of *branqueamento* further along. In any case, the Brazilian eugenics movement typified the modernizing strategy of the First Republic as well as the Vargas revolution (Stepan 1991, 162–69). Racial demographics were to be strictly monitored by the state in order to precisely achieve an intended effect: the elimination of a racial population in Brazil considered to be a drag on the modernizing process itself. Their modernizing project did not envision any open debate on or commitment to racial equality.

Gilberto Freyre offered Brazilian elites a different version of modernization. He argued that race did not have to be viewed as a drag on the elites' project of modernization. In fact, Freyre took the scientific racists and the eugenists head-on by proposing that Brazil had actually produced a singular solution to the question of racial conflict that had troubled so many other multiracial societies. He even argued for the modernizing elites to embrace the matter of race as a positive aspect in Brazilian development.

Freyre, nevertheless, cautioned the modernizers to take care not to abandon the institutions of the past that had held Brazilian society together. Here, Freyre almost lyrically extolled the virtues of the patriarchal plantation. In any case, Freyre's was a recasting of the vision of conservative, controlled modernization, in which that process might somehow preserve the paternalistic relationships that had been the hallmark of former regimes (Medeiros 1984).

REALE ON RACE

Reale's rather extensive writings include references to Brazilian race relations, suggesting the various dimensions through which Reale incorporates this subject into a larger, more complex philosophical scheme. In a brief essay on Freyre, for example, Reale (1962a) aims for no less than elevating the discussion of race to an abstract epistemological level. In effect, Reale attempts to lay a philosophical foundation for a discursive framework in which race becomes emblematic of Brazilian culture, society, and history.

Reale states a preference for a particular formulation of Brazilian race relations. He inclines his analysis toward the notion that Brazil exists as a racial democracy. Not unexpectedly, he expresses sympathy with the view that Brazilian race relations are unique among multiracial societies and that Brazil's professed system of race relations represents something of an achievement of national pride. Reale's are not merely ritualistic or superficial references. He appears to be highly aware of the intellectual tradition from which the notion of racial democracy stems. Moreover, he even acknowledges the polemics surrounding the development of the concept (Reale 1984, 66). On the occasion of his induction into the Brazilian Academy of Letters in 1975, for example, he pointedly referred to the notions of Fernando de Azevedo on the matter of *branqueamento,* one of the subsidiary tenets of the doctrine of racial democracy. Reale stated in his speech before the academy that he could not escape mentioning Azevedo's thinking about *branqueamento,* even if only for the sake of giving a full and honest intellectual account of the person whose chair he would be assuming there; nor could he ignore the recent contexts in which social historians had placed this notion. In fact, Reale quotes the English-language version of Thomas Skidmore's *Black into White* as the source of this observation. Despite Skidmore's somewhat critical and unflattering reading of the *branqueamento* notion, Reale extracts a summary quote from Azevedo's *A Cultura Brasileira* as a seeming gesture to acknowledge Azevedo's impact on elite thinking on the matter of race.

Yet Reale situates himself in an intellectual tradition that has regarded race and Brazilian identity in a particular and consistent way. Reale (1984, 33–38) offers suggestions of this intellectual tradition in an essay on the nineteenth-century jurist Jose Antonio Pimenta Bueno. Pimenta Bueno served in a number of national administrative and legislative posts, ending his public career on Brazil's Supreme Court. At one point, he assumed leadership of the Conservative Party in the National Senate during the debates over the slavery question. Pimenta Bueno would place his stamp on this debate. Reale attributes to him authorship of the first proposals regarding the gradual abolition of slavery. His proposals would eventually be codified as the Lei do Ventre Livre (Free Womb law). The revealing aspect of this particular event in Pimenta Bueno's career, and of Reale's insistence on highlighting it, is the character of reform in the measure. By any account, the Lei do Ventre Livre was an attempt to reform a regime whose moral strength and legitimacy were already beginning to wane. Pimenta Bueno, in authoring the initial draft of the law, was showing himself to be a reformer attempting to modernize a system that itself stood squarely as a monumental obstacle to the global and systemic project of modernization as a whole. This is the profile of reform to which Reale himself is most drawn and that he has replicated as intellectual architect of the conservative modernization pursued, even if somewhat loosely, by the military regime of 1964.

Reale grounds himself in the conservative tradition on Brazilian modernization and race relations in the most analytical and perhaps provocative way in a reflection on the writings of Freyre. Reale surveys the complete Freyrean oeuvre in an effort to extract what Reale considers to be the most abstract, universal, and philosophical problems to be found therein. He carefully builds his discussion on clear points of reference. Conceding that Freyre's are first and foremost works of sociology, Reale suggests that Freyrean sociology indeed attempts to answer some fundamental philosophical questions: What is the nature of society? Are conflicts natural attributes of societies? How do societies sustain themselves in an environment of ever-increasing, emerging, and intense conflicts?

Reale places Freyre in the Hegelian tradition on these matters. He notes that throughout Freyre's works the notion of a dialectic keeps appearing. And here, Reale captures the complexity of Freyre's thinking that is often lost in more cursory examinations. Reale admits to seeing in Freyre's works the premise of conflict and contradiction as an essential feature in societies. Specifically in the case of Brazil, the core of its contradiction stems from the coexistence of cultures with contrasting values and habits.

It would not be fair to say that Freyre, or for that matter Reale's reading of him, suggests a bland syncreticism of cultures. Both Freyre and Reale recognize the inherent conflicts in the ties juxtaposing African and European cultures in Brazilian society and history. In fact, positing this conflict is essential to the scheme that each would like to draw of Brazilian society. Nevertheless, the issue that becomes key at this point is the manner in which societies maintain themselves with conflicts at their base. It is at this analytical juncture that Reale asserts Freyre has made his most important sociological and philosophical contribution.

Proceeding in this manner, Reale arrives at what he plausibly considers to be the Hegelian core of Freyre's works. According to Reale, the philosophical contribution that Freyre makes is in his stress on the dynamic of the dialectic under which societies function. Referring back to Freyre's sociology, Reale points to the dialectical tensions in the master-slave relationship, and the pervasive establishment of the plantation during the colonial and imperial periods in Brazilian history as illustration of this dialectical dynamic. In Reale's reading of Freyre, the dialectical relationships in society are not necessarily resolved into a new synthesis, but nevertheless are preserved and kept in place through the functioning of social institutions. Social institutions, therefore, become the essential cement that allow for the inherent antagonisms of a society to play themselves out in some sort of permanent and stable way.

This reading of Freyre is not necessarily novel. Indeed, one commentator has observed that the structure of Freyre's sociology read in this way can be seen as a sophisticated defense of the mechanisms of domination and social control that characterize much of Brazilian society (Medeiros 1984). No doubt the high regard that Freyre gives to the particular institution of the patriarchal plantation lends credibility to this conclusion. In any case, Freyre's social philosophy evinces preference for a certain hierarchy of values and social forces; preeminence is given to institutions themselves. In Freyre's scheme, the patriarchal plantation assumes the role of the institution that gives vibrancy to the dialectic connecting the Luso and African cultures of the slave regime. In effect, the patriarchal institution of the slave plantation defines the configurations of a society and holds this configuration in place. If otherwise, and without the defining power of an institution such as the patriarchal plantation, the slave regime would have existed either as a meaningless and incoherent mixture of incompatible cultures, or at worst, in a situation of constant and degenerative violence.

Even if Freyre and Reale set out on different temporal paths—one in the patriarchal past, the other in the modern world—both nevertheless begin their inquiries at the same Hegelian starting point. Where Freyre sees the patriarchal institution of the slave plantation as the transcendent institution, Reale points to the modern state as the institution that enervates the inevitable conflicts that emerge in a modern society. Modernization imposes an added set of contradictory social forces on a given society. If it is to be adapted successfully, modernization must proceed, so the Realean logic runs, under the aegis of ancient and already tested institutions, which then give shape to the dialectical relationship between a modern present and a patriarchal past.

Freyre and Reale's visions of society are, in fact, uncannily complementary. For each of them, societal conflicts create the imperative for organizing societies around strong institutions whose purpose is to control conflicts in a manner that allows for the simultaneous existence of dialectical forces and a strong social order. In this regard, neither Freyre nor Reale would find the North American pluralist notions of politics very congenial. Instead, they would have greater sympathy for an interventionist state that would firmly regulate, if not suppress outright the wide range of political manifestations that, in pluralist terms, would arise naturally from a society's conflicting elements.

MIGUEL REALE'S POLITICAL PROJECT

The argument suggested in this essay is that the high degree of compatibility between Reale's positions on race and his general vision of Brazilian society illustrates the way in which conservative thinking on race fits closely into the project of national modernization pursued by Brazilian elites for much of this century. In other words, race comprises one of the tacit but essential elements on which the project of conservative modernization has been based. This approximates the Foucauldian notion of reform tending toward the greater management and control of social forces. It also implies preference for a certain method of organizing societies. Institutions in this scheme assume preeminence as buffers between the social forces that emerge as the products of modernization and the stability of societies themselves. Entire claims on the state must necessarily be suppressed or at least strictly regulated for the purpose of this stability. A brief sketch of Reale's political philosophy will hopefully place these assertions into clearer perspective.[6]

Throughout his career, Reale attempted to construct a coherent system to support his basic convictions about the individual, society, and politics. His work probably most closely approximates a Hegelian approach to fundamental questions. Reale is attracted to the patterns of opposites in ideas and actions that characterize the analysis of dialectics. Moreover, Reale assumes a phenomenological core in values and consciousness. Reale has written that values and consciousness exist in a state of bipolarity, in which each can be realized only through the match of subjective and objective worlds (Gracia 1986, 199; Reale 1984, 17–39).

Reale typifies in his writings the philosophical contrasts that are the hallmark of his works. He has been described, for example, as a practical philosopher. While he is quick to pose large questions, he will just as quickly claim that his purpose is to search for concrete solutions to the problems he lays out. He has invested a considerable amount of intellectual energy in constructing rationales for particular practical solutions to what he has perceived to be some of Brazil's more deeply rooted political problems. His blueprint for reform has consistently been based on the premise that Brazil requires a more thoroughgoing institutionalization of its public life.

Reale's is a philosophy of tension. Principles, arguments, and assertions, for all of their logical rigor, seem left unresolved. In large part, this may be due to Reale's own professed aversion to absolute abstractions. He may, for instance, assert that the state possesses an ethical character and carries out normative ends. He may be equally vigorous in claiming that particular states lose their relevance in defending to an abstract degree guarantees of individual rights, as he has done in his critical comments on liberal democracies (Reale 1978, 28–31). On the other hand, he contends somewhat strenuously that his criticism of liberal democracy should not be misunderstood as an endorsement of totalitarianism (Reale 1986, 90–93).

Reale's political philosophy stems from his assertions about the relationships that tie the individual, society, and state together. From this starting point, Reale arrives at his stated preferences for certain kinds of regimes and particular forms of social organization. In Reale's analytical scheme, the individual exists as a complex set of identities that encompass gender, ethnicity, class, and even the rational. These sources of identity are not necessarily compatible with each other, nor is the individual capable of reconciling these different attributes within a single personality. Reale moves on to claim that society's purpose and function is to stand aside from the individual so that society, through the institutions of the state, can establish a universal interest independent of the conflicts to which the individual is susceptible. A society is more than a collection of individuals in Reale's view. As such, it assumes a certain position outside the individual in order to create a common good (Reale 1981, 9).

Reale (1978, 1–21) defines the common good generally as the products of technology and prosperity. These societal goals confer on the individual a material security and freedom from the drudgery of labor; indeed, these are the ends for which the state is designed. By its very nature, the state assumes an interventionist and instrumental character by adopting a project of modernization that is defined as creating increasing prosperity and greater distribution of the products of technology throughout society. In axiomatic terms, Reale would say that the state exists to make people happy, yet not necessarily to guarantee their political freedoms. Reale (1978, 1–21; 1987B, 135–49), in frequent references, labels this the social democratic state and places great store in it as the political model for Brazil.

Modernization is the most prominent project that a state can carry out, according to Reale. If this project is derailed or threatened in any way, the state has the obligation to defend it. This, in effect, became the rationale for his support of the military coup of

1964. Reale, however, perceived that Brazilian modernization was being threatened by chaotic and haphazard institutionalization of public affairs. He advocated, first and foremost, that the military regime place a high priority on constitutional and political party reform in order to correct, as he saw it, the lack of institutional supports for the modernization project (Reale 1977). Here, Reale comes closest to resembling his conservative modernizing predecessors, who felt as well that modernization could be contained with sufficient social controls by stable institutions.

The sense in which Reale (1978) approximates the tradition of conservative modernization is spelled out in his essay on the republic of ancient Rome. It captures and underscores Reale's own preferences for the elements that comprise his political project. The themes, values, and political designs that he describes here are repeated in his other works, and while he speaks explicitly of ancient Rome, he suggests that his descriptions serve as a model for contemporary Brazil.

Among the values that Reale identifies as the essence of Roman political culture are those of utility and commitment to the common good. The hallmark of Roman culture, Reale contends, was its search for practical and concrete solutions to the questions of governance. In fact, the Roman commitment to pragmatic solutions to public questions allowed them to construct a republic, and later an empire, on policies that sought inclusion of the widest and most diverse of elements. Specifically, Reale asserts that the Romans were successful in tempering class conflicts within their society. Reale notes, for example, that class antagonisms were articulated by the plebeian class in the form of its claiming as universal the status of citizenship, which was meant to exist as a patrician monopoly. By continuously extending citizenship status, the patrician class was able to forestall, in Reale's reading, an eruption of class grievance that would have destroyed the patrician class in a thoroughgoing revolution. What Reale finds significant in all of this is the Roman's manipulation of the foundations of the state to preserve the existing social order. Reale's discussion of Rome also contains hints of what he perceives a modernizing society to be. His essay is peppered with references to Rome as a culture of action. It is a society dedicated to expansion and great building projects. Reale finds the source of Rome's values in these impulses: its drive to expand and construct was reinforced by its stress on the practical and empirical. These were also the source of the highest Roman value: social order. And as much through accommodation as coercion, Rome sought to reconcile as far as possible the conflicting interests of Roman society.

Ironically, Reale, the legal theorist, asserts that Rome's lack of a formal theory of law was one of its greatest virtues. According to Reale, Roman law was crafted to reflect Roman culture. A culture based on expansion and building enterprises did not have time for abstractions or doctrines, such as occupied the culture of ancient Greece. In other words, Roman culture as reflected in the law was highly consonant with the mission of the Roman state. As a modernizing society, Rome had successfully calibrated culture, society, and the individual's role in society in order to carry out the larger ambitions of the state.

Reale's description of ancient Rome encapsulates his version of the modernizing project. He has argued that, like Rome, Brazilian culture should place emphasis on the practical and empirical as a way of better aligning its culture with a national project of modernization.[7] Reale's vision of the Brazilian modernizing project leaves the core of conservative modernization intact. This vision stresses the interventionist role of the state in promoting modernization. As the primary engine of modernization, the state acquires the legitimacy to defend this project. The state may do so through coercion, or by setting loose those processes that paradoxically coerce the reconciliation of social forces and of the conflicting attributes and identities that reside in the individual. The myth of racial democracy and the patriarchal institutions of Freyre's *Casa Grande* become benign substitutes for accomplishing the ends of conservative modernization. Identities are suppressed, and accommodations are made for the purpose of promoting progress within the existing social order.

AFRO-BRAZILIAN POLITICS TODAY

As discussed earlier in this essay, Freyre and Reale complement each other in their visions of society. Where Freyre steeps himself in Brazil's racial history, Reale employs Freyre's materials to give greater shape to his paradigm of a future modernization. This compatibility is as much structural as it is empirical. Both Reale and Freyre employ the same philosophical structures in their respective works to arrive at their visions of society. In other words, their structural or philosophical compatibility represents the starting point of a discourse on the nature of society and the direction that social change should take. Michel Foucault has already shown how powerful philosophical discourses are in shaping modern society. In the case of Brazil, a specific conservative discourse on race relations and modernization has developed, with wide-ranging effects. This discourse, in large part, has defined the environment in which Afro-Brazilian politics function.

The implication to be drawn here is that an indispensable element of Afro-Brazilian politics certainly has to be the development of a counter discourse to replace the one based on the model of conservative modernization. This enterprise may perhaps extend beyond the normal discourses on Brazilian race relations. It will involve embracing issues that go to the heart of Brazilian culture. It would suggest, further, that fundamental political issues — such as questions about the attributes and implications of citizenship, or the nature of national identity — ought to be reexamined critically in light of the prevailing discourses that determine the kinds of national projects the Brazilian state will pursue and by what means the state will achieve the ends of a modernizing process.

This discussion ought not to conclude by conveying the impression that the conservative discourse is the sole perspective on Brazilian race relations. Brazilian intellectuals have, in fact, worked with other discourses to fully articulate systematic alternatives to the conservative model of social change. The works of Florestan Fernandes, Octavio Ianni, Fernando Henrique Cardoso, and a later generation of scholars, Carlos Hasenbalg among them, have contributed incalculably to the store of evidence and insight into contemporary Brazilian race relations.[8] Their perspectives conform much more closely to the political claims and aspirations voiced by Afro-Brazilians themselves. Still, the conservative discourse on race relations continues to be pervasive, if not dominant in Brazilian political culture.

The question that undoubtedly arises is this: how has the conservative discourse sustained its dominance? Several factors suggest themselves as clues to the riddle. The first has to do with the intrinsic power of discourses themselves. Discourses hold power precisely because they offer some tangible demonstration of their efficacy. Thomas Kuhn's (1970) often-cited work on scientific revolutions attests as much to this as it does to the fact of transformations in scientific paradigms. Modernization initially appealed to Brazilian intellectual elites because at the twilight of the First Republic, they confronted a political regime rife with corruption, inefficiency, and cynical disregard for the principles of republican government. A new intellectual discourse would help them discredit all vestiges of the decaying regime, including semifeudal oligarchical relations. Considered to be part of a servile, backward past, Afro-Brazilians would have to be thrown on the margins of modernization. Hence, scientific racism became the early embodiment of the Brazilian discourse on modernization.

Racism should have receded from Brazilian intellectual circles when new scientific canons replaced old ones with respect to race. Yet Brazilian intellectuals reinvented their notions of race and modernization in order to preserve the core of a conservative modernizing discourse. Freyre, of course, went farthest in crafting this reinvention.

A discourse's power is just one element that helps explain its durability; human agency is a vital element as well. Individuals actively promote a particular discourse and keep it alive. They do so for reasons of ambition, for example. Reale's career is a case in point. Although his own energies had a great deal to do with his success, he made shrewd decisions that drew him more closely into the precincts of influence, where he then exercised authority over significant phases of a modernizing project (his two tenures as rector of the University of São Paulo were efforts to modernize an intellectual institution). His strategic position in Brazil's intellectual establishment provided him the place from which to offer reassurance that the conservative modernizing project was the most authentic and practical for Brazilian political elites to follow.

There is another facet to this question. It has to do with the way in which the modernizing project has actually been carried out in Brazil. Ironically, the record of Brazilian modernization turns out to be the opposite of that outlined in the Reale-Freyre tradition. As modernization has evolved in Brazil, it has occasioned a series

of crises in political regimes along with periods of ideological incoherence. Elites have not always been able to convert critiques
of an old regime into a consensus program for reform. In fact, as
the work of Brazilian historian Sergio Miceli (1979) shows, political crises induced by modernization have led to ideological polarization, sometimes creating rifts between Brazil's elites. After the
collapse of the First Republic, for instance, the critics of the old
regime lost the institutional coherence of their opposition—as embodied in the Partido Democratico and, to a much lesser extent,
in the movement of the Tenentes—and split in centrifugal fashion into extremely polarized ideological movements. These movements plagued the first Vargas era, eventually compelling him to
suppress all opposition and install an authoritarian, semicorporat-
ist regime in 1937. Similarly, in the crisis of 1964, the Brazilian
military looked, however reluctantly or incompletely, to a conservative modernizing blueprint as the basis of the national project
for its regime. During particular crises, the conservative discourse
appears to hold greater attraction, if not outright coherence for
political elites. This no doubt is due, as Reale's career again shows,
to the strategic positions in the state and society held by intellectuals who subscribe to the conservative discourse.

A quick survey of the current scene in Brazilian politics suggests
some disturbing patterns. This period of democratic consolidation
in Brazilian politics exhibits patterns that stimulated the search for
new intellectual discourses in the 1920s and 1930s. Then as now,
democratic organizations appeared to be weak, political corruption
was considered to be widespread, and any consensus on a national
project had eroded. Today, this reflects an environment of public
criticism that nonetheless lacks a coherent political language out
of which a consensus plan of national reform might come. This
condition presents an opportunity for intellectuals linked to the
Afro-Brazilian community. The time may be opportune to stress
more strongly the importance of constructing alternative solutions
to Brazil's problems that place Afro-Brazilians more closely at the
center of national concerns. Intellectuals should at least underscore
that Afro-Brazilian politics is both a dynamic and urgent enterprise
that attempts a needed redefinition of the discourse out of which
national politics flows.

NOTES

1 The two major periods of modern black Brazilian political activity are, of course, during the time of the Frente Negra Brasileira in the 1930s and when the Movimento Negro Unificado achieved prominence as a major protest organization in the 1970s and 1980s.

2 In particular, this discussion draws from Foucault 1973, 1979. See also Miller 1993.

3 Foucault (1979) offers as evidence of this development the appearance of the penitentiary as an institution of reform in the nineteenth century. The clinic and the insane asylum are other institutions that, according to Foucault (1973), fit this pattern.

4 Reale's first tenure as rector was in the late 1940s and early 1950s. His later tenure occurred under the military regime during the 1970s.

5 Oliveira Vianna and Reale both collaborated on a journal named *Panorama*. Published in the 1930s and of short duration, *Panorama* served as an outlet of cultural and philosophical analysis and was associated with the Integralist Movement in Brazil. See Reale 1986, 86, 109–10, and Poletti 1981, 3.

6 In its own right, a full reading of Reale's works would be daunting. Nevertheless, the task can be made manageable by focusing on Reale's later writings, which were composed in the mid-1960s and 1970s. The following discussion draws mainly on these later writings.

7 It should be noted, however, that Reale is extremely dismissive of *jeitinho* as a reflection of this pragmatism; *jeitinho,* for Reale, is much too improvised and provisional to be considered a modern value. *Jeitinho* is the term that refers to the uniquely Brazilian skill at finding unexpected solutions to seemingly insurmountable problems.

8 For an evaluation of Fernandes's impact on Brazilian intellectual life, see D'Incao 1987.

REFERENCES

Azevedo, J. C. de A. 1981. Apresentacao. In *Miguel Reale na UnB*. Brasilia: Universidade de Brasília.

D'Incao, M. A. 1987. *O Saber Militante: Ensaios Sobre Florestan Fernandes.* São Paulo: Paz e Terra.

Fernandes, F. 1965. *A Integracão do Negro na Sociedade de Classes.* São Paulo: Editora Dominus.

———. 1972. *O Negro no Mundo dos Brancos*. São Paulo: Difusao Europeia do Livro.

———. 1976. *Circuito Fechado*. São Paulo: HUCITEC.

Ferrara, M. N. 1986. *A Imprensa Negra Paulista (1915–1963)*. São Paulo: FFLCH–USP.

Foucault, M. 1973. *Madness and Civilization*. Trans. R. Howard. New York: Vintage.

———. 1979. *Discipline and Punishment*. Trans. A. Sheridan. New York: Vintage.

Gracia, J., ed. 1986. *Latin American Philosophy in the Twentieth Century*. Buffalo, N.Y.: Prometheus Books.

Kuhn, T. 1970. *The Structure of Scientific Revolutions*. 2d ed., rev. Chicago, Ill.: University of Chicago Press.

Medeiros, M. A. 1984. *O Elogio da Dominacao: Relendo Casa Grande e Senzala*. Rio de Janeiro: Achiame.

Miceli, S. 1979. *Intelectuais e Classe Dirigente no Brasil (1925–1945)*. São Paulo: DIFEL.

Miller, J. 1993. *The Passions of Michel Foucault*. New York: Simon and Schuster.

Reale, M. 1934. *O Estado Moderno*. Rio de Janeiro: Jose Olympio.

———. 1962a. A Filosofia da Historia do Brasil na Obra de Gilberto Freyre. In *Gilberto Freyre: Sua Ciencia, Sua Filosofia, Sua Arte*, 405–11. Rio de Janeiro: Jose Olympio.

———. 1977. *Da Revolucao a Democracia*. São Paulo: Convivio.

———. 1978. *Politica de Ontem e de Hoje*. São Paulo: Saraiva.

———. 1981. *Miguel Reale na UnB*. Brasília: Universidade de Brasília.

———. 1983a. *A Formacao Politica da Burguesia Brasileira*. In *Obras Politicas: Primeira Fase, 1931–1937*. Brasília: Universidade de Brasília. First published in 1934.

———. 1984. *Figuras da Inteligencia Brasiliera*. Rio de Janeiro: Tempo Brasileiro.

———. 1986. *Memorias*. Vol. 1. São Paulo: Saraiva.

———. 1987b. *Memorias*. Vol. 2. São Paulo: Saraiva.

Poletti, Ronaldo. 1981. O Pensamento Politico de Miguel Reale. In *Miguel Reale Na UnB*, Miguel Reale. Brasília: Universidade de Brasília.

Skidmore, T. E. 1974. *Black into White: Race and Nationality in Brazilian Thought*. New York: Oxford University Press.

———. 1990. Racial Ideas and Social Policy in Brazil, 1870–1930. In *The Idea of Race in Latin America, 1870–1940*, ed. R. Graham. Austin: University of Texas Press.

Stepan, N. L. 1991. *"The Hour of Eugenics": Race, Gender, and Nation in Latin America*. Ithaca, N.Y.: Cornell University Press.

Peggy A. Lovell

WOMEN AND RACIAL INEQUALITY

AT WORK IN BRAZIL

Within Brazil, issues of gender and racial inequality emerged in the late 1970s as important rallying cries in the opposition to military rule.[1] Women and Afro-Brazilians were key actors in the new social opposition movements. In the struggle for democracy and social justice, their voices were joined by those of politicians, church officials, and union leaders in public dialogue on the role gender and race play in structuring opportunities and rewards in contemporary Brazilian society. Today, the Brazilian women's movement, like the black movement, is ideologically quite diverse. Members of both groups, nevertheless, are working to expand the parameters of their struggle, arguing that race, gender, and class shape the lives of all Brazilians in inseparable ways.

Women's groups first appeared in Brazil during the 1960s and early 1970s.[2] These early organizations were largely created through efforts by the Catholic Church to mobilize mother's clubs into community self-help groups. Neighborhood- and church-linked associations were concerned primarily with practical issues, such as the cost of living or urban services, rather than strategic gender issues. Feminist groups began to publicly organize in the mid-1970s following the United Nation's commemorations of International Women's Year in São Paulo, Rio de Janeiro, and Belo Horizonte (Alvarez 1994, 20–21). Yet it was not until the late 1980s that activists and scholars concerned with gender inequality started to include race in their analysis of the life chances of Brazilian women.

Brazilian feminists' delayed attention to race was for two reasons. In the 1970s and early 1980s, the prevailing debate among feminists centered on the orthodox marxist primacy of class oppression. Race, due to the priority accorded to economic relations, was relegated to secondary importance. Feminists' indifference to race was also associated with the long-standing belief that Brazil was free from the racial violence and discrimination that plagued other multiracial societies. Brazil's absence of racial discord was thought to stem, in large part, from three distinctive features of race relations in that country: a history of widespread miscegenation; a resulting dynamic system of multiracial classification; and the absence of postslavery, legally sanctioned discrimination. These unique characteristics helped create the myth that, in Brazil, skin color did not determine one's social position.[3] To challenge this myth of racial democracy—and also to contest the subsumption of their struggle for racial equality within the larger class struggle—black militant groups organized in the late 1970s and early 1980s.

Afro-Brazilian women militants initially shunned predominantly white feminist groups, which seldom addressed the specificity of their situation. Similarly, some Afro-Brazilian women felt that their needs and concerns were not being adequately considered by the male-dominated black movement. The combined effects of racism in the feminist movement and sexism in the emerging black movement led Afro-Brazilian women across the country to found autonomous black women's groups (Alvarez 1994, 50–51; Hanchard 1994, 129–33).[4] Since the early 1990s, there has been a growing awareness of and attention to race and gender issues within feminist and black discourses. A diversity of approaches, organizational forms, and strategic priorities around race- and gender-based concerns has emerged.

INEQUALITY AND DISCRIMINATION

Among the first researchers to challenge Brazil's myth of racial equality were scholars from what has come to be known as the São Paulo school, particularly Florestan Fernandes (1969), Fernando Cardoso (1962), and Octavio Ianni (1978; 1987; Ianni and Cardoso 1960). These Brazilian scholars examined the persistence of racial antagonism and inequality within Brazil's capitalist development. Today, few social scientists disagree with the general proposition that racial discrimination exists in Brazil. Yet, prior to the late 1970s, research on the sharp variations between the white and Afro-Brazilian populations was confined to nongeneralizable case studies, or limited to historical research on slavery and abolition. The hypothesis that racial discrimination exists—all other things being equal—was, up until the past few years, difficult to substantiate. The study of contemporary racial inequality was greatly enhanced by the availability of large national-level census and survey data sets that could reach beyond the case study approach in order to identify tendencies otherwise not subject to empirical assessment.

The first estimates of contemporary racial inequality in Brazil were works by Nelson do Valle Silva (1978; 1985) and Carlos Hasenbalg (1979; 1985). These studies showed that 100 years after the abolition of slavery, Afro-Brazilians continued to predominate in the lowest economic strata. These findings of racial inequality are consistent with the results of more recent analyses of differential child mortality rates (Wood and Lovell 1992), residential segregation (Rolnik 1989; Telles 1991), and educational inequality (Hasenbalg and Silva 1985; 1991), which all show pervasive and persistent racial discrimination.

Likewise, studies of gender differentials demonstrated that Brazil's prevailing style of uneven economic development did not favor the equitable incorporation of women into the economy. As in advanced industrial countries, women in Brazil are paid less than similarly qualified men (Miranda 1977; Bruschini and Rosemberg 1982). Women are not only handicapped by the gender gap in earnings, they are also disproportionately concentrated in the lowest-paying economic sectors (Faria 1989).

Analysts have shown that labor market inequalities between whites and Afro-Brazilians (Andrews 1992) and between women and men (Saffioti 1985) have actually increased with economic growth and modernization in Brazil. Lured from the northeast and rural areas by industrialization in the 1950s, Afro-Brazilians and women migrated to the dynamic urban metropolises. The spatial redistribution of the population was accompanied by notable racial and gender gains in urban employment. Between 1950 and 1980, the proportion of individuals of African descent employed in cities increased from 36 to 62 percent (Oliveira, Porcaro, and Arajuo Costa 1985), and the proportion of women receiving a wage increased from 13.6 percent in 1950 to 33 percent in 1983 (Martins 1985). Yet, at the same time, wages for women and Afro-Brazilians continued to lag behind those of white men.

These findings of racial and gender inequality in the Brazilian labor market have significantly advanced our understanding of the social costs of uneven economic development within Brazil. With respect to racial differentiation among women, however, these efforts remain deficient. Previous analyses of inequalities in the Brazilian labor market have, for the most part, focused either only on gender differentials—without disaggregating by race—or, when attention was turned to racial inequality, exclusively on men.[5] The goal of this study is to test the hypothesis that the profound social, economic, and demographic changes that have taken place in Brazil since 1960 have had different workplace outcomes on Afro-Brazilian and white women.

ANALYSES AND FINDINGS

Data and Methods

My empirical analysis relies on data from the 1960 and 1980 public use samples of the demographic censuses. From these data, I constructed files by occupation and urban geographic region in which both white and Afro-Brazilian (*preta* and *parda*) women aged eighteen to sixty-four were gainfully employed.[6] The individual-level data made it possible to estimate mean socioeconomic and demographic characteristics of the urban workforce. Regression equations predicting average monthly wages by race were then estimated in order to arrive at indicators of labor market inequality.

Region of Residence and Schooling

Analysts of labor market inequalities often observe racial differences in geographic location and educational attainment. Region of residence and schooling completion rates are related inasmuch as they determine access to better-paying jobs. This is particularly true in Brazil, where Afro-Brazilians are disproportionately concentrated in the impoverished northeast, where social and economic

TABLE 1

Region of Residence and Years of Schooling by Race, Employed
Women Aged 18–64, Urban Brazil, 1960/1980

	White			Afro-Brazilian		
			1980			1980
	1960	1980	1960	1960	1980	1960
	(1)	(2)	(3)	(4)	(5)	(6)
Region of Residence						
NE	14%	9%	.64	35%	30%	.86
SE	86	91	1.06	65	70	1.08
Years of Schooling Completed						
0	14%	5%	.36	43%	17%	.40
1–4	51	30	.59	50	42	.84
5–8	17	18	1.06	4	19	4.75
9+	18	47	2.61	3	22	7.33
N	11,917	28,108		6,392	15,119	

Source: Brazilian Census Public Use Samples, 1960 and 1980.

opportunities are scarce. In table 1, I present mean 1960 and 1980
estimates of regional and education distributions for women aged
eighteen to sixty-four.

The results shown in table 1 indicate substantial geographic disparities by race. While in both 1960 and 1980 the majority of
women in both racial categories were employed in the urban southeast, a disproportionate number of Afro-Brazilian women were
working in the less-developed regions of the northeast. In both
decades, about one-third of Afro-Brazilian women worked in the
northeast, while white workers were concentrated (86 percent in
1960 and 91 percent in 1980) in the highly developed urban regions
of the southeast.

Corresponding to the skewed geographic distribution of the population were differences in education. In 1960, Afro-Brazilian women were three times as likely as white working women to have no formal schooling. Women of African descent were also less likely than whites to have completed middle or high school. Hence, urban white women by 1960 had a sizable educational advantage; 35 percent had completed eight or more years of schooling compared to only 7 percent of their Afro-Brazilian counterparts.

Over the next two decades, women in both racial categories achieved substantial gains in education. In many cases, the gains for Afro-Brazilians were greater than those for whites. For example, we find that Afro-Brazilian women increased their representation in the highest education category 7.33 times (column 6), compared to an increase of 2.61 for whites (column 3). Despite such absolute gains, the relative disparity between the two racial groups remained virtually unchanged. By 1980, Afro-Brazilian women remained concentrated in the lowest educational categories. This gap is reflected in the finding that 47 percent of white female workers had better than a middle school education, compared to only 22 percent of working Afro-Brazilian women. The conclusion we can draw from these findings is that both Afro-Brazilian and white women achieved absolute gains in schooling attainment, yet the racial gap persisted.

Occupation

Changes in the occupational distribution of working women are presented in table 2. The findings show that occupations were clearly stratified by race. In 1960, the majority—about 68 percent—of Afro-Brazilian women were employed in the lowest-status occupation of domestic workers. The equivalent figure for white women was approximately 28 percent. Professional and clerical jobs, in contrast, were the domain of white women; slightly over 48 percent of urban white women (compared to about 12 percent of Afro-Brazilian women) were employed in white-collar jobs.

The biggest shift for women over the next two decades was the exodus from blue-collar jobs, particularly domestic employment, and the entrance into white-collar occupations. Again, rates of change among Afro-Brazilian women were the greatest, partly be-

TABLE 2

Occupational Distributions by Race, Employed Women Aged
18–64, Urban Brazil, 1960/1980

	White			Afro-Brazilian		
			1980			1980
	1960	1980	1960	1960	1980	1960
	(1)	(2)	(3)	(4)	(5)	(6)
White Collar						
Manager/Administrator	0.7%	3.9%	5.57	0.1%	1.5%	15.0
Professional/Technical	26.4	26.7	1.01	8.1	14.3	1.7
Clerical	21.2	32.5	1.53	3.7	18.3	4.95
Total White Collar	48.3	63.1	1.31	11.9	34.1	2.87
Blue Collar						
Skilled manual	15.8	17.5	1.11	13.8	21.9	1.59
Transportation/						
Communication	0.3	0.2	.67	0.3	0.4	1.33
Domestic worker	27.9	14.8	.53	67.6	36.5	.54
Other personal services	7.8	4.5	.58	6.4	7.0	1.09
Total Blue Collar	51.8	37.0	.71	88.1	65.8	.75
Total	100%	100%		100%	100%	

Source: Brazilian Census Public Use Samples, 1960 and 1980.

cause in 1960 they were so underrepresented in nonmanual jobs.
Among clerical workers, for example, Afro-Brazilian women increased their representation from 4 to 18 percent. Nevertheless,
in 1980, we again observe a substantial racial lag. A little over 63
percent of all working white women were employed in the better-
paying white-collar occupations as compared to only 34 percent of
Afro-Brazilian women. Despite the gains of Afro-Brazilian women,
by 1980, the greatest proportion (36.5 percent) remained concentrated in domestic labor.

The improvements that were made in occupational distribution among women in both racial groups were the result of two factors. First, the expansion of jobs in Brazil from 1960 to 1980, and the accompanying urbanization and economic growth, meant that there was a higher demand for female labor. As a result, both white and Afro-Brazilian women were able to move into the urban workforce. Second, as demonstrated in the educational gains shown in table 1, women were better qualified for these jobs. Yet despite improved levels of educational and occupational distribution, evidence in tables 1 and 2 shows that by 1980, Afro-Brazilian women were still disproportionately concentrated in the least-favorable regions, lowest educational categories, and lowest-paying occupations.

Wages

As argued by conventional theorists, these gaps in regional, educational, and occupational distributions are what lead to overall black-white earnings differences. As a result of the persistence of these unequal opportunities among women in Brazil, we can expect differences in wages by race. Data in table 3 compare average monthly wages by race and occupation for women in 1960 and 1980.[7] Overall, the findings show that Afro-Brazilian and white working women achieved absolute increases over time in wages.[8] Still, in every occupation, and in both decades, white women earned more than Afro-Brazilian women. The racial wage gap actually increased over time among nonmanual workers. For instance, Afro-Brazilian women employed in white-collar occupations averaged Cr$3,368 less than white women in 1960; by 1980, this gap had increased to Cr$4,747.

Additional data suggest wages also differed by sex. Table 4 presents women's 1960 and 1980 average monthly wages as a percentage of men's by race and occupation. Comparing white women and men, columns 1 and 2, we find that women's median earnings were lower than men's in every occupation. Among white-collar workers in 1960, for example, white women earned 55 percent of that of men. Over time—and similar to the change in the racial wage gap among women—the gender gap in wages increased among white-collar workers.

A comparison of Afro-Brazilian women and men shows a similar pattern. Afro-Brazilian women were paid less than Afro-Brazilian

TABLE 3

Average Monthly Wage[1] by Occupation and Race, Employed
Women Aged 18–64, Urban Brazil, 1960/1980

	White			Afro-Brazilian		
	1960	1980	1980 – 1960	1960	1980	1980 – 1960
Occupation	(1)	(2)	(3)	(4)	(5)	(6)
White Collar						
Manager/						
Administrator	17,026	22,285	5,259	9,437	13,586	4,149
Professional/						
Technical	9,152	15,499	6,347	5,644	9,249	3,605
Clerical	9,962	10,308	346	7,504	7,498	6
Total White Collar	9,624	13,240	3,616	6,256	8,493	2,237
Blue Collar						
Skilled manual	5,815	5,726	89	3,944	4,906	962
Transportation/						
Communication	5,433	7,247	1,814	4,338	5,462	1,124
Domestic Worker	2,065	3,674	1,609	1,779	3,543	1,764
Other personal						
service	5,075	5,789	714	3,093	4,806	1,713
Total Blue Collar	3,676	4,921	1,245	2,222	4,147	1,925

Source: Brazilian Census Public Use Samples, 1960 and 1980.
[1] In constant 1980 Brazilian cruzeiros.

men in all occupations. Similar to the findings among whites, the shift over time was an increase in the gender gap among workers in the more prestigious jobs. Between 1960 and 1980, Afro-Brazilian women's wages decreased from 61 to 57 percent of that of men in white-collar occupations. Among blue-collar workers, however, Afro-Brazilian women's share of earnings actually increased from 37 to 48 percent.

These patterns of wage differentials suggest an interplay between race and gender in determining earnings in Brazil. Lower wages

TABLE 4

Women's Wages[1] as a Percentage of Men's[2] by Race and Occupation, Employees Aged 18–64, Urban Brazil, 1960/1980

Occupation	White		Afro-Brazilian	
	1960 (1)	1980 (2)	1960 (3)	1980 (4)
White Collar				
Manager/Administrator	63%	55%	78%	57%
Professional/Technical	45	43	54	46
Clerical	67	69	76	73
Total White Collar	55	49	61	57
Blue Collar				
Skilled manual	73	54	67	59
Transportation/Communication	61	63	63	53
Unskilled manual	35	47	36	54
Total Blue Collar	45	46	37	48

Source: Brazilian Census Public Use Samples, 1960 and 1980.
[1] In constant 1980 Brazilian cruzeiros.
[2] White women are contrasted to white men; Afro-Brazilian women are contrasted to Afro-Brazilian men.

for women relative to men indicate gender inequality in wages. Afro-Brazilian women, therefore, suffered the effects of both racial and gender inequality. The findings presented so far imply that the structural transformations that took place between 1960 and 1980, which increased labor market opportunities for women and raised wages, did not for the most part reduce either racial or gender differentiation.

Measuring Racial and Gender Discrimination

To further analyze the racial wage gap among women, I applied a technique commonly used in economics to estimate labor market inequalities. The objective of this analysis was to investi-

TABLE 5

Decomposition of White/Afro-Brazilian Wage Gap,[1] Employed Women Aged 18–64, Urban Brazil, 1980 (Base Group = White Women)

| | 1960 | | 1980 | |
| | Cz$ | % | Cz$ | % |
Component	(1)	(2)	(3)	(4)
Total difference	3,847	100	4,539	100
Composition	1,562	41	1,613	36
Discrimination	−362	−9	820	18
Interaction	2,647	69	2,105	46

Source: Brazilian Census Public Use Samples, 1960 and 1980.
[1] In constant 1980 Brazilian cruzeiros.

gate whether—net of differences in region, education, and other wage predictors—Afro-Brazilian women were paid less than white women. Wage discrimination is said to occur when similarly qualified workers in the same job category receive unequal pay on the basis of racial differences.

The first step in the decomposition analysis was to estimate separate wage-regression equations by race.[9] I chose a set of individual-level variables, traditionally employed in models of earnings, for the analysis: job experience, years of schooling, region, occupation, and migrant and marital status. Results from these equations served as input into a decomposition model. This technique partitions the earnings gap between two groups into three parts: composition, discrimination, and interaction.[10]

Decomposing the wage differential for women in 1960 and 1980 (table 5), we find the following: In 1960, 41 percent of the wage gap between Afro-Brazilian and white women was due to compositional differences. Composition represents the amount of the earnings differential due to unequal levels of human capital. This component reflects the racial gap demonstrated in regional, schooling, and occupational placements.

The second component, discrimination, accounted for −9 percent of the wage gap between white and Afro-Brazilian women in 1960. Discrimination is substantively interpreted as the amount of the wage differential resulting from unequal pay among equally qualified workers. The negative sign of the discrimination component indicates that Afro-Brazilian women, in 1960, actually received greater wage returns for their individual characteristics than did similarly qualified white women.[11] The third portion, interaction, accounted for 69 percent of the earnings differential. Interaction reflects the combined effect of both differential qualifications and pay.

By 1980, these relationships had changed. A partitioning of the wage differential shows that compositional differences decreased to 36 percent, representing the gains in educational and occupational attainment won by Afro-Brazilian women. Yet discrimination tripled. Eighteen percent of the wage gap between Afro-Brazilian and white women was now due to unequal pay. Despite the human capital achievements of Afro-Brazilian women, in 1980, they were paid less than similarly qualified white women.

THE INTERSECTION OF GENDER AND RACE

Three important conclusions arise when we examine racial differences among women during this period of rapid transformation in Brazilian society. First, comparing the profiles of urban working women, we find that by 1980 both Afro-Brazilian and white women achieved absolute gains in schooling and entrance into more prestigious occupations. The opportunities and economic rewards of such gains, however, were not equally distributed. White women gained access to higher education and better-paying occupations in much greater numbers than Afro-Brazilian women. After two decades of economic development, the largest single job opportunity for Afro-Brazilian women continued to be that of a domestic servant.

Second, analyses of wages among the urban female labor force showed persistent inequalities. In every occupation, white women were paid higher wages than Afro-Brazilian women, although wage inequality afflicted all women in Brazil. A comparison of men's and women's wages by occupation showed gender differentials; men's wages were consistently higher than women's. Additional analysis of wages through regression-based decomposition techniques suggested that, by 1980, the racial wage differences among women could not be explained solely by unequal levels of educational or occupational placement. Rather, after controlling for sociodemographic differences, Afro-Brazilian women continued to be paid less than white women. Hence, Afro-Brazilian women suffered the combined effect of gender and racial wage inequalities.

Finally, the results suggest that the structural transformations that took place between 1960 and 1980—which increased labor market opportunities for all women—appear to have done little to reduce racial differentiation among women. On the contrary, those Afro-Brazilian women who rose to the top of the occupational hierarchy experienced increased inequality.

The analyses presented here reveal that during the period of Brazil's rapid industrialization, working women confronted an urban labor market in which their position was clearly conditioned on the basis of their sex. Yet women did not share a common experience of gender inequality. A central factor determining the life chances of Brazilian women was race. Gender and race—in addition to social class—intersected to differentiate women's work lives in Brazil.

NOTES

1 For a discussion of Afro-Brazilian protest during the *abertura,* see Andrews 1991, 191–207 and Winant 1992. For a similar discussion on the role of women in the political transition, see Alvarez 1990.

2 This discussion of the history of the women's movement in Brazil draws on the work of Sonia Alvarez (1994; 1990).

3 Proclaiming a benign experience with slavery, low levels of racial prejudice among Portuguese colonists, and a dearth of colonial European women, the author of Brazil's racial democracy thesis—Gilberto Freyre—argued that the resulting extensive miscegenation created race relations that were "probably the nearest approach to paradise to be found anywhere in the world" (Freyre 1946, 9).

4 To address the specific concerns of Afro-Brazilian women, activists have formed organizations such as: Geledes, a black women's institute founded in 1990 in São Paulo to confront issues of reproductive rights, labor market discrimination, and other health concerns; and Agbara

Dudu, a group established in 1982 in Rio de Janeiro to address issues of basic needs, health care, and violence.

5 Notable exceptions that analyze racial differences among women include Carneiro and Santos 1985; Patai 1988; and Oliveira, Porcaro, and Arajuo Costa 1987.

6 Women not receiving a wage were excluded from the analysis.

7 Wages are presented in constant 1980 Brazilian cruzeiros. Using deflators—provided by Fundacao Getulio Vargas—that correct for inflation, wages for 1960 were set at 1980 values.

8 Two exceptions are white women employed in skilled manual occupations and Afro-Brazilians employed as clerical workers.

9 Two unreported preliminary steps led to the separate wage analysis by race for women. The first was to estimate earnings models that included race as a dummy independent variable. The results showed that the race coefficient was both statistically significant and negative, indicating that controlling for human capital, the earnings of Afro-Brazilian women were lower than those for white women.

To test whether the equations for white and Afro-Brazilian women differed greatly from one another, the second step was to estimate an interaction model that introduced multiplicative terms for the race variable with each independent variable. The result showed significant interactions between race and several independent variables. In addition, results of general F-tests rejected the null hypothesis that a pooled model should be fitted.

The conclusion from these tests is that the relationship between wages and the prediction of wages differ for each racial group. Specifically what this means is that increases in experience, education, and employment in higher-salaried occupations, and being a migrant and married yield higher wage returns to white women than to African Brazilian women. Simply put, this means that Afro-Brazilian women earned less for performing the same jobs as similarly qualified whites.

10 The decomposition model is:

$$(Y^h - Y^l) = [(a^h - a^l) + \Sigma X^l) (b^h - B^l)] + \Sigma b^l (X^h - X^l) + \Sigma (b^h - b^l) (X^h - X^l)$$
$$\quad\quad (a) \quad\quad\quad\quad\quad (b \quad\quad (c)$$

11 This may reflect the fact that so few women of either race were employed in the urban labor market in 1960.

REFERENCES

Alvarez, S. E. 1990. *Engendering Democracy in Brazil: Women's Movements in Transition Politics.* Princeton, N.J.: Princeton University Press.

———. 1994. The (Trans)formation of Feminism(s) and Gender Politics in Democratizing Brazil.

Andrews, G. R. 1991. *Blacks and Whites in São Paulo, Brazil, 1888–1988.* Madison: University of Wisconsin Press.

———. 1992. Racial Inequality in Brazil and the United States: A Statistical Comparison. *Journal of Social History* 26, no. 2: 229–63.

Bruschini, M., and F. Rosemberg. 1982. A Mulher e o Trabalho. In *Trabalhadoras do Brasil,* eds. M. Bruschini and F. Rosemberg, 9–22. São Paulo: Editora Brasiliense.

Cardoso, F. H. 1962. *Capitalismo e Escravidao no Brasil Meridional.* São Paulo: Difusao Europeia do Livro.

Carneiro, S., and T. Santos. 1985. *Mulher Negra.* São Paulo: Nobel/Conselho Estadual da Condicao Feminina.

Faria, V. 1989. Changes in the Composition of Employment and the Structure of Occupations. In *Social Change in Brazil, 1934–1985: The Incomplete Transition,* eds. E. Bacha and H. S. Klein, 141–70. Albuquerque: University of New Mexico Press.

Fernandes, F. 1969. *The Negro in Brazilian Society.* New York: Columbia University Press.

Freyre, G. 1946. *The Masters and the Slaves.* New York: Alfred A. Knopf.

Hanchard, M. G. 1994. *Orpheus and Power: The Movimento Negro of Rio de Janeiro and São Paulo, Brazil, 1945–1988.* Princeton, N.J.: Princeton University Press.

Hasenbalg, C. A. 1979. *Discriminacão e Desigualdades Raciais no Brasil.* Rio de Janeiro: Graal.

———. 1985. Race and Socioeconomic Inequalities in Brazil. In *Race, Class, and Power in Brazil,* ed. P.-M. Fontaine, 25–41. Los Angeles: University of California, Los Angeles, Center for Afro-American Studies.

Hasenbalg, C. A., and N. d. V. Silva. 1985. Industrialization, Employment, and Stratification in Brazil. In *State and Society in Brazil: Continuity and Change,* eds. J. D. Wirth, E. d. Oliveria Nunez, and T. E. Bogenschild, 59–102. Berkeley, Calif.: Westview Press.

———. 1991. Raca e Oportunidades Educacionais no Brasil. In *Desigualdade Racial no Brasil Contemporaneo,* ed. P. A. Lovell, 241–62. Belo Horizonte: CEDEPLAR/UFMG.

Ianni, O. 1978. *Escravidao e Racismo.* São Paulo: HUCITEC.

———. 1987. *Racas e Classes Sociais no Brasil.* São Paulo: Editora Brasiliense.

Ianni, O., and F. H. Cardoso. 1960. *Cor e Mobilidade Social em Florianopolis: Aspectos das Relações entre negros e brancos numa Comunidade do Brasil Meridional.* São Paulo: Companhia Editoria Nacional.

Martins, T. 1985. Ainda na Base da Piramide. *Mulherio* 5:21.

Miranda, G. V. d. 1977. Women's Labor Force Participation in a Developing Society: The Case of Brazil." *Signs* 3, no. 1: 261–74.

Oliveira, L. E. G., R. M. Porcaro, and T. C. N. Arajuo Costa. 1983. *O Lugar do Negro na Forca de Trabalho.* Rio de Janeiro: IBGE.

———. 1987. Repensando o Lugar da Mulher Negra. *Estudos Afro-Asiáticos* 13:87–99.

Patai, D. 1988. *Brazilian Women Speak.* New Brunswick, N.J.: Rutgers University Press.

Rolnik, R. 1989. Territorios Negros nas Cidades Brasileiras (Ethnicidade e cidade em São Paulo e no Rio de Janeiro). *Estudos Afro-Asiáticos,* no. 17: 29–41.

Saffioti, H. I. B. 1985. Technological Change in Brazil: Its Effect on Men and Women in Two Firms. In *Women and Change in Latin America,* eds. J. Nash and H. Safa, 109–35. South Hadley, Mass.: Bergin and Garvey.

Silva, N. d. V. 1978. Black-White Income Differentials: Brazil, 1960. Ph.D. diss., University of Michigan.

———. 1985. Updating the Cost of Not Being White in Brazil. In *Race, Class, and Power in Brazil,* ed. P.-M. Fontaine, 42–55. Los Angeles: University of California, Los Angeles, Center for Afro-American Studies.

Winant, H. 1992. Rethinking Race in Brazil. *Journal of Latin American Studies* 24, no. 1:173–92.

Wood, C. H., and P. A. Lovell. 1992. Racial Inequality and Child Mortality in Brazil. *Social Forces* 70, no. 3:703–24.

Carlos Hasenbalg and Nelson do Valle Silva

NOTES ON RACIAL AND POLITICAL

INEQUALITY IN BRAZIL

Two themes run throughout academic studies of race relations in Brazil during the last two decades.[1] The first is that of racial inequality in contemporary Brazil.[2] Research on this problem has served to show the great discrepancy between the level of idealization — that is, the supposed absence of prejudice and racial discrimination — and the reality of the social situation for the black population in Brazilian society. The second identifiable theme refers to the ways in which the experience of inequalities and racial discrimination are manifested in the political arena.

Studies on these issues, the first type directly associated with traditional sociological analysis and the second more related to political science, are unequally developed. The investigations of racial stratification and inequality have not only fully documented the socioeconomic position of groups of color, but have also detailed the social processes that tend to keep the nonwhite population at the bottom of the social pyramid. In the explanation of inequalities, recent research has tended to de-emphasize the "legacy of slavery" to focus instead on the role of contemporary mechanisms of racism and discrimination.

Studies of how racial inequalities manifest themselves in the political realm are more recent and less numerous. In general, they strive to explain why race, as a socially constructed category, has not been transformed into an important source of identity and collective action. With a comparative look at other multiracial societies, this line of investigation tries to account for the limited role of racial conflict in Brazilian society.

This chapter has two limited objectives. The first is to provide a brief review of racial inequalities in contemporary Brazil. The second is to offer some observations about the relationship between race and politics in Brazil by presenting data pertinent to the topic that have not previously been analyzed.

The data that follow, based on estimates from the National Housing Survey (PNAD) of 1987, can serve as a succinct outline of the pattern of inequalities in Brazil. For this purpose, we analyzed the distribution of groups by color—white, black, and brown (*pardo*)—according to a set of social and economic parameters. (The category "yellow" and those who did not declare color have been excluded from the analysis.) Table 1 provides an overview of the data.

For historical reasons associated with the economic cycles of the system of slavery and international migrations during the decades prior to the abolition of slavery, groups of color in the population today show an extremely unequal geographic distribution. Three-quarters of the white population are concentrated in the south and southeast regions, the most developed parts of the country, compared to almost three-fifths of the nonwhite population, who live in the less-developed northeast, north, and central-west regions. This geographic disadvantage of the nonwhites, most accentuated in the brown (*pardo*) group, results in fewer educational and economic opportunities. Differences in *geographic distribution* and *racial discrimination* constitute two explanatory factors for racial inequalities in Brazil.

In terms of educational achievements, one observes that in 1987, the illiteracy rate among nonwhites (36.3 percent) was still two times greater than that of whites (18 percent). The proportion of whites who have completed the compulsory eight years of elementary schooling, 29.5 percent, is more than double the 13.6 percent of nonwhites. Finally, whites have an almost four and a half times greater probability than do nonwhites of completing college-level studies.

In the decades prior to abolition, the access of blacks and mulattos to the best agricultural jobs in coffee production and employment in the nascent industry was limited; this was particularly the case in the southeast, where most of the foreign immigrants were settling. An increase in the number of nonwhites in the modern

TABLE 1

Racial Inequality in Brazil, 1987 (in Percentages)

	White	Black	Brown	Nonwhite[1]
Population in southeast/south	75.3	62.8	37.1	40.5
Urban population	78.1	73.4	62.9	66.6
Illiterate ten years	+18	35	36.5	36.3
Completed elementary school	29.5	11.5	14	13.6
Completed high school	9.2	1.2	2.3	2.1
Average years of study	4.1	2.2	2.6	2.5
Social security registration	57.3	43.1	37.4	38.2
Nonmanual labor	26.9	6.7	12.6	11.6
Signed Worker's License	52	47.5	42.5	43.3
Average monthly salary (Cz$)	10,615	4,326	4,984	4,888

Source: National Housing Survey: Color of the Population, vol. 1, 1987.
[1] Nonwhite includes black and brown (pardo) and excludes yellow.

urban economy began only after 1930. Today, urban nonwhites are overrepresented in manual labor. At the same time, they are disproportionately represented in the worst jobs in the informal sector, as is suggested by the smaller percent of nonwhites who hold a signed Worker's License as compared with the total number of persons involved in nonagricultural activities. Based on the same means of estimation, the proportion of whites employed in the formal sector compared to nonwhites would be 52 and 43.3 percent, respectively. Currently, discriminatory barriers seem to have been displaced to a higher level of the occupational structure.

This is suggested by the unequal proportions of the two groups in nonmanual occupations, the latter serving as a proxy indicator for the new middle class. In 1987, the rate was 26.9 percent for whites, but only 11.6 percent for nonwhites. The variation itself in the percentage of blacks (6.7 percent) and browns (12.6 percent) in these occupations indicates that differences in phenotype are important factors for gaining access to these positions.

As one would expect, racial inequalities in educational opportunities and employment have had strong effects on the distribution

TABLE 2

Possession of Documents by Persons Eighteen Years of Age and Older, according to Color, Brazil, 1988 (in Percentages)

	White	Black	Brown
Bank account	40.6	16	18.7
Contributor's Identification Card	75.7	64.7	64.4
Voter Registration Card	90.4	85.2	88.6
Birth certificate	60.9	66.8	64.3
Marriage certificate	67	49.8	55
Identification card	82.3	71.9	73.4
Driver's license	33	10.9	13.3
Worker's License	74.1	77	71.9

of income. In 1987, the average monthly income of nonwhites was a little less than half (46 percent) than that of whites.

A supplement to the PNAD of 1988, titled *Political-Social Participation,* attempted to trace the profile of Brazilians in terms of their use of civil, political, and social rights. A questionnaire was given to a subsample of people eighteen years of age and older. We have selected two items from this study to illustrate racial inequalities in areas different from those socioeconomic variables represented in the demographic census and household research of the Brazilian Geographic and Statistical Institute (IBGE). The first item refers to the possession of documents associated with different aspects of the exercise of the rights of citizenship (see table 2).

It is worth pointing out the characteristics associated with these documents. To have a bank account is a direct indication of high economic status and the logical result of a well-paid job in the formal economic sector; it is required for some types of contracts and for buying on credit. The Contributor's Identification Card (CIC) is a taxpayer's ID card held by all salaried workers. It is required to open a bank account and to finalize any contract. Since voting in Brazil is obligatory for all literate citizens between the ages of eighteen and sixty-nine, a Voter Registration Card is required of all adults, that is, all except the illiterate, for whom voting is optional. This ID card—which consists of a photograph, signature, and fingerprint—is required by the state, and is necessary for various legal and contractual procedures. Finally, the Worker's License, when signed, works as a guarantee of workers' coverage under federal legislation. Traditionally, this is the document that the police have demanded from lower-class citizens, as a way to distinguish between "workers" and "vagrants" or "bums."

The distribution of these documents by color illustrates the clear disadvantage of nonwhites. The only exception to this tendency is that of black people who possess a Worker's License. In the absence of another explanation for this exception, one may suppose that black people know that is the best ID card to have. The Worker's License is more important than the Voter Registration Card, as it proves one is a worker. In all other aspects, a greater proportion of nonwhites are excluded from these minimal indicators of citizenship. This exclusion is greater in economic indicators (bank accounts and the CIC), but it is also present in the exercise of the political right to vote (Voter Registration Card).

The supplementary questionnaire on sociopolitical participation also contained questions to determine the number of people who had been victims of physical assault during the preceding year (October 1987 to September 1988), and to identify the assailant in the most recent incident. The data, classified by color, are shown in table 3.

These data on physical assault indicate, first of all, that black people are subject to a greater probability of violation to their physical bodies. Second, the attacks suffered by nonwhites appear to originate to a greater extent from family and acquaintances. Third, confirming what is well known, black men have a significantly greater probability of being victims of police violence than either white or brown men. Finally, less known is the fact that nonwhite women are more often subject to the possibility of suffering physical assault within the family circle.

The lower socioeconomic position of blacks and mulattos in contemporary Brazil has been explained in terms of the different starting points of these groups from whites at the time of the abolition of slavery. The counterargument to this is that the relevance of slavery as the cause of social subordination of blacks and mulattos should decrease over time. The claim that contemporary racial

TABLE 3

Victims of Physical Assault (in Percentages)

	White	Black	Brown
Men	1	1.4	1
Women	0.7	0.9	0.6
Total	0.8	1.1	0.8

	Assailants of Men (in Percentages)		
	White	Black	Brown
Relative	10.1	8.7	12
Acquaintance	40.8	52.2	46.2
Police	5.5	10.8	5.3
Stranger	41.9	27.4	34.7
Other/unknown	1.9	0.9	1.5
Total	100	100	100

	Assailants of Women (in Percentages)		
	White	Black	Brown
Relative	25.7	39.5	41.1
Acquaintance	34	35.8	33.9
Stranger	38.5	22.9	21.9
Other/unknown	1.8	1.9	3.1
Total	100	100	100

inequalities are only residually tied to the legacy of slavery is predicated on the continued existence of racist principles of social selection. Recent studies comparing the social mobility of whites and nonwhites clearly indicate that these two groups encounter different social opportunity structures (Silva 1981; Oliveira, Porcaro, and Arajuo Costa 1983; Hasenbalg and Silva 1988). Discriminatory practices and the symbolic violence inherent to a racist culture have limited the available educational opportunities for nonwhites much more than for whites of the same social origin (Hasenbalg and Silva 1990). Consequently, the educational achievements of nonwhites translate into proportionately fewer occupational advances and lower incomes than those of whites. One can therefore conclude that Brazil will not achieve greater equality between racial groups through a process of individual social mobility.

A recent work by George Reid Andrews (1992) is extremely relevant for situating racial inequalities in Brazil in comparative perspective and in terms of change over time. Andrews compares a large body of statistical indicators of racial inequalities between whites and nonwhites in Brazil and the United States from the turn of the past century until approximately 1988. The areas examined include the spatial distribution of whites and nonwhites, demographic indicators, education, employment, and income. The various measures show that until 1950, racial inequality tended to be greater in the United States than in Brazil. After this date, however, the indexes of inequality began to decline in the United States, while in Brazil, they remained stable and in some areas worsened. According to the majority of indicators available, by 1980 the United States had become a more racially equal society than Brazil.

In his explanation of this change, the author emphasizes three principal factors: the migration and regional distribution of racial groups, the effects of income concentration ensuing from economic growth, and federal government policies on race. Andrews (1992) concludes that each of these factors contributed to reducing the racial inequalities in the United States between 1950 and 1980, while at the same time leaving these inequalities untouched in Brazil. This points to the centrality of racial issues in the political life of the United States during the last decades and the marginal place these issues still hold in the Brazilian political arena. These findings are particularly interesting if one considers that Brazil's self-image, as a society characterized by harmonious and equal race relations, was formed to a large extent in contrast to the North American racial reality.

If, as we have seen, racism as a mechanism of social selection places nonwhite Brazilians at a disadvantage in the competitive process of social and individual mobility, confining them to the bottom of the social hierarchy, then the question arises as to the role of race in the formation of collective identities geared to political action.

In a pioneering work, Amaury de Souza (1971) formulated questions appropriate to the study of the relationship between race and politics in Brazil.

In the first place, it would be worthwhile to investigate to what extent the experience of social inequalities on the part of an ethnic group is expressed in differential attitudes and political behavior; in the second place, and if the response to the first question is positive, under what conditions does this experience transfer into a racial solidarity capable of expressing itself as collective political behavior; and in the third place, how does the political system operate in a multi-racial society to demobilize the potential of collective political behavior (Souza 1971, 63).

Unfortunately, the challenge made more than twenty years ago did not have much of an impact on the agenda of Brazilian political scientists. They had other priorities, and this is not the place for speculation on the matter. At any rate, the questions proposed by Souza allow us to organize a short review of the literature on this topic.

In reference to the first question, it is worth recalling that the most recent works published on prejudice and racial attitudes of groups of color came out in the 1950s and 1960s (Martuscelli 1950; Cardoso and Ianni 1960). More specifically, there are very few studies about the electoral behavior of whites and blacks.

Souza's article itself analyzed data from electoral research conducted in 1960 in the former state of Guanabara during the presidential elections of that year. His research showed that blacks (that is, blacks and browns) favored the Brazilian Workers Party to an extent beyond what would be expected from their social class position. This may be attributed to the identification of black people with the poor and, in the case of middle-class blacks undergoing social mobility, a continuing political loyalty (Souza 1971, 70).

In another work, Soares and Silva (1985) did a sociological analysis of the official 1982 election results of the state of Rio de Janeiro. Their findings showed that race divisions played an important role —cutting across class lines—in the election of Leonel Brizola as governor; this was particularly the case in the metropolitan area of Rio de Janeiro. The percentage of mulattos in the electorate arose as a significant structural variable accounting for votes for Brizola.[3]

Finally, from a study based on electoral survey data gathered from four Brazilian cities in the period prior to the presidential elections of 1989, Mônica Mata Machado de Castro (1992, 17) hypothesized that:

the social disadvantages of non-white groups would result in demonstrations of political nonconformity exemplified by votes for leftist candidates and parties, or those perceived as representatives of popular interests; yet it is also likely that these disadvantages would be associated with isolation, a lack of interest in politics and a feeling of alienation from the electoral process.

A regression analysis of the data showed a correlation between the nonwhite voters and two predicted tendencies: a greater electoral indifference and a greater tendency to vote on the Left.

It is difficult to formulate generalizations based on such a limited empirical base. It does seem possible, however, to assert that the variable of race has an influence on voting choices, even when social class is controlled for or taken into account. This is definitely an area of research that remains almost completely unexplored, despite the availability of data generated by a small electoral survey industry that has come into being in the country over the course of the political opening and redemocratization, that is, 1979 forward.

Answers to the second question proposed by Souza, on collective political behavior, can be found in the newly developing literature on black social movements, particularly studies on the rebirth of this movement since the mid-1970s, after some decades of relative inactivity (Fontaine 1980, 1985; Nascimento 1989; Andrews 1991a, 1991b; Monteiro 1989; Santos 1992; Hanchard 1994). A noteworthy feature of these studies is that they have developed outside the institutionalized area of research on social movements. Indeed, the black movement has been excluded from the issues covered by investigators specializing in social movements.

At the same time that recent studies on the black social movement have emphasized questions and challenges posed by the movement to the dominant concepts regarding race in Brazilian society—those associated with the idea of racial democracy—there has been a consensus among scholars as to the serious difficulties the movement faces in increasing the social bases for mobilization aiming to eliminate discrimination and race inequalities. These studies constitute an important perspective for observing the clash between denunciations of racism made by the movement and the commonsense view of race that still appears to be formed by the ideology of racial democracy.

A review of the history of the political mobilization of black Brazilians in the twentieth century is outside the scope of this discussion. Yet it is worth mentioning some contrasts between the black protest of the 1930s, which culminated in the Brazilian Negro Front (Frente Negra Brasileira, or FNB, 1931–1937), and that of the contemporary black movement, revived in the 1970s.[4]

The FNB was created under favorable political conditions brought on by the end of the First Republic. The work and discourse of the leaders of that time were essentially assimilationist. In the assessment of the social situation of blacks at the time, whites were held responsible for the centuries of slavery, the abandonment of ex-slaves, left to fend for themselves, and racial prejudices. In this assessment, however, part of the responsibility was placed on the black population itself, which in the perception of the leadership, was submerged in a state of moral apathy. The project of creating "new blacks," and of going through a second abolition, was to be achieved by redemption and the moral uplifting of the race through education and work. Integrationist thinking was less given to desires for social ascent than to the incorporation of blacks into the working class. In what has been viewed as an element of the "whitening ideology," the model of the "new black" was the white who had already been incorporated into the workforce and class structure.

As Andrews (1991a and 1991b) observes, even though it did not generate a politically significant impact in São Paulo—the major stronghold of the FNB—and it failed from an electoral point of view, the movement did attain a relatively wide positive image among the urban black population, particularly in its early stages. Among the major reasons for its later decline, which culminated in the closing of the FNB in 1937, Andrews identifies internal divisions, specifically those between a faction characterized by extreme-right chauvinism and proximity to Integralist Party ideas, and a minority faction inspired by socialism. In so doing, the movement of the 1930s would have replicated internally the same divisions that existed in the political system of Brazil in that period.

The contemporary black movement was revived in the mid-1970s, in the final years of a period of heightened authoritarianism in Brazilian politics. Like the other social movements that flourished at this time, its discourse has been radical and combative.

The rebirth of the movement has been associated with the growth of an educated sector of the black population that, for reasons of race, encountered barriers to their aspirations for social mobility. To this must be added the impact of changes in the international arena on this group, which functioned as a source of ideological inspiration: the civil rights and black power movements in the United States, and the struggle for national liberation in the Portuguese colonies of Africa (Andrews 1991b; Hanchard 1994).

This phase has broken with the assimilationist values that guided the 1930s' movement. The white integrated into society (and to its values) is no longer a model. Elements of cultural nationalism are manipulated with the intent of creating a positive identity for black Brazilians. From this grounding, there is a criticism of the ideals of the Eurocentric world and a rejection of the "whitening" ideal; at the same time, there is a "back-to-our-roots" orientation, an adherence to negritude, and a revalorization of African origins.

Along with this work on the cultural front and on identity, racism and the myth of racial democracy in Brazilian society are vehemently criticized. Indeed, racism is held responsible for the social subordination and inequalities experienced by the black population in this century.

Discounting the differences of historical time periods, there is little doubt that the FNB and the movement of the 1930s were more successful than the contemporary black movement in promoting awareness and mobilizing sectors of the black population. Various factors might be suggested to explain the decreased success of the contemporary movement in achieving support from the masses. Among these, we would like to emphasize two that appear to be particularly relevant.

The first has to do with the growing social differentiation of the black population as a result of the structural changes that have occurred in Brazilian society during the last few decades. This social differentiation created an increasing social and educational distance between the minority of activists and the majority of the black population, characterized by their poverty and low level of education.

The second factor is of an ideological nature. While the movement in the 1930s promoted a "revolution within the system," and its objective was not incompatible with the prevailing ideologies and racial values in the country, the rhetoric of the contemporary movement exhibits a racial opposition to the dominant values on race, especially those that espouse harmony and the avoidance of confrontation between racial groups.

The third question posed by Souza, relating to how the political system operates to contain potential collective political behavior, brings us to the problem of racial power and domination. Historians and sociologists who have examined postabolition republican race relations in Brazil offer interpretations of interest to this question, even when such interpretations were not the central focus of their research (Fernandes 1965, 1972; Degler 1971; Skidmore 1974; Hasenbalg 1979; Andrews 1991b). Among the factors most frequently mentioned in the literature as a source of containment of black protest are: the racially biased intervention of the Brazilian state until the 1930s, particularly in regards to immigration policy and the formation of a free labor market; the "whitening" doctrine or ideal that, together with the social perception of race as a color continuum, fragments racial identity and promotes aspirations for social mobility; the notion of racial democracy itself as an ideological recourse that tends to disguise racial divisions and inequalities through symbolic forms of integration; and the poverty, illiteracy, and low education levels that affect a large portion of the nonwhite population, limiting their available options for political mobilization.

Political science has made very few contributions to this issue. The recent work of Michael Hanchard (1994), which is from this discipline, is one of the most provocative from the point of view of interpretation. The author combines a critical analysis tracing the black movement from 1945 to 1988 with one revealing the mechanisms of racial hegemony in Brazil. He finds historical antecedents of this hegemony in the ideologies of racial exceptionalism and racial democracy, while at the same time showing the everyday mechanisms of this hegemony at the levels of popular culture and the institutions of civil society.

With the exception of election research, the academic literature on race and politics in Brazil has been developed without the benefit of knowledge of the general public's attitudes on matters of race relations. We know much more about what the elite think about these matters, whether they be black or white, than we know about the general public.

The best example of this is the overused ideology of racial democracy, an idea invented by intellectuals and appropriated by the government—which made it the official story of race relations in the nation. It has been presumed to constitute the common sense about race in the population. Yet the ways in which this ideology is translated into concepts and attitudes among white and black Brazilians continue to be largely unknown.

At this point, it is worth recalling some results from research on prejudice and discrimination in Brazilian society, the majority of which come from studies sponsored by UNESCO in the 1950s. In these studies, the most significant results were obtained in São Paulo. For example, in the study undertaken by Lucilla Hermann, designed to determine the norms of race relations in the São Paulo middle class, and later analyzed by Roger Bastide and Pierre Van den Berghe (1957), 580 white students from five different schools were interviewed. The data revealed some relevant characteristics: first, stereotypes against blacks and mulattos were quite widespread. Those referring to mulattos were slightly more favorable than those referring to blacks, although they were generally quite similar. That is, when presented with the same characteristics, mulattos were judged inferior or superior to whites at a slightly lower percentage than were blacks. The most accepted stereotypes against blacks among respondents were: lack of hygiene (91 percent), physical repulsiveness (87 percent), superstitious (80 percent), lack of financial planning (77 percent), lack of morals (76 percent), aggressiveness (73 percent), laziness (72 percent), lack of diligence at work (62 percent), sexual perversity (51 percent), and exhibitionism (50 percent). The authors point out that "the similarities with North American stereotypes are more common than differences, particularly with respect to the association of racial prejudice and sexuality" (Bastide and van den Berghe 1957, 691).

Also in regard to stereotypes, it is worth emphasizing that of the total interviewed, 268 considered blacks and mulattos in the same way; exactly that same number was more favorable to mulattos than to blacks, while just 43 of those interviewed were more favorable to blacks than to mulattos. An in-depth analysis of this last group revealed a *greater general level of prejudice against blacks and mulattos* than the group that was more favorable to mulattos, suggesting a more virulent level of racism. One finds similar results with respect to this preference for blacks as compared to mulattos in Costa Pinto's study of Rio de Janeiro (1953).

A somewhat anomalous fact, and one that interests us more, is that the answers given by these same respondents to questions on ideal norms of behavior conflict with their generalized acceptance of stereotypes against nonwhites. Thus, equal opportunities for whites and nonwhites is approved of by 92 percent of those interviewed, and more than 60 percent accept casual relationships between individuals of different colors. In all, the normative standard appears to largely follow the creed of racial democracy.

A third dimension is that of actual behavior, segregation being especially noteworthy. A good percentage of those interviewed said they had no contact with either blacks or mulattos, and their rejection of interracial marriage was quite high: 95 percent would not marry a black and 87 percent would not marry a light-skinned mulatto.

The results of this research appear to bring out a paradox: on the one hand, there is a large adherence to the normative social canon of racial democracy in Brazil, and on the other hand, a high level of stereotyping and segregation at the level of interpersonal relationships. This ambivalence constitutes, in the perceptive phrase of the authors, the very essence of the "Brazilian Dilemma" as opposed to the "American Dilemma."

The last part of our discussion focuses on some attitudes in the population concerning race problems. From there, we hope to assess the possibilities and difficulties for mobilizing on the basis of race in Brazilian society. For this purpose, we use the only data that, to our knowledge, contains information relevant to this topic, namely, information collected in a study called *Collective Identities and Democratization: The 1986 Elections in São Paulo.* This research was based on interviews from a sample of 573 residents of the city of São Paulo, eighteen years of age and older. The interviews took place during the thirty days prior to the elections of November 1986. The identification of color of those interviewed was assessed in two ways. First, color was determined by the interviewer, using the conventional categories of the Instituto Brasileiro de Geogra-

TABLE 4
Identification of Color (in Percentages), by Those Interviewed

Interviewer determination	White	Black	Mulatto	Dark	Other	No answer	Total percentage	Total number
White	82.1	1.4	4.1	10.9	0.6	0.8	100	407
Black	18.3	48.4	28.9	2.7	1.7	0	100	34
Brown	9.4	14.1	39.4	32.9	0	4.1	100	118

fica Estatistica (IBGE): white, black, yellow, and brown. Second, those interviewed indicated their own color, choosing between the following categories: white, black, oriental [sic], mulatto, and other. We decided to use the identification of color made by the interviewers for classification purposes because of the large number of ambiguous responses in color attribution made by those interviewed. According to the first criterion for grouping the data, 408 (71.2 percent) of those interviewed were white, 27 (4.7 percent) were black, 14 (2.4 percent) were yellow, and 124 (21.6 percent) were brown. Since only a small number of those interviewed were black or brown, for analytical purposes, the data for the two groups were joined together into one category: nonwhite. The "yellow" group was excluded from this analysis.

Taking into account the unequal distribution of whites and nonwhites in the social stratification system, we used the education of those interviewed as the control variable for social position. Those interviewed were divided into two groups: those with "low education," including all with primary education (up to the fifth grade), and those with "high education" (from the sixth grade through a university).

The first problem to be pointed out regarding the process of mobilizing based on race is the fluidity and ambiguity of Brazilians' racial identity. This can be seen in the data comparing the identification of color from the interviewers and the self-identification of color from those interviewed, as table 4 illustrates.

Even though the identification of color made by the interviewers followed similar categories to those used by the IBGE—that is, white, black, and mulatto—a significant proportion of informants avoided these alternatives, declaring themselves to be "dark" (*moreno*). To be dark is perfectly ambiguous: it could mean to have dark hair, so there are whites who are dark in this sense, or it could mean to have dark skin. Note that among the people that the interviewers identified as black, less than half identified themselves by this color: 18.3 percent declared themselves white and another 28.9 percent called themselves mulatto. The greatest possible discrepancy occurs among those identified as brown by the interviewers: 9.4 percent of these identified themselves as white, 14.1 percent as black, and 32.9 percent as dark.

The problem of racial identity in Brazil stems from a referential ambiguity in the categories used to express differences in color: the case of the designation "dark" is paradigmatic in this ambiguity. It has been observed time and again that in Brazil there is no clear rule of identification, such as exists with hypodescent, for example, in the United States.

The linguistic racial terms used by Brazilians are different from those used by the black movement, which tends to operate on the basis of a dichotomy of black versus white in an effort to construct an identity that can engage in collective political action. The number of people that identify themselves as black is ridiculously small when the total population of the country is taken into account. This does not mean, however, that the categories used by the IBGE, as well as those used in this research, do not capture real differences in the location of these groups in the structure of Brazilian society.

With respect to analysis of the attitudes of the people interviewed, we turn now to what the answers given to three questions tell us about the perception of racism and racial discrimination.

Rights

Currently, we hear a lot about the problem of racism in Brazil. In general, do you feel that blacks and mulattos have the same rights as whites or not?

| | Low Education | | High Education | | Total | Non- |
	White	Nonwhite	White	Nonwhite	White	white
Yes	88.8%	77.7%	73.8%	75.1%	79.9%	76.4%
No	11.2	22.3	26.9	24.9	20.1	23.6
Total percentage	100	100	100	100	100	100
Total number	(170)	(74)	(233)	(73)	(403)	(147)

The abstract way in which the question was formulated opened up the possibility for respondents to answer at different levels of interpretation: in formal legal terms, in which equality is guaranteed by law; in terms of concrete social life, or the actual enjoyment of the benefits of citizenship; and at a normative level of how things ought to be. Since it refers to rights, the question probably tended to be interpreted at a formal legal level. As such, there was almost a consensus (around 75 to 80 percent) that rights are equal. Differences between the most frequently given responses from whites and nonwhites, and from those with high and low education levels, were minimal.

The second question is placed in the context of social interaction, referring specifically to the rules by which the labor market operates. It should be recalled that the socioeconomic differences among racial groups, which the recent literature has systematically demonstrated, are precisely the result of the functioning of this labor market.

Discrimination

Some people say there is discrimination against blacks and mulattos in employment—that it is much more difficult for them to get a good job than it is for whites. Others feel that to progress in life, everything depends on the person and has nothing to do with the color of one's skin. In your opinion, is there discrimination against people of color, or is the opportunity to advance in life equal for whites and blacks?

| | Low Education | | High Education | | Total | Non- |
	White	Nonwhite	White	Nonwhite	White	white
Discrimination exists	50.6%	62.7%	79.5%	70.9%	67.3%	66.9%
Opportunities are equal	49.4	37.3	20.5	29.1	67.3	66.9
Total percentage	100	100	100	100	100	100
Total number	(170)	(74)	(234)	(73)	(404)	(147)

First of all, this contextualized form of the question verifies that approximately two-thirds of the respondents believe that racial discrimination exists in the labor market. Second, the perception of discrimination increases with the educational level of those interviewed, notably among whites, where the percentage of those that believe discrimination exists jumps from approximately 50 to 80 percent, as we move from the less educated to the more educated group.

In the case of the nonwhites, the perception of discrimination can be seen as based on personal experience. The effects of a higher education suggest that it enables one to learn or grasp experiences at a remove from personal life, improving the perception of the mechanisms at work in society. One can also see that the perception of discrimination increases more among whites than it does among nonwhites, as we move from the lowest educational level upward. This is possibly due to the rudimentary way in which the term education was used as a control variable, distinguishing between only two levels: in fact, whites classified with high education enjoy a higher level of education than do nonwhites in this category. Within the category of high education, 40.6 percent of whites

but only 23 percent of nonwhites have completed high school– or
university-level instruction.

On more concrete matters of social life, the next question deals
with one of the most basic elements of civil rights: the question of
differential treatment of whites and nonwhites by the police.

Police Treatment

Some say that blacks and mulattos are much more targeted by the police
than whites. Others say that the police investigate any suspicious person,
no matter what their color may be. Do you feel that blacks and mulattos
are more readily targeted, or that a person's color has nothing to do with
police activity?

| | Low Education | | High Education | | Total | Non- |
	White	Nonwhite	White	Nonwhite	White	white
They are more targeted	59.1%	71.3%	84.4%	75.6%	73.5%	73.1%
Color does not matter	36.7	27.4	14.2	24.4	23.7	26.2
Do not know	4.2	1.4	0.5	—	2.2	0.7
No response	—	—	0.9	—	0.6	—
Total percentage	100	100	100	100	100	100
Total number	(170)	(74)	(234)	(73)	(405)	(147)

This question focuses on part of the daily experience of the population. These answers follow the same pattern as those of the previous question, only more overtly. Almost three-quarters of the
respondents agree with the fact that blacks and browns are more
readily targeted by the police. Once again, the perception of discrimination increases with the educational level of the respondents;
this is particularly strong among whites, moving from 59.1 to 84.4
percent.

The answers to the last two questions suggest that differential treatment and discrimination based on race are not practices that escape the attention of whites and nonwhites. Information such as this raises doubts about the hegemonic character of the idea of racial democracy.

Given the fact that the notion of racial democracy must be qualified to account for the perception of the existence of differential racial treatment based on a person's color, one might expect that race could be the basis for a movement demanding equal rights and the adoption of corrective politics.

The next question deals with strategies to be adopted by the group discriminated against. This question was put only to those respondents who had perceived discrimination in the labor market.

What to Do

In your opinion, what should blacks and mulattos do to defend their rights?

| | Low Education | | High Education | | Total | Non- |
	White	Nonwhite	White	Nonwhite	White	white
Each one demand individually that their rights be respected	8.2%	10.9%	8%	11.8%	8%	11.3%
Organize a movement in which only blacks and mulattos participate	3.5	6.5	5.8	7.2	5.2	7.2
Organize a movement in which whites who worry about this problem can						

	Low Education		High Education		Total	Non-
	White	Nonwhite	White	Nonwhite	White	white
also participate	80.1	69.5	84.6	80.4	83.1	75.3
Don't know	8.2	10.9	—	—	2.6	5.2
Total percentage	100	100	100	100	100	100
Total number	(85)	(46)	(188)	(51)	(273)	(97)

The answers to this question indicate a clear rejection of the possibility that the problem could be resolved on an individual level, which therefore implies that the solution should be reached through collective mobilization. The percentage of all respondents that endorsed the idea of solving the problem individually is approximately 10 percent.

Yet there is also a strong rejection of the idea that this collective movement should be restricted to the group discriminated against. The solution proposed by the great majority is that of a wide-ranging movement with an interracial and interethnic character; that is, one based on empathy on the part of whites to the problem of racism. This implies a rejection of the possibility of a movement based on the confrontation between racial groups. On the road to a solution, harmony should prevail. As to the responses according to racial or color groupings, there is a slight difference in the sense that whites tend to favor a joint solution to a greater extent than do nonwhites. This does not mean, however, that nonwhites tend to more often support an individual solution or a racially exclusive movement.

To conclude, harmony and the avoidance of racial confrontation seem to be the translation, or natural expression, of the racial ideology in Brazil. There exists a racial problem and it demands collective action to be corrected, which qualifies the notion of racial democracy. On the other hand, there is certainly a value or ideal of harmony between races, an ideal shared by whites and nonwhites. In this context, strategies that suggest racial confrontation are rejected. The path has to be one of sensitizing people to the problem and motivating all Brazilians to action, independently of their color.

It is appropriate at this point to ask whether harmony is a general value within Brazilian society, that is, whether it is a norm or rule applicable to all areas of social interaction. In this light, it is interesting to see the answers to a question about using strikes as a legitimate form of dealing with class conflict.

Worker Strikes

Are you in favor of or opposed to worker strikes as a form of pressure in salary negotiations?

| | Low Education | | High Education | | Total | Non- |
	White	Nonwhite	White	Nonwhite	White	white
In favor of	37%	65.6%	67.2%	55.1%	54.2%	60.4%
Neither for nor against	1.3	2.1	3	8.1	2.3	5.4
Against	56.5	29.1	29.4	36.8	40.7	32.8
Do not know	5.2	3.2	0.5	—	2.8	1.4
Total percentage	100	100	100	100	100	100
Total number	(171)	(74)	(234)	(73)	(405)	(147)

A strike is largely considered a legitimate mechanism to settle conflicts between a company and its workers. With the exception of whites with a low level of education, more than half the respondents in the other three groups were favorable to strikes as an instrument of pressure in salary negotiations.

This takes us back to the question of whether harmonious relations are an expected norm for sociality. The impression one has from the available data is that the idea of harmony is something restricted to Brazilian racial ideologies.

This emphasis on the necessity of harmonious racial relations, ones without a confrontational character, brings us back to the difficulties found within the black social movement in moving ahead with its specific demands and in increasing its social base.

NOTES

1 The authors thank Ana Caillaux of IUPERJ for her help in processing the data in this chapter.
2 For general references on racial inequalities, see Hasenbalg 1979; Oliveira, Porcaro, and Arajuo Costa 1983; Fontaine 1985; Hasenbalg and Silva 1988; Lovell 1991; and Silva and Hasenbalg 1992.
3 We also note the work of Valente (1986) on blacks and the 1982 elections in São Paulo. The study exemplifies the points of contact, and what is even more common, the lack of cooperation between the black movement, black voters, political parties, and black candidates and politicians.
4 The fundamental cultural and educational character of the black initiatives in the 1940s and 1950s can be summarized as follows: "In the 40's and 50's the integration of the black population into the industrial work force and the formation of new populist parties that actively tried to support blacks, failed to adhere to a racially defined political movement. As a result, the Second Republic did not result in any political black movement that compared with those of the 1880's, 1930 or 1980." See the English-language version of the text in Andrews 1991a, 40.

REFERENCES

Andrews, G. R., 1991a. *Blacks and Whites in São Paulo, Brazil, 1888–1988.* Madison: University of Wisconsin Press.

———. 1991b. O Protesto Politico Negro em São Paulo, 1888–1988. *Estudos Afro-Asiáticos,* no. 21.

———. 1992. Desigualdade Racial no Brasil e nos Estados Unidos: Uma Comparação Estatistica. *Estudos Afro-Asiáticos,* no. 22.

Bastide, R., and P. L. van den Berghe. 1957. Stereotypes, Norms, and Interracial Behavior in São Paulo, Brazil. *American Sociological Review* 22: 689–94.

Cardoso, F. H., and O. Ianni. 1960. *Cor e Mobilidade Social em Floriánópolis.* São Paulo: Companhia Editora Nacional.

Castro, M. M. M. d. 1992. Raça e Comportamento Eleitoral. IUPERJ, trabalho não publicado.

Degler, C. N. 1971. *Neither Black nor White: Slavery and Race Relations in Brazil and United States*. New York: McMillan.

Fernandes, F. 1965. *A Integração do Negro na Sociedade de Classes*. 2 vols. São Paulo: Editora Dominus.

———. 1972. *O Negro no Mundo dos Brancos*. São Paulo: Difusão Européia do Livro.

Fontaine, P.-M. 1980. Transnational Relations and Racial Mobilization: Emerging Black Movements in Brazil. In *Ethnic Identities in a Transnational World*, ed. J. E. Stack Jr. Westport, Conn.: Greenwood Press.

———. 1985. Blacks and the Search for Power in Brazil. *Race, Class, and Power in Brazil*, ed. P.-M. Fontaine. Los Angeles: University of California, Los Angeles, Center for Afro-American Studies.

Hanchard, M. G. 1994. *Orpheus and Power: The Movimento Negro of Rio de Janeiro and São Paulo, Brazil, 1945–1988*. Princeton, N.J.: Princeton University Press.

Hasenbalg, C. A. 1979. *Discriminação e Desigualdades Raciais no Brasil*. Rio de Janeiro: Graal.

Hasenbalg, C. A., and N. d. V. Silva. 1988. *Estrutura Social, Mobilidade e Raça*. São Paulo: IUPERJ.

———. 1990. Raça e Oportunidades Educacionais no Brasil. *Estudos Afro-Asiáticos*, no. 18.

Lovell, P. A., ed. 1991. *Desigualdade Racial no Brasil Contemporâneo*. Horizonte, Brazil: MGSP Editores.

Martuscelli, C. 1950. Uma Pesquisa sobre Aceitação de Grupos Nacionais, Raciais e Regionais em São Paulo. *Psicologia* (Universidade de São Paulo), boletim no. 119.

Monteiro, H. 1989. O Ressurgimento do Movimento Negro no Rio de Janeiro n Decada de 70. Master's thesis, University of São Paulo.

Nascimento, M. E. 1989. A Estrategia da Desigualdade: O Movimento Negro dos Anos 70. Master's thesis, University of São Paulo.

Oliveira, L. E. G., R. M. Porcaro, and T. C. N. Arajuo Costa. 1983. *O Lugar do Negro na Força de Trabalho*. Rio de Janeiro, IBGE.

Pinto, L. d. C. 1953. *O Negro no Rio de Janeiro*. São Paulo: Companhia Editora Nacional.

Santos, G. G. 1992. Dos Partidos Politicos e Etnia Negra. Master's thesis, University of São Paulo.

Silva, N. d. V. 1981. Cor e o Processo de Realização Socio-Economica. *DADOS*, no. 24.

Silva, N. d. V., and Hasenbalg, C. A. 1992. *Relações Raciais no Brasil Contemporâneo*. Rio de Janeiro: Rio Fundo Editora.

Skidmore, T. 1974. *Black into White: Race and Nationality in Brazilian Thought*. New York: Oxford University Press.

Soares, G. A. D., and N. d. V. Silva. 1985. O Charme Discreto do Socialismo Moreno. *DADOS,* no. 28.

Souza, A. d. 1971. Raça e Política no Brasil Urbano. *Revista de Administração de Empresas* 11, no. 4: 61–70.

Valente, A. L. F. 1986. *Politica e Relaçoes Raciais: Os Negros e as Eleições Paulistas de 1982.* São Paulo: FFLCH/USP.

Benedita da Silva

THE BLACK MOVEMENT AND

POLITICAL PARTIES

A Challenging Alliance

My political activity started very early on in life because of the social conditions, as well as the willingness we have in Brazil to make things happen. My parents were extremely hardworking people: my father used to work in civil construction, my mother was a washer. They were illiterate but had a political conscience, and this oriented us toward the possibility of growing politically, of struggling for things, of studying because it is important to study in order to grow. My parents helped us a lot in this direction and there is something they said that I will never forget: blacks have to be people.

At first, my militancy was directed more toward community issues than a national perspective, as was the struggle against racism. The struggle was primarily community-oriented, and I was also looking to help the community, the poor community. So when I became officially involved in the project of electoral participation in the Partido dos Trabalhadores (PT) in 1982, it was more in the name of the community movement than the black movement per se; but the fact that I was involved with the black movement, and everybody recognized me as a black woman, helped me quite a bit, I believe. I have yet to see anyone succeed in winning political elections just with discussions of racism. I benefited from starting with the community struggle together with the racial struggle, but the community struggle had to take shape first. Once that happened, I could run for elections, talking about myself as a black woman favelada. Being a favelada was my first point. It made people associate my community struggle with the black and women's movements. This was and is such a strong combination that until today, even when I run for elections or tackle a new topic, the black woman, the favelada, is always at the forefront. People ask me more about this than anything else.

Social movements involving the poor from the slums were a success at the level of the grass roots, but did not receive any sympathy from the government. As a result, we thought the following: as long as we are not elected, it will be difficult to tackle our issues. But we knew the other parties and that they would not take into account what we wanted. Ordinary women, ordinary men, and workers would not be allowed to be candidates for elections. As we were facing this situation, we realized that we needed something else besides the church that worked with us, besides our organization. We needed something else to help us. Thus, we got involved with the PT.

The PT emerged because unionized workers were also always struggling and they saw the necessity of creating a political party. Their idea coincided with the feeling in the favelados movement that we needed to be represented in some way. Because of our common interests, we helped to build the PT and became candidates for this party. In Rio de Janeiro's 1982 municipal elections, nearly all of the faveladas leadership that was represented in the PT had candidates running under this party's banner. I was the only one to be elected. That is why I belong to the PT—it is a party that I helped build and it has various popular sectors. At the same time that I assisted in developing the party, it has also helped me get ahead in electoral races. I was a councilor in the municipality, then federal deputy twice; I was a candidate for mayor of Rio de Janeiro and was almost elected. Now, I have been elected senator.

The party was founded in 1979–1980, and I have been a member since the beginning. In 1982, the party understood that everybody had to be involved in the electoral process and that the various leadership groups, whether it was the black movement or the community movement, of the PT should have a candidate. It was under these circumstances that I became a candidate for the PT. Yet I was somehow worried because all my life I saw that political parties were not directed toward the questions that I was defending; historically, the Left has not paid attention to the racial question in its organizational structure. In Brazil, none of the parties—whether from the Right, the center, or the Left—make race their reference point, and I wanted to raise and tackle this racial question with much emphasis. But to the extent that the representation was present, I thought that this would bring a contribution; we could give rise to that debate inside the party.

Through my activism and the party itself, I thus became involved with the struggles against racism and apartheid. There were various campaigns: for the release of Nelson Mandela, for cutting relations with South Africa, for a boycott and sanctions against South Africa, and then, for the rights of blacks in Brazil. We worked on the question of the rights of blacks in Brazil, and today the PT knows that I am committed to this issue, and that I have brought to the party a great contribution in the debates and proposals that were presented in front of the legislature.

At the time of the Constituent Assembly for the constitution in 1988, there was general ignorance regarding the racial question. That is not the case today. Now, many of our supporters raise the issue. The fact that racial questions were brought up at the Constituent Assembly, however, made it a watershed event. Previously, no one dared to talk about these questions. At the assembly, no one said anything against blacks because they were afraid of being considered racist. Also, no one had any prior experience in this area, so we had many ideological confrontations. It was said that the question was social and that if we solved the social problem, we would solve the racial problem. There was a great battle over this topic. We insisted that it was also a racial question, arguing that the established theories about the relationship between capitalists and workers had not taken into account the sex and racial origins of workers. It was important to discuss this, especially in the PT, because the prevailing factor in the party was social class, yet the slaves in Brazil had been either Indian or black. Why those populations? Because they were poor? In fact, slaves were from various social classes. So what was the reason? It was the color of their skin—and we had to deal with this racial question. The Indians did not disappear: they had a whole culture, a way of living, their own organization. There were obvious economic interests, however, from the bourgeois class at that time, who wanted to explore Indian lands, and the Indians would disturb those interests. Brazilian capitalism is a capitalism that, in spite of the theories, for us has its origin in the racial question, in the enslavement of black and Indian peoples. It was this slave labor, highly colonized, that built the country. Brazil itself has its origin in the racial question as well. The debates at the Constituent Assembly were quite rich, and today we can accept this as being one of the strongest points within the Partido dos Trabalhadores. We don't have to impose this issue anymore. The party now understands the necessity of partaking in this debate.

REFLECTIONS OF A BLACK POLITICIAN IN BRAZILIAN SOCIETY

Even with our statist view, we have often really viewed the state as a powerful enemy. This is something we need to get past. The black movement needs to have a better understanding of the relationship between civil rights and state power. In Brazilian society, for example, we need a strategy in which the state's presence will be important for the racial struggle, at least in my view. The black movement should not just confront the political state, but should strive to democratize it with regard to public policy that is relevant to the interests of the black population, which is predominantly poor in Brazilian society. I raise this issue because I see it as my role —as a political representative of the black movement, the political movement—to discuss the state's relationship to social movements, black social movements, blacks, and society's institutions.

In Brazil, we have political as well as social movements, but there is a lot of confusion in this regard. All of us are identified as social movements and, at least in the perceptions of political scientists, are sort of seen as the types of movements that used to be called inorganic movements. This is due to the fact that the views prevailing in Brazil are incapable of seeing that there has never been any movement that was not political because it is an organized movement. We have an idea that political movements are the traditional ones—such as education, health, housing, and union movements—and that no other movements are organized. This was a mistake that we made in the black movement, not recognizing in the other movements that there was room for furthering the racial struggle. We didn't see the need to establish ideological alliances.

For me, the black movement is still one that has its academic supporters and is extremely ideological, so that we might make more blacks a part of it. I do not believe that religion is a unifying theme for blacks. Still, we need to have a strategy that will enable us to act in concert with the religions that incorporate blacks. Political parties also do not bring blacks together. Because of the ideological component of every political party, all of us are in different political parties. We need a strategy for blacks to guarantee their participation in their own political parties, within their own view of what it should be. This is an exceptionally difficult thing to bring about in Brazil because blacks are disassociated, because the movements are disassociated.

The black movement and consciously black politicians have a leadership role to play, but it has not yet been realized. There is disagreement among us, and it is not just over the state, which we've nearly named as the main enemy to be opposed. Blacks are pointing to other blacks with a different way of seeing things as adversaries. For example, blacks *from the black movement* will spend twenty-four hours arguing with you and will end up not voting for you because, from an ideological perspective, they can't find qualities in you that lend themselves to your representing them. This results from being disassociated ideologically.

We see the relations between black women, labor, and capital as the base of exploitation of the black Brazilian woman. With all due respect, the writings of Marx, Hegel, and others like them, in my estimation, were not able to perceive these ethnic and gender differences in labor-capital relations. These relationships were enough, however, to install the capitalism that is currently bringing Brazilian society the highest rates of inflation, hunger, misery, exterminations, violence, and other things. I face these issues and debates with the militants within my own party because in Brazil there are no black leftists who have engaged in an ideological struggle within their parties, so the racial issue has become a touchstone. But Brazilian society doesn't see our examples of political education buzzing about in its daily life. We must therefore have a clear vision if we are to work on these conceptions. I believe it is important to devote a little more effort to understanding black participation in Brazilian politics.

The tensions between the black movement and political parties is quite serious, and it's important to raise the issue here. When

I was elected to Congress, and was appointed as part of the congressional Constitutional Assembly charged with drafting our *new* constitution, there was much discussion about whether I was competent enough to be a congresswoman. Many thought that holding a seat in Congress was a more difficult thing, that I would have to understand a lot of subjects. In short, people felt that this was really a job for whites, the elite, and not a candidate identified with the racial cause, supported by a social movement that wasn't the black movement.

Racism still exists in Brazil. We cannot assume that because today I am a senator, racism has ended and that I do not suffer. Quite the contrary. The more elevated the social position of the black in Brazil is, the more uncomfortable this black feels if he or she keeps being a black and keeps defending the black cause. Blacks become a threat and, as white elites do not want to yield anything, blacks present a concrete target for racists.

I have had personal experiences with racism. On several occasions, I have been sent through doors other than a building's main entrance. I have even been searched. My husband, Antonio Pitanga, was stopped twice during the recent army searches on the *morros*. They searched his car. I was also stopped but not searched. Another example of the racism that I have encountered is the reception that I once received from newly hired elevator operators in the Parliament's chambers. I arrived one Monday, greeted everyone, and entered the elevator to be informed by the new operator that the elevator is "only for Parliament members."

As one can see, those of us in the PT face many difficulties in dealing with what is traditionally meant by a black movement in order to meet black expectations. As a black woman, I am not there to represent the militant wing of the black movement, but rather, underpaid blacks who live in the slums, blacks from cultural blocs, blacks from samba schools, blacks from Candomblé rites, Protestant blacks, Catholic blacks, and blacks who are not a part of anything at all. Because these blacks aren't a part of that thing called the black movement, they vote on the basis of skin color or platform. They see my black skin and decide, here's somebody who's black and who'll stand up for me.

The other issue in dealing with the movement is foreign policy, or international relations. If you have no notion of foreign policy or international relations, you'll have a difficult time coming up with any sort of policy at all. From a politician's point of view, there is nothing better than to have all these colored folks do nothing more than simply confirm and reaffirm their cultural values, while *they*, the people in power, take care of everything else. Here, the issue of foreign policy becomes an extremely important card in the black struggle. Brazil's foreign policy has significant ramifications for the lives of its black women citizens. For example, the issue of the extermination of black children is one where black women need to be involved in and made aware of foreign policy. When our children are being bought on the streets for a measly $100, the time has come for us to be educated about foreign policy! We must understand foreign policy on the issue of extermination, because it basically implies that poor people mustn't be born.

This is the conception I offer: the widest view of blacks and the black situation in Brazil. I consider preserving cultural values as extremely important, because I don't want a loss of identity, but I also want to increase my range of claims and strategies, so as to make the power and decision-making structures realize that blacks must be trained to occupy all positions. I don't want to see blacks badmouthing blacks anymore, and I don't want to compete against blacks for a place in the seats of power that we do not yet have. But we can, as brothers and sisters, create the possibility of greater strength in positions of state and organizational power with all necessary rebelliousness, because I don't want to be a candidate in an election where I might have to see all our contradictions raised.

RACE, RACISM, AND ELECTORAL POLITICS IN RIO

The state of Rio de Janeiro is racist. In the mayoral election contest in Rio de Janeiro in 1992, from the viewpoint of the black movement, blacks kept arguing about what we should and should not do politically—and all the while, white society thumbed its nose at us. They called me a monkey in the middle of the street! They said they'd have to plant banana trees so that I could live in the palace, that I'd fit in an oven, and they would make gorilla pantomimes in front of me. Also, some of my white campaign people were threatened.

Because of an emerging phenomenon, however, Rio de Janeiro gave me 2,249,861 votes (or 32 percent) when I ran for mayor. There are three points to this Brazilian electoral phenomenon: the electorate votes for the party, for the person, and for the "wave." I believe that I received these three forms of votes. First, people voted for me for my life story, for the struggles that I had led. They also voted for the party that I represent, to which I identify myself. And they voted for the "wave": I represent the emblem of the poor, of the blacks, of the unprivileged, and they saw in me what they wanted to see. I did not receive only black votes, but I received many more votes from blacks than from nonblacks. This was because black people could see me and say: "I am going to vote for you because you are black." This vote was a very conscious one.

Racism has not ended and prejudice still exists, but my candidacy and the votes that I got demonstrate that there is an increasing awareness of this in the black community and among the Democrats. Democrats, even when they are not black, know that the political role of the black is important. The election, therefore, gave them the opportunity to say: "If Benedita can do it, the other black people can do it." We are working for this.

THE NECESSITY OF A BLACK INTELLIGENTSIA

The Brazilian government has among its executives only one black, Pelé. This black person, however, is not there as an intellectual, a mentor. He is there because of his success as a football player, because he is a well-off black man economically, and because he gave international recognition to our country through his athletic achievements. The other "black man," the intellectual, does not yet have representation in the Brazilian government. I think that this is due to the fact that blacks in Brazil lack academic knowledge, and in Latin America, academic knowledge is a big boost for those in power. Yet it is necessary to produce black intellectuals, and for this intelligentsia to have a prominent role, not only for Brazil but for the black world.

The poor Africans, the Afro-Americans, the Afro-Brazilians, the diaspora: we have to help each other, we have to have a strategy, we need to develop common actions to benefit black people wherever they are. A dialogue needs to be initiated among those interested in creating a black intelligentsia, which is why I found the theme of racial discrimination and the exchange of ideas at the Racial Politics in Contemporary Brazil conference to be so important, so profitable. First, it allowed us not only to exchange ideas and find out about each other's experiences, but also to look for paths for integrated action. It is important to maintain this dialogue and exchange of ideas so that people can become acquainted with black academics.

In Atlanta, Georgia, I believe, a museum was constructed in order to gather together all the knowledge of blacks—what blacks had discovered, what they had researched, and so on. I am going to suggest to the Brazilian government that a museum like this be built in Brazil. In reality, you have an academic world of the best quality in Brazil, yet blacks are not able to constitute a force in this realm. One of the strengths of the United States, for example, is that it has a black academic world, including black universities. We do have black intellectuals, but nobody has their books in the libraries; those books are not even suggested to the academic world. We have to create the conditions for a black intelligentsia in Brazil, such as exist in other countries. I want to prepare myself to lead this issue because I want the black race to feel complete about the intellectual question. We have to create the conditions to create possibilities.

Thereza Santos

MY CONSCIENCE,

MY STRUGGLE

How many times in the course of my life, as a black, did I question the path for black conscience? Many times that questioning emerged together with rebellion: when in extreme cases of discrimination and racial violence, I saw blacks who were passive, some with the fear of reacting, others even finding this normal and using to that effect the stigma of the race; or at other times, in the meetings of the black movement, when I realized that the leadership did not manage to have a political conscience about the reality of Afro-Brazilians.

Many times, I felt lost, even desperate. It seemed that I was stuck to a wall by a knifepoint until I discovered that it was a privileged experience that my life improved and what I call my black conscience crystallized. But in order to understand all of this, it is necessary to go back in time. To remember the childhood in a middle-to-lower-class neighborhood in Rio de Janeiro, but even so a street with few blacks, a small street made up of two blocks. There were the games with the white kids and, consequently, name-calling: monkey, black bird, urubu (a black vulture). The magnanimous mothers who, to show that they were not prejudiced, passed their hands through my hair and said: She is black, but she is very educated! She is a real black with a white soul!

That irritated me. As I did not understand the dichotomy between black and white, nor the prejudice of racism, I wanted to know how I could possibly be black outside and white inside. According to what I understood, the soul was within me and it was black like me. I know today that the majority of black Brazilians lose their racial identity on this path, taken away by the whites who are around them or their own families, who do not have any conscience of being black.

But I remained with the curiosity aroused by a color, and I had to discover how it was possible to have one color outside and another one inside. I did not have any problem being black, due to what my grandmother had taught me. She always said that to be black was a reason to be proud, not to be ashamed. On the other hand, I had lived previously in a neighborhood where there were only black kids, but it was close to other members of our big family and there was an attitude not only of pride, but also of provocation in relation to the whites. But pride did not answer the question of being two-colored, and it did not answer either to the fact that the girls thought that I always had to do everything that they told me to do and, when I disobeyed, I was called monkey.

Questions and more questions, with no answers. My mother was the only one who could answer, but she never did. Sometimes my mother would lose her patience with me and shout: "Why, why, why! You'd better watch it and be quiet for a while. You want an answer to everything. Your name from now on will be Thereza *porque* (why)!" I became Thereza *porque*. But I remained with no answer. In reality, it must have been very difficult for my mother, who was not like my grandmother at all.

In my school, where the students were almost exclusively white, the situation was not much different. There, I started to discover that I was different, but I did not want to be called monkey, black bird. I wanted to be called by my name, and I no longer wanted to be a puppet in the hands of the children. I began to withdraw and to play on my own at home. Coming back from school, or when I would go and buy sweets from the store nearby, I started to notice that there were some black kids who would walk by in the street going to school or carrying buckets of water on their heads. This arose my curiosity and I wanted to know where they came from. I looked around me and discovered the slum (*morro*) that was at the end of our street. When I walked to the hill where the slum was, I found that 90 percent of the kids were like me. Some of them already knew me; I was called the-black-girl-who-lived-down-the-street. The kids really treated me well, and I perceived a certain reverence on the part of the adults. I was equal, but at the same time, I was better because I had a house. The slum on the hill became my refuge, and I discovered poverty and separation. I still didn't know what discrimination and prejudice was.

With this discovery, I started to regain my self-esteem, although I did not know what that was at that time. Transformation. I brought my little friends from the hill to play in the villa, and noticed the reaction of the mothers and the withdrawal of the white kids.

I didn't care. Maybe it was a form of aggression; I don't really know. I only knew that I was happy and that the white kids' annoyance left us more room. The women from the slum on the hill who had never gotten close to my house, would come and ask for water. My mother responded, but would not allow them to get too close. She didn't complain about my new friends, but she increased my study hours. There was less time to play.

I did well enough in school over the years to attend a university, a rarity for a black in Brazil. When I entered the university, there were only two blacks. Both were light-colored, and one never even mentioned prejudice. I suspected that she did not know that she was black.

There, I became a member of the Popular Center of Culture (CPC) of the National Union of Students in 1961, which at the time was closely linked to the Communist Party of Brazil. I discovered the difference of class, which was valuable, but nothing about blacks. Whenever I would ask questions about the racial issue, I would hear a lecture about my ideological deviations, as there was no racial question but only the question of social class. If the social question could be solved, I was always told, everything else could be solved. I needed to learn that the real issue was social inequality. Prejudice and discrimination did not exist.

In order to fit in, I had to read a lot of Marx and Lenin to improve my knowledge and end my ideological deviance. At first, I tried to convince myself that they were right; indeed, the CPC gathered the intelligentsia of the Brazilian Left at the time, all of whom were white. Who was I to question people like Oduwaldo Viana Filho, Ferreira Gular, Jose Serra, Dias Gomes, Francisco de Assis, Carlos Estevam, Carlos Lira, and others? Some of these people, like Oduwaldo, have died, but others, like Carlos Lira and Jose Serra, are important figures in their respective political parties.

Nevertheless, I realized that these people had a very condescending relationship with me, as well as with the other blacks who were on the Left. It was a kind of paternalism, as if we were more or less stupid, and they were in charge of protecting us, of guiding us. In the meetings, many times when I expressed an opinion, somebody would interrupt and speak in my place to translate what I was thinking. At that time, that would bother me, although I did not know how to identify what was happening, but a little while after, I discovered what that meant: racism, prejudice, and tutelage. In the course of all these years, after the political opening, tens of books were written about the CPC, but none of them ever mentioned a single one of us, the blacks who were working side by side with them and who were caught together with them by the police. It is obvious that we were superfluous. In the end, we were blacks and not the children of the bourgeois class, like them. The reality I discovered later is that we were "honorary whites" to them. As black people with distinct political concerns and issues, however, we were invisible; they could not see us and, consequently, did not respect us. I think that for the Brazilian Left at this time, in the 1960s, we only served as symbols and metaphors for their "class struggles," evidence to the rest of the world that they were not prejudiced, that they were democratic. We were not supposed to have an agenda of our own. Ironically, their treatment of us was living proof that they were racists.

Nonetheless, I learned a bit more from my experiences in the CPC and broadened my conscience. I would read everything I could find about blacks, and their history in Brazil and the world. I discovered Africa in general and the Portuguese-speaking countries in particular; as well as the Popular Movement of the Liberation of Angola (MPLA), the African Party for the Independence of Guinea-Bissau and Cape-Verde (PAIGC), and the Front for the Liberation of Moçambique (Frelimo). I learned to speak about and discuss politics, and gained the courage to call racism by its real name. I no longer accepted the excuse of class inequality to cover up the reality of racial discrimination, and I learned to fight in search of racial equality because I was in search of my own dignity.

In spite of everything that I lived, and in spite of the fact that I perceived that we were considered and used as objects by the white Left, I was still committed to their vision for a more just and democratic society, so I resisted the impulse to leave the CPC altogether. Still, I was determined to struggle to transform this situation.

A few other Afro-Brazilian activists and I decided to take advantage of the auditorium of the National Union of the Students (UNE) and turned it into a theater. We were all in the UNE, trying to resist the dictatorship. Haroldino de Oliveira, a black activist, was shot in the chest. The doctors decided that it would be too dangerous to remove the bullet and, to this day, it rests next to his heart. This is one token of the black contribution to bringing true democracy to Brazil. This was in 1964, the year of the coup.

An incident occurred in 1966 that finally ended my relationship with the white student movement. Along with a group of nine white university friends, I went to a celebration at the Federal Club, a club made up of Jews, developers, and chief judges—in a word, the cream of the crop in the justice system of Rio de Janeiro. It was a ball before Carnival, invitation only. After entering the club, however, I was told to leave by the manager, who said, "Blacks are allowed here only as servants!"

I left, but decided to fight. I believed in justice and had, in fact, nine witnesses, my university friends. I started legal proceedings based on the 1951 Afonso Arinos law, an ineffective law against racial discrimination, but the only recourse available. The press of Rio gave me its support, an Italian television channel did a long interview with me, and *LIFE* magazine published a leading article about the case. All of this, because it was the first time that a black Brazilian woman had the courage to sue in a court of justice for racial discrimination. And to complicate the discrimination case, the trial took place in the neighborhood of some justice members.

The outcome is easy to guess. They managed to turn the lawsuit into a nonsuit, even with five lawyers accompanying the case. At the height of these proceedings, the first thing my university friends did was praise my courage with a round of applause and then offer a piece of advice: I should look for the company of people like me, my own kind, so to speak, so that I don't get hurt.

I followed their advice faithfully—no longer associating with them, their politics, or their political or social parties—and went to work in the samba school of Mangueira, of the *morro* of Mangueira in Rio de Janeiro. I created the Feminine Department of the samba school with fifty women and was elected as its general executive secretary. I was named the cultural director of the school, and started to offer classes in Portuguese, mathematics, and other subjects to children in the school yard.

Soon, I became known as the "little professor" in the favela, and would provide literacy courses to older people and people who had just come from prison. I could go up and down there at any hour of the early morning and nothing happened to me; I was protected. When there was a lack of books, I asked the president of the favela to assist me in obtaining more for the classes. He had a vegetable stand on the street market and, when he placed cardboard signs in it requesting donations, it started to rain books. In less than two months, we managed to open a library. At the same time, I discovered what a school of samba was all about, as well as its social implications. I learned more about blacks from the slum on the hill than I had learned in various books. Because I was much closer to the Afro-Brazilian reality, I changed my focus of struggle.

My work there increased and my old "friends" from the white Left reappeared. They wanted to convince me that all the work invested in the favela should be credited to the party. I didn't accept this, and made it clear to them that this was a job from a black for blacks, favelados (slum blacks), which did not fit the profile of the party.

In January 1969, I was arrested by the Marinha (navy) police and interrogated daily. The police saw me as a stupid, misguided black woman with no mind of her own, who was being used by white communists. While I could not possibly have a movement of my own, I could be of some use to the police to denounce the people with whom I had had contact and with whom I had worked. In this daily questioning, they did not want to know anything about me, what I had done or was doing, but instead, wanted information about the people to whom I was connected. It was not difficult to see what they wanted and how they saw me; it was quite obvious that their attitude was tainted with racism.

If before this, I had the belief that I could not collaborate with the police, the anger that I already felt increased. At the first opportunity, I escaped to São Paulo.

I discovered in that city a prejudice that was clearer and more deeply rooted. Once there, I started working with the late Eduardo Oliveira de Oliveira, one of the most striking figures of the black movement in the 1970s, a conscious fighter. First, we found that it was possible to develop a theater oriented toward blacks and soon created the Cultural Center of Black Arts (CECAN). We wrote and staged a play, entitled *And Now, We Speak . . .* , about the history of Afro-Brazilians, their optic, their perspective. It had a cast of thirty-two black actors. The show turned into a trademark and a reference for us. This gave us courage because it confirmed what we thought, namely, that the path to follow in search of our identity and self-esteem was culture, and theater was our weapon.

We staged the play *Ongira um Grito Africano* by Estevao Maya-Maya and Antonio de Padua, two blacks. I then worked in the Cultural Department at the School Mocidade Alegre. I wrote various narratives for Carnival, all of them based on the sociocultural participation of the black in Brazil, as another way to disseminate research. We consolidated our work, thirty-five of us, without any organizational structure or money, but with the conscience of what we had to do. These were three years of struggle and apprenticeship for each one of us. But my past came back to haunt me; my "comrades" from the Communist Party, who had made no attempt to contact me since I left Rio, appeared. They needed my apartment to shelter people who had to be hidden and decided that my home was ideal. I was black, hence beyond suspicion; I was working as an actress on television, hence more or less famous. Once again, I could not say no and submitted.

There were tensions at the time between our group and the more traditional, conservative black groups in São Paulo, who did not like our politics or the fact that we were attracting young people with our work. Their discovery of my role in helping Communist Party members led to my name once again being put on the list of the political police. I had two ways out: either leave Brazil or go to jail. In 1972, I decided to go into exile.

I went to Africa, working first with the African Party for the Independence of Guinea-Bissau and Cape-Verde for thirty months. For eighteen of these months, I organized literacy campaigns and developed theater pieces, alongside armed guerrillas. It was a life of learning, of political and human experience. I spent the rest of my time with PAIGE in the capital after independence, helping to create national cultural projects. Afterwards, I worked for twenty-nine months in Angola, establishing a theater school, a music school, and a school of dance.

All this time, I was still affiliated with the Brazilian Communist Party and was supposed to send part of my wages to party refugees in Paris. I started to learn to say no. The learning was enormous. My days seemed tripled due to the amount of information and formation that I received. I was a professor and also a student, the star of the first theater show, the *History of Angola,* in the independent nation on 11 November 1976, the day of the first anniversary of independence. The show was also presented at the second Festival of Black Art in Nigeria in January 1977, and in the cities of the interior of Angola as well.

I participated in Angolan radio and television shows: *Africa Liberty; Angola, People, Culture; Che Guevara;* and *Kuenha.* It was a lot of work, but it was done with pleasure, a strong will, and the certainty of contributing to the formation of a new world.

My euphoria during this period would soon end, though, due to internal struggles over racial discrimination with members of the Angolan government. Our production of the show had a cast of seventy-eight people, including three whites. All were Angolans, born and bred. I was told that in the attack of 4 February — the beginning of the armed struggle in Angola against the Portuguese — there were no whites among the guerrillas. In fact, there were whites who participated in the armed struggle, I explained, and I cited some names, adding that this was not important but that it was instead necessary that we struggle to build a country free from any forms of prejudice. The individual responded with: "You are black, but you are a foreigner!" I decided to go back to Brazil, not wanting to submit myself to this type of violence.

I asked for permission to return and, in answer, received the voice of prison. I, who went to Africa to flee prison in Brazil, spent eighty-five days in an Angolan cell, in the same jail that fifteen years before, the revolutionaries of the MPLA had attacked to liberate the prisoners of conscience.

These were eighty-five days of despair, anxiety, hatred, a hunger strike, discredit of the struggle. The MPLA, in an attempt to break the deadlock, invited me to go on working in Angola, so I could leave the prison. I refused in order to defend the values for which I struggled, but I had fears of dying, of disappearing. There were rumors running around of prisoners who disappeared from one day to another. Fortunately, students who I taught in various theater projects held a vigil for me in front of the jail, against the wishes of the newly independent regime.

The officials responsible for the prison were worried for my health because of the hunger strike and feared they would have to take me to a hospital. How would people react? I was well known, respected, and cherished by the population. At the same time, I would not accept an agreement to get out and the situation became unbearable. Finally, they decided to expel me from Angola, in 1978. I had to return to Brazil.

Once expelled, I traveled on the same flight as the delegation commanded by the current president and my old friend, Jose Eduardo dos Santos, at the time of the vice prime minister. All eyes were on him, and he lowered his head. I arrived in Brazil on 28 June 1978, with no document except for the identity card that I hid in my pants. I had to take off my clothing and shoes, and remain only in my underwear. The federal police threatened to imprison me for lack of a passport. They allowed me to make a phone call, which I used to call home. My family, in turn, called the press. They soon arrived, taking photographs and conducting interviews, which led to better treatment by the police. I asked the press to stay; it was the only way to remain free. You must remember that it was still the time of the dictatorship. I had arrived at 7:15 A.M. and was finally released at 4:00 P.M.

Free, but falling apart; free to start all over, but from scratch. I need a job, but how? Without a single piece of clothing to wear, and my heart in shambles and my convictions on the ground, I cried day and night. The days went by, yet I could not manage to do anything else. July 7 arrived, my birthday, and I despaired. I had been in Brazil for ten days and still could not put my act together; my mind did not offer me any escape. In the mist of this mental chaos, the phone rang. It was for me, from Angola. My students were celebrating my birthday. All fifty-two of them were gathered together with thirty others to wish me happy birthday. It was as if the whole country talked to me for more than two hours. They sang "Happy Birthday" over the phone and then told me to blow hard to extinguish the candles. They also explained that they had a decorated bottle ready with my name inside, into which they were going to put the first piece of cake and then throw it in the ocean to come to me. I cried more than I spoke; I cried with sadness, pain, anxiety, but I learned to cry with hope and love.

I discovered in those few hours that, in spite of it all, it was worth an average of fifteen hours of work a day, the dedication to do it all:

to write, direct, do scenarios, models. It was the only way to produce anything in the cultural sphere. Even the miserable days spent in a little cubicle in jail had been worth it because I realized that I had planted something, and more important, there was love between us and every day the work and the effort were done with love.

This discovery, the care that my students gave me, was the spring that was missing. I started to piece my life together. I looked for friends; through some friends, I succeeded in finding work in São Paulo. At the end of eight months, I realized that to find myself, I had to struggle on my own, without my family as protection.

The attitude was the same: culture as a form of resistance. A basis was necessary, and I looked for my old friends at CECAN, but most by then were gone. So I began to work with members of the new generation of black militants in São Paulo, those who came of age during the 1970s: Ismael Ivo and Luiz Carlos-Cuti, a poet and a dance artist respectively, conscious blacks. We participated in the thirty-third Brazilian Society for the Progress of Science, abandoning all the formal aesthetic standards of roundtables and academic lectures. We opted for the theatricalization of our issues and from there decided to create a traveling group of black-consciousness shows in the interior. We performed and gave lectures, such as: "The Black in the Brazilian Society," "The Black Woman: Triple Discrimination," "Culture as a Form of Resistance," "The Black Movement in the 1980s," and "Black Culture in São Paulo." This enabled us to forge linkages between black entities within the state of São Paulo, from the interior to the exterior. With some difficulties, black groups started to emerge. We also lost one of our brightest lights during this time, Eduardo Oliveira de Oliveira, after a long period of isolated self-destruction. His death is painful, essentially because of the way it happened.

We diversified the work with samba schools like Nene of Villa Matilde and Green and White Shirt. It was necessary to provoke face-to-face discussions about the reality of racial discrimination against Afro-Brazilians. The work in the interior kept going on, in places like Taubate, Jacarei, Campinas, São Jose dos Campos, Ribeirao Preto, and so on.

In the periphery of the city of São Paulo, mothers were losing their children to the assassins of Rota 66, the special unit inside the military police whose duty was to kill first and ask questions later.

An overwhelming majority, I'd say about 90 percent, of those assassinated were black men. We initiated an uprising in coalition with the mothers whose kids had been assassinated. We couldn't count on the participation of the black Movement because its members wanted to be of the middle class. Many were and are from the periphery, but refuse to return.

During this period, we also addressed women's issues in the black struggle. The feminist movement had started to gain ground in Brazil, but with little discussion of the black woman. It was necessary to look for our own space. The government of the state of São Paulo created the State Council of the Feminine Condition in 1982, during Franco Montoro's tenure as governor, but made no room for us. We struggled and fought with the council until we were granted representation. I was chosen by the group Black Women as their representative. Though the white women of the council often ignored or personally attacked me, I didn't play the game and demanded that all projects focus on the problematic of the black woman. Two years after the formation of the council, which consisted of thirty-two members, we demanded four seats and, in the end, were refused.

State elections were near, however, and the governor's office was not interested in getting into trouble with blacks. We received the four seats. Sueli Carneiro, Ilma Fatima de Jesus, Vera Lucia Saraiva, and myself were the four activists who represented the black women's group. Afterwards, I was appointed as a cultural adviser to the municipal secretary of culture in 1983. There, I participated in the creation of projects like Culture and Popular Resistance, the Profile of Black Literature, an International Presentation of São Paulo, and the International Meeting of Black Music in 1984.

In 1986, the group Black Women wanted to put forward a candidate for councilor, and I was chosen. I lost the election, but managed to get 9,000 votes in a campaign with no resources. And yet, I found out that 95 percent of the votes I received were from the black electorate. This ended the myth that the black does not vote for the black. My votes came from blacks. I made a new discovery: black voters, if they believe in their own people, will vote for black candidates.

My struggle went on in the samba schools, in the periphery, in the interior, with women, at the Ministry of Culture. Sometimes I got tired and felt like giving up. I realized many times that I had dedicated my whole life to this cause. I don't know whether I am right or wrong, but I also realize that I could not behave in any other way.

Many times, the black militants have called me a radical. What does it mean to be a radical? For the past few years, I have had to invade the Office of Public Safety because of the murdering of black youth, who were killed like animals just for the sin of being black. In the beginning, I would ask the "leadership" of the black movement to join me in the struggle and demand from the office a new attitude from the police. They never showed up. They folded their arms and did not react.

It is difficult to understand this attitude on the part of the black movement, but I understand that the destruction of racial identity together with the values of a violent society, in the capitalistic sense, has a lot to do with this reality. It is also difficult and complicated, however, to keep my supposed coherence, and yet I won't change. My life experiences have helped me tremendously in the search for my path and what I call my conscience. Facing the incoherence of the black movement, I kept asking myself: If I learned to live with whites, and if the reality of the black in Brazil is not that different, how come they did not learn?

Violence is a constant in black people's lives. Conscious Afro-Brazilians are well aware that they are on their own, without support. Yet everyone needs a source of support for something. By the confidences and the requests that came to me by chance, I realized that I had turned into a source of support. I accepted the role and looked for a solution, this meaning constant confrontation. It seems daring, but I am convinced that this is the only way to preserve our black dignity: the fact of knowing that one has to and can fight. Conscience taught me this path and, for this reason, I'll keep going.

Ivanir dos Santos

BLACKS AND POLITICAL

POWER

I am the son of a peasant woman. My mother came out of the rural zone of Rio when she was very young, more or less fourteen years old, and when coming through Rio, met a man from Bahia, a black professional mechanic. To be a mechanic in the 1950s, one had to be highly qualified; it was considered an important profession because there was no auto industry in Brazil at the time. In the course of their relationship, she ended up pregnant. In 1954, the year in which I was born, she was living in the "favela of the *esqueleto*" (skeleton), an important favela in Rio, close to Maracana; she was living on her own. He was living with another woman in the area of Nilopolis, in the *baixa fluminense*.

She had to support me, and one of the activities she ended up having recourse to was prostitution, so I am the child of a prostitute. For a long time, she prostituted herself in order to feed me. My mother lived in the "favela *esqueleto*" and then she lived in the "favela of Comandante Mauriti," which was a zone of prostitution quite well known in the "favela *do mangue*" (swamp), here in the center of the city. Then we lived in the "*Morro da Mangueira*," where I live today. According to what people tell me (and I believe I remember a little bit also), I joined some children and we formed a group. Whenever the prostitutes were taken by the police, we protested at the door of the precinct in order to get them out. Together with the relatives of the prostitutes, we alleged that we were the prostitutes' sons, uncles, mothers, and so forth. From that time on, we became familiar with the police violence that was common in the milieu of the prostitutes.

They say that in the years 1958–59, I was kidnapped by the police because of the pressure that was made by the children to have their mothers released. I was put in an official institution for minors called Servico de Assistencia ao Menor (SAM). We discovered later that my mother looked around for me in all the schools and did not find me. The documents in the archives of the SAM do not say where I was. My father, who was embittered (he accompanied my mother in her search), went away to São Paulo, and my mother committed suicide shortly thereafter. She burned herself to death. I discovered this when I was fourteen. So I was placed in a school in Teresopolis.

That school was very hard, very small. There was much physical abuse—for instance, you had to walk on your knees—and when we got to eat rice, it was cause for celebration. We had music and we would sing, "Today we have rice, rice, rice, rice." Ordinarily, we would eat *canjiquinha* (the corn given to chickens) and soup at night. Soup and bread; I had so much of it that, today, I never eat soup. I stayed in that school until I was eleven or twelve when, unexpectedly, some buses showed up one day and we were transferred to another school in Rio de Janeiro. I believe that the first school I attended was called Santa Teresinha, and the second Sao Geraldo in Jacarepagua. At Sao Geraldo, I experienced some type of leadership, I had some privileges: I would go out to buy bread for the other kids, I would help make the meals, I would work in the kitchen. That's what they called "privileges." I remember that I was not literate because there had not been much support for scholarly pursuit at my first school. Still, I managed to do primary school in two years. It was very intensive and the pace was too quick.

In 1968, I passed the "Vestibular," a competitive exam for students in the state boarding schools, which allowed me to go to a model school called "15 de Novembro." When you got into that system, you lost the identity of your name. You were given a number. The collective identity prevailed over the individual one. School "15" was a better school with better food, although it was disciplined in a military fashion and was more formal.

As school "15" students, we were alienated from the social events that went on around us. I discovered later, after I got out of the school of the Teresopolis, that the military coup of 1964 had occurred. The military regime then founded Fundacao Nacional do

Bem-Estar do Menor (Funabem). The model school that I was in, "Quintino," was considered the model school by the military. I was in the midst of student agitation in 1968 and did not know what was going on. We had a few more privileges; for instance, we had permission to go to the Maracana Stadium and watch soccer games on weekends, where we sold *mariolas* (candies). Interestingly, I observed that 95 percent of the students in that school were black. The few whites who were there were being punished; some of them came from important families of the middle class and the rest were poor people.

That same year, I met a young boy whose mother also lived in the "Comandante Mauriti" district. He used to go home every weekend and asked if I would like to come along during one of his visits, as I talked a lot about the neighborhood. I went, and the minute I turned the first corner, all the prostitutes recognized me. They knew whose child I was, even though I did not know who they were. I got to talk to a few people, people who had lived with my mother. They were reluctant to talk to me about her, but suggested that I talk with somebody who was supposed to be my godmother. I went to Rocha. Rocha told me about the tragedy of my mother's suicide, and that my father traveled and had left a card with the address of a hotel with her, just in case she found me, but she had lost it. From that moment on, I started to perceive reality, I understood that I had no relatives left. I was all on my own, isolated, and I discovered that I was the son of a prostitute. With all the emotions that this realization involved, I went back to school.

I carried on with my studies. I studied music because I played the clarinet. I was leaning toward music, the saxophone and the rest, and kept studying until I graduated from primary school. In my last year of primary school, we had various extracurricular activities and, through them, I became aware of the struggles that existed in that school. I not only organized the Festas Juninas (June celebrations) for the school, but also produced a newspaper with other companions called *O Grito* (The Scream). The newspaper was authorized by the school administration, but when we wrote a criticism about it, the newspaper was eliminated. Then, in 1973, we created the *Sombra* (The Shadow). I was then in my first year of high school. We would write the newspaper at night and then distribute it in the classroom during the day. The *Sombra* caused an upheaval in the school; it sounds funny, but I was not aware that all this was occurring while we were under a dictatorship.

When I was eighteen years old, I had to start the process of graduating from school. I was full of doubt and didn't know where I was going, especially since I didn't have any family. It was a hard experience, but at the moment of my graduation, I met a boy who lived in the town of Villa Kennedy. I had a name that I always kept on me; it was the name of someone who had been my mother's husband and had lived with her. He was the *dono do morro,* as we called him in slang, who had moved from the "favela *do esqueleto*" to go to Villa Kennedy. The boy from Villa Kennedy said that he knew this man's mother, Dona Abigail, who lived in Villa Kennedy, and that I should go there with him. I graduated and agreed to go, but instead, managed to get my first job.

I went to Ilha Grande, where I met Broto, my father. He did not know me well, but was emotional when he saw me because he thought I was his son. He said that he was able to recognize me after all these years because when he was caught at the "*Morro da Mangueira*" by the police, I was in his arms and that was the only reason why he was not killed. I was quite young at the time, only three or four, yet he still recalled the incident with much emotion.

After the encounter with my father, I met with a few companions who had been classmates of mine at the Funabem. They had never transgressed the law, but had been arrested and, for this reason, were prisoners. I delivered a speech that now sounds extremely infantile. I told them that the same opportunity that was given to me had been given to them; however, I had managed to make more of my opportunities. I had followed the right path and they had chosen the wrong one. I was naive then, but with a strong determination. What struck me was that these men had not been delinquents when they were minors and I wanted to create an instrument that could be of some help to those students.

My first job was as an assistant to the General Services (GGS), a civil servant position with a pompous name. I went through a phase of self-questioning because I had finished primary school and Funabem had led us to believe that we would be doctors or bank managers. It was not true. In fact, I ended up being a technician. This first job, working for the GGS, consisted of cleaning up the typographic machines. After nine months, I was dismissed. I started to mobilize and work with my companions to establish the Association of the Ex-Students of Funabem. In 1974, I proposed the idea to the Funabem's Board of Directors and they asked me to gather a group of ex-students to talk with them. The ex-students that I brought together were resentful toward the Funabem because they thought that they were thrown into society with no support, no protection. This created a problem with the board. The directors, in turn, became resentful and said that they no longer wanted to meet with us. Afterward, although I did not have a great political conscience, they started to persecute me, calling me a communist and other types of names, like marijuana-smoker. I didn't even know what that meant and certainly didn't know why they were doing this. I went to various places looking for jobs at the time; I had managed to apply for work at the Funabem, but the application was never approved and I didn't really know what had happened.

Then a man came into the picture who turned out to be significant. He was a black professor of music, an ex-student of the SAM, and he always discussed with me the question of difference, how society treated blacks and whites, and the importance of political struggle. His name was Master Pires.

I went to work at Sano, which built water reservoirs, as an office assistant, my highest achievement. I also performed in theaters and gave music lessons, exchanging my salary and work for scholarships to allow students to study in that school or participate in theater. Coincidentally, in 1976, there was an election for a city council position and the school owner was a candidate for the MDB, the party of the opposition. We helped him a lot, and he won. The first thing he did after the election was to fire me. At the time, I didn't understand why. I later realized it was because I coordinated the cultural nucleus of the faculty of communication.

I pursued the struggle for the Association of the Ex-Students of Funabem until 1977, when I found a job teaching in a college called ITU, owned by a guy called Luis Carlos Cruz. The first day of class, when I entered his room, he asked me how the Left was doing. I raised my left arm and he said, "No, the Left." I really had no notion about the Left and Right, but still I was labeled a leftist because of my attempts to found the association. I had managed to gather and coordinate people from the Funabem by the end of

1973. In 1974, I got in touch with the black movement after Jorge Carlos, an ex-student (we went to several schools together) who was then involved in the Modern Art Museum's effort to create a Research Institute for Black Culture, took me to meetings. He was on the first board of directors for the new research institute; we could see the effervescence, and kept struggling in the direction of organizing theater and music projects.

In 1978, after passing another "Vestibular," I approached the faculty of education at the Funabem and was taken to meet the higher-ups at a dinner, like those students who were going to the university and were shown the good path to follow. I told the directors that I had applied several times for a job there and they decided to make me an employee without putting me through complex tests. So, I ended up teaching music for Funabem. It was during this time that my first son was born. At the end of this period, in 1979, the presidency of the Funabem changed. There was an "opening" left by President Figueiredo and a new person came to Funabem, Claire Gazelle. She initiated a critique of the prison system of Funabem. I met with her and the board of directors to again propose the creation of an association, and she agreed to it.

In February 1980, I gathered an assembly of ex-students and we finally established the association. At that time, I didn't want to be its president and, instead, was elected president of the council; we elected a sergeant of aeronautics as president. The whole thing was quite intuitive, not the result of a great strategy. We had this vision that we would remove students from their misery, that we would find employment for students, but I soon came to realize that this whole endeavor was quite ephemeral, very small. We could only get jobs for ten or fifteen students, while more than a thousand needed work, and the students started to put pressure on the association with their own problems. The students didn't understand. The problem that I had finding people jobs led to serious reflection on my part. Between teaching classes at the Funabem and directing the association, I saw that 97 percent of the students were black. Only 3 percent had transgressed the law, and the great majority of them were poor, the children of single mothers. They came from communities that did not improve their way of living. The Funabem would take you away from your community and would offer, in return, better living conditions—because you ate every day—

and then throw you back into a situation of misery. I started to think that what was important were the rights of children. If the children's rights were respected, obviously one would not need the Funabem or such institutions or associations.

In 1984, we organized the first demonstration in the history of the movement in Rio. It was a demonstration protesting against violence directed at adolescents and for the defense of their rights. More press than demonstrators attended and, shortly after, I was dismissed from the Funabem because the demonstration criticized its direction. That same year, I also graduated from a university. It was there that I had begun to implement my struggle with the black movement; my interest in and awareness of the racial question also increased there.

In 1985, an experience that really struck me occurred: a group of ex-students from the Funabem disappeared in Baixada Fluminense. They had a co-op called Descuido; they would steal from markets and resell the products at a lower price to the community. They "disappeared" at the hands of the death squads. We made all types of requests to Governor Brizola to find the children, or to account for them, but nothing happened. It was discouraging to see how the state treated a crime against the poor.

Around that time, some people from the Partido dos Trabalhadores, the labor party, contacted the association, and we started to understand a bit more about society, the injustices that affect our population, our youth, our children. In 1988, the centennial of the abolition of slavery was celebrated nationwide and denunciations by the mass media and government of the assassination of the teenagers in Baixada Fluminense. This was the first report in Brazil about the assassination of children and, for most people, it was startling news that 75 to 79 percent of the kids who were killed were black and between fifteen and seventeen years of age. Later, IBASE wrote other reports, but this was the first one in Brazil. It was translated and distributed throughout the world, and this increased worldwide the pressure on the Brazilian government; it showed how it treated its children and that there were organized groups killing these teenagers.

I traveled to Europe during that period and received a request from an international organization to do a report about street children. As a deputy candidate for the labor party in 1986, I had had the opportunity to speak with various segments of society. From that experience, I learned that one cannot resolve societal problems from an isolated point of view; one has to understand the social structure and the central problems of society. It was not just the problem of the ex-students, it was the problem of the blacks, of the favelados, the single mothers—of all of them.

By 1989, we were able to start the Center of Articulation for Marginalized Peoples, a bigger center with a definite program in direct connection with the struggle against the violence toward children—in this case, the violation of human rights. In Brazil, people do not associate the racial question with human rights, and unfortunately, other parts of the world also see it this way. They think that "human rights" is just "beating activists," and that murdering youth and black people is not a human rights' violation because these people are delinquents and criminals. The question of race is tightly linked to the question of criminality. We were the first black organization to focus on this connection and its relation to the violation of human rights. We created important international alliances and, at the same time, led a campaign against the mass sterilization of black women. The majority of sterilized women in Brazil are black and we saw this as a strategy of genocide against the black population. The separation of race and criminality, and ending of forced sterilization of women, were two important convictions (*bandeiras*) in 1989. Our campaign, called "Don't Kill Our Children," was the basis for us to start building the *primeiro encontro nacional de antidades negros* (first national meeting of black groups).

In Brazil, we hope to develop unity within the movement of black Brazilians, which has been very difficult. I participate in debates and go to conferences to obtain information that I can't get in Brazil. From outside, you learn to look at Brazil more closely, to understand why you live in a country where 3 percent of the population dominates nearly 70 percent of the economy there, to understand why the great majority of the population—which is mostly black—doesn't get the benefits from the richness that was built by their ancestors. I came to realize that if we don't associate the racial question with the social question, we will be creating a corporative movement that does not grow much; we have to relate the racial question to the question of misery and poverty that today affects the great majority of the population and also what happens to our youth. As our conscience sought new paths, our militancy developed.

Through my election experience in 1986, I learned that a black man with a conscience within a political party dominated by a white intellectual middle class of students is never well accepted, especially in a party where everything is just a question of class struggle, where everything gets resolved in this way, and where the question of "ethnie," of race, is beyond the class struggle. The class struggle is important, but it shouldn't cover up differences; it does not help to create a new man, trying to suppress the cultural differences that he may have. Such discourse was new for the Partido dos Trabalhadores (PT) in 1986, as this was a discourse that did not belong to the party but to a social movement. We had difficulties, but in 1987, at the first national encounter of PT, we contributed by introducing the racial question, clearly articulated by us and people from other states. We met in Brasília with about 150 black militants and, for the first time in a political party in Brazil, the racial question was discussed, not in a populist way but as a party policy. Interestingly, no major leader of the party showed up at that meeting. In 1988, a black city councillor, Benedita da Silva, was elected in Rio, and we had a meeting that was not well attended to write a document for the party. It was a novelty for the party to have a black woman from a favela became one of the policy makers. Even the media treated this exceptionally, with the purpose of favoring real integration.

From 1989 on, we started to work on another important phase. Besides the convictions that were taking shape, one of the richest moments from a political point of view was when society was confronted with the racial question and we started to propose Benedita da Silva as a vice-presidential candidate for the PT. First, we won conventions in various states to get her name listed for vice president. There were several blacks who had good connections in various states and I traveled around as well to build support for this proposal. Second, PT found itself with a big hot potato in its hands; in spite of their politics of alliances, they could not ignore us. The white leaders treated us very harshly, because they considered us too bold, and I believe that this determined fundamentally Silva's ascent within the party. We proposed the following: It was good that Silva was the vice president, but she had to be allowed to talk to the national PT convention. It was one of the most beautiful speeches that I ever heard her deliver. It was about the racial relations with the blacks and favelados. The party had to give her a standing ovation. I believe we altered the convictions of the party, to some extent—a party that had once considered this question insignificant.

Still, it was not enough to change the party's mind on the racial question. There was too much conflict, too much battling. It is obvious that the Center of Articulation for Marginalized Peoples (CEAP), since it is like a nongovernmental organization, had nothing to do with the party in any way. The convictions that it created in the popular camp ended up influencing the party. That's how the mass sterilization of women occurred, the extermination of teenagers, the "funk" parties. The party has this fear of finding out about the so-called disorganized sectors. The party branches talk about the "chosen," that we have to find them, and the party does not understand that the reason for the first failure and the failure of Lula's campaign was due to our incomprehension of those who are not in the organized sectors. They are not disorganized, they are just sectors that have a different form of organization. I believe that the leninist "instruments" that people learn to read do not explain this. Possibly Gramsci illustrates this, when he writes about culture and counterculture, about groups that have different cultures and aren't the hegemonic culture. Even if you have a leftist discourse, you still read by the hegemonic culture of society, the culture that maintains the status quo. So you are never going to understand the black population and someone in the party with the understanding of the identity of this segment is always going to be regarded at least as being strange. He will be treated in a different way by the party; he won't be taken seriously. What is missing is the capacity of an internal theoretician to understand that we are talking about a new segment, a historical segment, which is beyond the comprehension of most. It's not in the formal market as labor class, but it's not the peasant class, either. Consequently, it feeds the formal market with the resources it gets. This is the political understanding that is missing and it is obvious, as the biggest part of this segment is black, that it has its own way of dressing, speaking, walking, and expressing itself. It is distinctive, although society tries to impose a unique behavior on it.

We see this in the explosion of African blacks, which go some-what in this direction; the *candombles* are forces of resistance. Dur-ing Lula's campaign for president, for the first time in the history of this country, a presidential candidate came inside a *candomble*. It was somewhat of a scandal, but the movement managed to suc-cessfully organize it. At that time, there was a battle between the Evangelists and the Catholics because the *candomble* religion of blacks had never been formally acknowledged and dealt with in public by a politician. Politicians go to *candomble* houses to get elected, but they go in secretively, using the back door. Lula went there publicly, however, and the media was forced to take it well. But Lula didn't go there to win votes. He went to talk to *candomble* leaders. There was an encounter between the *candomble* leaders and him, and they handed him their claims. From this experience, I also discovered that several marxist-leninists had been involved with the *candomble* in the PT itself. There was a series of liaisons, but they did not have the courage to admit this because it is a reli-gion that they were ashamed of, from a public point of view. We in the black movement felt that the moment the Protestants at-tacked the *candomble* religion, it was important that a presidential candidate who was then first in the polls give a public expression of support to that religion, showing that he had no prejudice. This was one more contribution that the black movement made to the party. The tension behind the scenes was serious, and the only way that we were able to work through it was due to the work that the CEAP did in this area.

Two important personal political experiences have influenced my thinking about the movement: acting as the coordinator of Lula's governmental program for children and adolescents in 1989 and working as a strategist on Silva's vice presidential campaign. I was the only black involved in the coordination of Silva's campaign, and what interested us was the future. At the time, we were trying to make Silva palatable to the white middle class; the black middle class already fervently supported her during the elections. Yet we could only win if we radicalized her campaign, emphasizing her defense of the poor and the slum dwellers. People thought, "No, we have to compromise." We put on a gigantic demonstration next to the prime real estate in Rio de Janeiro, the beaches of Ipanema and Cobacabana. During the demonstration, people from the surrounding apartments said "Macaca"; they insulted Benedita. We did not win anything with this gesture. In the "South Zone" we would have lost anyway, but we also lost in the suburbs, in the popular area where we could have won. This was a campaign that had all the means to be great. It gathered all the concrete conditions to win, but we lost it because of a strategy mistake. The strategy, however, was not ours; it was that of the middle class, the white middle class. The white middle class needed a way of explaining back home, in their white homes, that Silva represented a conflict of classes, not races. The Right knew this and was tranquil; the conservatives knew that the conflict at the beach was really over the fear of blacks invading and taking away the tranquility of the working white middle class. There was a confrontation and they knew how to exploit it, and this entered even in the black sectors. So, we lost the elections, but it was a rich experience.

I was a bit surprised, however, that we did not create a black political picture, but rather, a picture of symbolic representation. That would have been enough for us to have our own strategy, a strategy that would be exclusive to the blacks' point of view. In the future, we have to learn how to make alliances with the white progressive petite bourgeoisie, but according to a policy that we need to determine ourselves, not trying to disguise it as if we want to become white. We still haven't produced a picture with this political clarity. We have produced a picture that is brilliant, like Silva's campaign—a symbolic picture that touches, that makes you emotional, that is charismatic. But charisma does not explain everything, and there are profound limitations to charismatic leadership. Charisma must be endowed with a project; that is, it's no good if Silva or, for that matter, Jesse Jackson is charismatic unless there are people behind them who think and contribute. Unless a leader is willing to listen to the people behind them, to accept their contributions, to work in a team, to work together, that leader will not be successful. This has been one of our difficulties over the past few years within the PT. If only we had a brilliant black picture from the trade union point of view. But it is much more than the logic of trade unionism. Even if a candidate is sensitive to the racial question and talks about the racial question, it is not in the sense of comprehending a political project in relation to the majority of the black masses, which do not belong to trade unions.

So we have this problem: it is obvious that you will be nominated secretary of the government if you win the elections, but I think that we need to understand the social actors in the other existing black groups. There should be a common strategy that we can follow. We need blacks that have a good knowledge of urbanization, of population settlement. We are missing key components of analysis of contemporary Brazilian society. Silva could make a great contribution if she understood this, but she cannot stand on her charisma alone.

In order to truly benefit the masses, there are three forces in Brazilian society that need to be united. First, there are the black intellectuals, who are presently dispersed and trying to survive within white institutions. Then there is the emerging black middle class, which is ashamed of joining a collective project. Lastly, there are the militants, the activists. We lack a project that successfully brings these elements together, where no one needs to fight for space and nobody wants to take anybody else's space. I believe that there is not a leadership that with all its charisma could produce politics in this direction.

Certainly, we can be proud of Silva's election to the Brazilian Senate. And she's not alone; a black woman named Marina Silva was elected to Congress from Acre, a novelty in this rural area. These small gains are important for us. It is not enough, however, merely to be represented in Congress. We need to think of what can we do from our position in Congress. We also need to work on bringing more blacks into the realm of public affairs. Otherwise, in spite of everything we do against racism, people will say, "What are you complaining about? You have Bene who is a Senator, Marina who is a Senator, Pitanga who is a city councillor," as if these were considerable and concrete steps. In addition, liberals often explain away racism in terms of competence: "The problem is yours, not ours. Society gives space to those who are truthfully competent." But we know that defeating racism is not just a matter of competence.

Nor is racism a problem to be solved by one person. We need a collective project to answer the needs of the great majority of the population. This necessitates new ways of thinking and a critical mass to advance this project. We need to bring people together with the understanding that one person, on their own, will neither achieve the redemption of a people nor represent a people in its aspirations for the future. We are missing collective action and instruments that can provoke this collective ascent.

In Brazil, the academic world has thought about the racial question, even with some of the black academics, but this has not contributed effectively to the movement. It has differed little from the trade union movement, where the production of knowledge has primarily helped the organization and the progression of the movement itself. The women's movement also contributed to the production of new knowledge. Academics have generally remained distant from activists and the actions of the movement in Brazil. On the other hand, it is a mistake on the part of the black movement to think that it can explain itself on its own, to seek self-sufficiency. It is egocentric to think that one can solve all problems, work on all questions, and know all the paths on one's own. The black movement needs to view academia with less prejudice, and academia has to cease being so omnipotent and begin to make contributions. It is a path that must be explored. At the same time, more militant activists, youth, and blacks of the new generation must succeed in making it into academia. They must succeed in studying our problems and our questions, and give us an efficient contribution.

The movement needs to initiate a direct dialogue with academia —much like the trade union movement, entrepreneurs, and all the social sectors have done—to promote relationships between academia and the movement. We need to initiate a dialogue with those who research questions that are related to the Black movement; with those who can contribute and help blacks to improve not only the movement's discourse, but also its vision and political maturity. We should not be worrying so much about being the objects of research; if you are an object, you can also be a subject, you can influence fundamental things. The conference in Texas was important for this reason. I believe that this was the first conference from an international point of view, the first one in the United States, that initiated a dialogue from this perspective: it not only considered the work of academics, but also that of activists. This space must be maintained, it must be open. It was a piece of news for the academic sectors that never had access to or an understanding of the activists who are not in the so-called "official circles." On the other hand, there are also blacks who are not really academics, but act as if they are. Some want to be in academia, but they are not prepared because academia has a sophistication and rituals that must be understood first. A duality also exists in Brazil, where the academic thinks he represents the movement because he has studied the movement. A definition of roles and the space of cooperation is important, and the conference opened a path in this direction; let's see if people will be able to enlarge it.

If academia and the movement had got together five years ago, not to say ten, Silva would have won the vice presidential election. Her campaign lacked the academic indications regarding the path to follow. We know that the Right has its own organic intellectuals, who help it reflect about its direction. We don't have this. Even more, we believe that this is not important, that this does not exist. Or we fear being directed. I believe this is a matter of discussing the spaces of contribution, rather than rejecting the idea of direction itself. Right now, when society raises all the prejudiced discourse with which the middle class identifies itself unconsciously, it was an intellectual who gave them such discourse. We need to know how to neutralize this in our speech on television. We need to speak with emotion and forget that the objective, rational facts are missing.

CONTRIBUTORS

Richard Graham is Frances Higginbotham Nalle Centennial Professor of History at the University of Texas at Austin. His books include *Britain and the Onset of Modernization in Brazil* (1968), *Escravidão, reforma e imperialismo (Slavery, Reform, and Imperialism)* (1979), *Patronage and Politics in Nineteenth-Century Brazil* (1990), and (as editor) *The Idea of Race in Latin America* (1990). He is currently at work on a project on economic liberalism and the local economy in the early nineteenth century, particularly as it affected the provisioning of the city of Salvador, Bahia.

Michael Hanchard is Associate Professor of Political Science and African American Studies at Northwestern University. His publications include *Orpheus and Power: Afro-Brazilian Social Movements in Rio de Janeiro and São Paulo, Brazil, 1945–1988* (1994).

Carlos Hasenbalg is Professor of Sociology at the Instituto Universitario de Pesquisas do Rio de Janeiro (IUPERJ). He is the former director of the Center for Afro-Asiatic Studies at Candido Mendes University in Rio de Janeiro. He is the coauthor, along with Nelson do Valle Silva, of *Estructura Social, Mobilidade e Raca* (1988) and *Relacoes Raciais no Brasil Contemporaneo* (1992) and several articles on race relations in Brazil.

Peggy A. Lovell is Associate Professor of Sociology and Latin American Studies at the University of Pittsburgh. She has published widely on issues of social inequality and is currently working on a book manuscript on race and gender in Brazil.

Michael Mitchell is Associate Professor in the Department of Political Science at Arizona State University. He has authored various articles on race and Brazilian politics. Among his publications are "The Ironies of Citizenship: Skin Color, Police Brutality, and the Challenges to Brazilian Democracy," with Charles Wood, *Social Forces* (forthcoming); "The Social Bases of the Transition to Democracy in Brazil," with Thomas Rochan, *Comparative Politics* 21, no. 3 (1989); "Blacks and the Abertura Democratica," in *Race, Class, and Power in Brazil* (1985); and "Cafundo: Counterpoint on a Brazilian African Survival," *Centennial Review* 28, no. 3 (1984).

Ivanir dos Santos is executive secretary and founding member of the Center for the Articulation of Outcast Populations (CBAP) in Rio de Janeiro, Brazil.

He is also a member of the Worker's Party. CBAP is an independent, nongovernmental organization founded in 1989 to focus on policy and popular mobilization on issues of racial inequality and race-related violence, street children, and the conditions of black women in Brazil. In 1997, CBAP was awarded the National Human Rights Prize in the nongovernmental organization category for the organization's popular programs.

Thereza Santos, an actress, playwright, and cultural activist based in São Paulo, Brazil, is currently director of the Afro-Brazilian relations office for the city of São Paulo.

Benedita da Silva's political life constitutes a number of firsts. A member of the Worker's Party, she was the first black woman elected to the Brazilian congress in 1986 and was reelected in 1990 from the state of Rio de Janeiro. More recently, she was elected senator from the state of Rio de Janeiro in 1994. She has also held the office of assemblywoman and was a candidate for mayor for the city of Rio de Janeiro in 1992. She is currently a candidate for vice governor in the 1998 state elections.

Edward E. Telles is the Human Rights Program Officer for the Ford Foundation in Rio de Janeiro and is currently on leave from UCLA, where he teaches sociology. His work at Ford includes supporting activities that strengthen antiracist jurisprudence and public policy in Brazil. He is also writing a book on miscegenation and race relations in Brazil.

Nelson do Valle Silva is Professor of Sociology at the Instituto Universitario de Pesquisas do Rio de Janeiro (IUPERJ), and senior researcher of the Laboratorio Nacional de Computação Científica (CNPQ). In addition to the two coauthored books with Carlos Hasenbalg, do Valle Silva is author of various articles on race relations.

Howard Winant is Professor of Sociology and Latin American Studies at Temple University in Philadelphia. He is the coauthor (with Michael Omi) of *Racial Formation in the United States: From the 1960s to the 1990s* (1994); he has also written *Racial Conditions: Politics, Theory, Comparisons* (1994) and *Stalemate: Political Economic Origins of Supply-Side Policy* (1988), as well as numerous articles on racial theory and politics, the comparative sociology of race, and problems in political sociology.

INDEX

Library of Congress Cataloging-in-Publication Data

Racial politics in contemporary Brazil / edited by Michael Hanchard.
p. cm.
Includes index.
ISBN 0-8223-2252-8 (cloth : alk. paper). — ISBN 0-8223-2272-2 (paper)
1. Blacks—Brazil—Politics and government.   2. Brazil—Race relations—
Political aspects.   3. Brazil—Politics and government—1985—
I. Hanchard, Michael
F2659.N4R25   1999
323.1′196081—dc21   98-27734